New Directions in Physical Education
Change and Innovation

Edited by
Neil Armstrong

CASSELL

To the memory of Joy McConachie-Smith (1936–1994)

Cassell
Wellington House
125 Strand
London WC2R 0BB

215 Park Avenue South
New York
NY 10003

British Library Cataloguing-in-Publication Data
A catalogue record for this book is available from the British Library.

Library of Congress Cataloging-in-Publication Data
New directions in physical education : change and innovation / edited
  by Neil Armstrong.
    p. cm.
   Includes bibliographical references and index.
   ISBN 0–304–33450–2 (alk. paper). — ISBN 0–304–33449–9 (pbk. :
alk. paper)
    1. Physical education and training — Great Britain. 2. Physical
education and training — Great Britain — Curricula. 3. Educational
change — Great Britain. I. Armstrong, Neil.
GV245.N495 1996
796'.07'041–dc20

95–34030
CIP

ISBN 0–304–33450–2 (hardback)
     0–304–33449–9 (paperback)

Typeset by Mayhew Typesetting, Rhayader, Powys
Printed and bound in Great Britain by Redwood Books, Trowbridge, Wiltshire

Contents

Preface

New Directions in Physical Education was initiated by the Physical Education Association Research Centre and edited by the Centre Director in association with the Physical Education Association of the United Kingdom.

New Directions in Physical Education includes relevant contributions from recognized leaders in the field of physical education on topics of current interest in sport, dance, and physical, health and outdoor education. Contributors were selected by the editor following consultation with the officers of the Physical Education Association but, of course, the views expressed are those of the authors and not necessarily those of either the editor nor the Physical Education Association of the United Kingdom. Suggestions of suitable topics worthy of inclusion in future volumes and of potential contributors would be welcomed by the editor. Correspondence should be addressed directly to Professor Neil Armstrong, Physical Education Association Research Centre, University of Exeter, Exeter EX1 2LU, United Kingdom.

Introduction

The Education Reform Act (ERA) (1988) represented the most significant piece of education legislation to have issued from central government in the UK for over forty years. In Chapter 1 of this volume Professor John Evans, Dr Dawn Penney and Professor Brian Davies examine some of the ERA's major legislative measures and consider their impact upon the provision of Physical Education (PE) and sport in schools. The authors question whether ERA has created the conditions by which all teachers can provide forms of PE that are both equitable and of a high quality.

In April 1993, the Secretary of State for Education commissioned Sir Ron Dearing to conduct a review of the National Curriculum. Following wide consultation, Dearing produced two reports (an interim report in July 1993, and a final report in December 1993) and recommended slimming down the National Curriculum, reducing its prescriptiveness, limiting assessment through national tests to mathematics, science and English, and improving the associated administration and documentation. The Secretary of State accepted Dearing's recommendations and initiated a review by the Schools Curriculum and Assessment Authority (SCAA) of all National Curriculum subjects. Advisory groups for each subject and each Key Stage were established and the review was carried out in spring 1994 with the revised subject Orders released for consultation in May 1994. The consultation period ran until the end of July 1994 and SCAA's final recommendations were delivered to the Secretary of State on 30 September 1994. Copies of the final Orders were distributed to schools in January 1995 for implementation from August 1995 for 5–14 year olds, and from August 1996 for 14–16 year olds.

New Directions in Physical Education has been prepared during this period of uncertainty and the subtitle *Change and Innovation* reflects the opportunities and challenges currently being addressed by the PE profession.

In Chapter 2, Professor Neil Armstrong and Dr Alison McManus analyse the anatomical and physiological development of the child as s/he progresses through the four Key Stages of the National Curriculum. They comment on gender issues and emphasize that, in the interpretation and implementation of the National Curriculum, physical educators must recognize the individual differences in the rate of growth and maturation of young people and the influence of these changes on their capabilities and aspirations. Dr Martin Lee, in Chapter 3, addresses the psycho-social development of children as it influences, and is influenced by, the PE process. He focuses specifically on the nature and development of self-concept, developmental patterns of play, the demands of group interaction, and changing perceptions of ability during childhood. Together Chapters 2 and 3 underpin the subsequent pivotal chapters on PE in Key Stages (KS) 1–4.

Carolyn Jones sets out the role of PE at KS1 and addresses the issues of enhancing the status of PE at KS1, improving the quality of PE at KS1, and developing a strategy for promoting physical activity in the early years. In the following chapter, Dr

Anne Williams suggests that successful PE provision at KS2 requires an understanding of a range of developmental factors of how they relate to the KS2 pupil and of their implications for good practice. Anne emphasizes the value of partnerships with outside agencies and their potential for enhancing the curriculum experience of the KS2 pupil. In Chapter 6, Brin Martin argues that KS3 is a transitional phase in which the teacher must enable independence and inform choice. He outlines the difficulties facing the KS3 teacher but concludes that KS3 should prove to be both challenging and rewarding for the teacher, and purposeful and inspirational for the learner. Joy McConachie-Smith reviews the major issues which need to be addressed by those planning the 14–16 curriculum. In Chapter 7, Joy carefully considers how KS4 relates and interfaces with the academic route of GCSE and subsequent A levels and the vocational competences as assessed in GNVQs and later NVQs as well as common core skills. She provides insightful comments on the potential of PE to bridge the academic and vocational routes and addresses the issues arising from this challenge.

In Chapter 8 Dr Kenneth Fox presents the concept of the 'active school'. He provides a contextual analysis of the emergence of interest in physical activity and health, and outlines the rationale underpinning recent public health initiatives relating to physical activity promotion. Ken then demonstrates how schools might develop and implement a policy which fosters the adoption of active lifestyles.

The National Curriculum has given impetus to the view that all children should not only have entitlement to a mainstream PE curriculum but also that this entitlement is translated into access. Professor David Sugden and Helen Wright advocate that presenting a curriculum for all children is simply an extension of good professional practice. In Chapter 9, they describe the needs of various groups of children and the demands made by them on a PE programme. They conclude by proposing that diversity in the resources children bring to the movement situation should not be looked upon as threatening, but should be viewed as absolutely normal – indeed they are.

The complex topic of gifted children in PE and sport is addressed by Dick Fisher in Chapter 10. He outlines the issues associated with identifying and developing gifted young athletes and explores schemes which have evolved in other countries. Dick considers the pressure for excellence and success and the responsibilities of parents, teachers and the world of sport in relation to the needs and interests of the gifted child. He concludes by describing some successful approaches and discussing principles which should guide the development of schemes for promoting gifted youngsters.

In Chapter 11, Rod Thorpe develops further the theme of partnerships with outside agencies. He states that curriculum time is insufficient to educate the child physically and explores ways of supplementing the experiences offered in the PE curriculum. Rod draws upon his experiences of Aussie Sport and Kiwi Sport as well as his understanding of PE and youth sport in the UK to present the case that, there has never been a better time to resolve issues of sport within the curriculum, while recognizing and promoting those aspects of sport which extend education beyond the curriculum.

Dr Andrew Sparkes draws upon life history data to examine the continuing search for self by two PE teachers as they move through various stages in their life cycle and career. In Chapter 12, he suggests that the quality of life in the school as a workplace is experienced by teachers in very different ways and that these differences have a powerful influence upon who becomes a teacher, what kind of teacher they become, and who stays as a teacher. Andrew presents an insightful case which proposes that in a post-modern world an acceptance of heterogeneity and a celebration of difference are essential for the creation of a positive school environment in which all teachers can work.

Recent central government intervention has not been restricted to schools and the reform of teacher education has been high on the government's agenda. In Chapter 13, Chris Laws examines the nature of teacher education in the context of current government policies and assesses the implications of recent developments for PE teacher education. Chris indicates new directions for teacher education and proposes a rationale for a continuing role for higher education while at the same time endorsing a move towards more experientially based professional learning.

Following the introduction and revision of the National Curriculum, the government has promised no further changes for the next five years. In the final chapter of this volume, Len Almond argues that, after a period of change and upheaval, this respite provides an opportunity to reflect critically on current practice. Len introduces and develops the concepts of active living, cultural practices of significance, and physicality. He considers the content and context of PE and suggests that although they can generate significant opportunities for promoting well-being this can only be achieved by creating a community in which it can unfold. His vision of PE is one in which teachers help young people to make informed choices about what to do with their lives, through the initiation of activities within PE which can generate satisfactions that help to enrich the quality of life.

The publication of this volume would not have been possible without the support of the contributors, the PEA Research Centre team, Naomi Roth of Cassell and my secretary, Alison Husband who kept the project on course. A special thanks to Professor Elizabeth Murdoch who kindly collated Joy McConachie-Smith's contribution following Joy's tragic death in December 1994.

Neil Armstrong
PEA Research Centre
University of Exeter, UK

Contributors

Len Almond FPEA Senior Lecturer in Physical Education, University of Technology, Loughborough LE11 3TU.

Neil Armstrong PhD, FPEA, FIBiol, FRSH, President of the Physical Education Association, Professor of Health and Exercise Sciences, University of Exeter, Exeter EX1 2LU.

Brian Davies PhD, Professor of Education, University of Wales, Cardiff CF2 4YG.

John Evans PhD FPEA, Professor of Physical Education, University of Technology, Loughborough LE11 3TU.

Richard Fisher PhD FPEA, Past President of the Physical Education Association, Head of Physical Education and Sport Sciences, St Mary's College, Twickenham TW1 4SX.

Kenneth Fox PhD FPEA, Senior Lecturer in Education, University of Exeter, Exeter EX1 2LU.

Carolyn Jones FPEA, Vice-President of the Physical Education Association, Lecturer in Physical Education, University of Newcastle Upon Tyne, Newcastle upon Tyne NE1 7RU.

Christopher Laws FPEA, Vice-President of the Physical Education Association, Head of Teacher Education, West Sussex Institute of Higher Education, Chichester PO19 4PE.

Martin Lee PhD FPEA, Principal Research Fellow, University of Brighton, Trevin Towers, Gaudick Rd, Eastbourne BN20 7SP.

Joy McConachie-Smith FPEA, Deputy Head of Department, University of Brighton, Trevin Towers, Gaudick Rd, Eastbourne BN20 7SP.

Alison McManus PhD, Research Fellow, Centre for Physical Education and Sport Science, University of Hong Kong, Hong Kong.

Brin Martin FPEA, Member of National Curriculum Review PE Group, Advisory Teacher, South Suffolk Professional Development Centre, Ipswich IP2 0AN.

Dawn Penney PhD, Research Fellow, Department of Physical Education and Sports Science, University of Technology, Loughborough LE11 3TU.

Andrew Sparkes PhD, Senior Lecturer in Education, University of Exeter, Exeter EX1 2LU.

David Sugden PhD AFBPsS, Professor of Special Needs in Education, University of Leeds, Leeds LS2 9JT.

Rod Thorpe, Senior Lecturer in Physical Education, University of Technology, Loughborough LE11 3TU.

Anne Williams PhD, Senior Lecturer in Education, University of Birmingham, Birmingham B15 2TT.

Helen Wright, Research Scholar, University of Leeds, Leeds LS2 9JT.

Chapter 1

Back to the Future: Education Policy and Physical Education

John Evans, Dawn Penney and Brian Davies

THE SOCIAL CONTEXT OF TEACHING AND TEACHER EDUCATION

These are difficult times for teachers and teacher educators. Indeed, they are pretty unsettling for anyone involved with the education of children irrespective of whether they work inside or outside schools. The work of teaching and parenting is changing because the world in which we work is also changing and, in some ways, dramatically so. Some argue that the age of modernity is in terminal decline, bringing 'new times', variously called 'high' or 'post' modernity, post industrial, or post liberal (Giddens, 1991; Featherstone, 1988; Hargreaves, 1994). Certainly, economic flexibility, techno-logical complexity, cultural and religious diversity, moral and scientific uncertainty and national insecurity characterize the contemporary socio-cultural terrain. These changes, as Hargreaves (1994) has argued, spread far and run deep; inevitably, they have a bearing not only on what children and young people bring to school in the form of attitudes, interests and expectations, but also on how and what teachers and teacher educators think and teach. It is therefore perhaps unsurprising that sometimes it seems that just about everyone wants those involved in education to change. As Hargreaves (1994) reminds us, the public wants teachers to change and educational administrators are endlessly exhorting them to do so. 'Meanwhile, teachers themselves are already experiencing change, lots of it; arguably more than at any time before.' In our view, Hargreaves (1994, p. 95) is not far off the mark when he states: 'For teachers, change is mandatory. Only improvement is optional.'

We, too, would argue that changes in the structure of the economy and the workplace are generating significant changes in the social and cultural domain. The growth of economic diversity, together with the revitalization of local and regional identities is having profound implications for knowledge and belief systems, and the expertise that rests upon them. At the same time, we live with unacceptably high levels of unemployment. Relationships between paid work, unpaid work and leisure are altering their form. More women want paid employment; more want access to leisure; and men, husbands and partners, still find it very hard to adjust to this state of affairs. Young women and men are choosing not to marry; instead, they live alone or cohabit, and are attempting to create ways of living that make sense to them individually, whatever the dictates of tradition (McRae, 1993, p. 107). Relationships are altering their form, and some are under strain. In some cases, this means less stable and less secure communities. In society as a whole, there is evidence of a shift – though never as widespread as some theorists of the post-modern would have us believe (Hargreaves, 1994; Kellner, 1988; Evans, 1995a) – from a small number of stable singularities of knowledge and belief to a fluctuating, ever-changing plurality of belief systems. This, as Hargreaves (1994) and others (Giddens, 1991; Evans and Davies, 1992) have argued, is giving rise to a crisis of moral purpose (what do we believe? where are we going?) and of cultural identity (who are we?) and generating an orientation to the self (forms of individualism). On the one hand, this may be a source of creativity, empowerment and change (in theory we can all be as we want to be); on the other, it may be a source of alienation, 'uncertainty, vulnerability and social withdrawal' (Hargreaves, 1994, p. 103). Some see these socio-cultural changes as a threat and a crisis, as evidence of social and moral degeneration, of the fabric of society coming apart. According to some Conservative Ministers of State, for example, parents, teachers and schools are to blame for the nation's social and moral decline, and 'traditional' order must be restored (Jenkins, 1993; Evans and Penney, 1995).

On the surface, these socio-cultural changes can seem remote from the work of physical education (PE) teachers or teacher educators. In our view they are not. Teachers and teacher educators are, unavoidably, implicated in the construction of authority, morality and social order. Large-scale social changes and forces within them such as racism, sexism and elitism are not abstractions. They may be resisted and modified but they cannot be removed from the daily practices of educationalists which are inevitably constituted and constructed by them. As Apple (1993) has demonstrated, their effects are visceral. Indeed, it is partly because of these changing cultural conditions that PE has gained such a prominent place in the public eye. Historically, the construction of masculinity, femininity and other cultural identities of class and ethnicity have been caught up with the process of teaching and teacher education and especially with the practices of PE and the way in which the body is schooled. As Shilling (1993, p. 73) has argued, the body has traditionally been used as a metaphor of society as a whole. Consequently, in times of economic and social crisis, when national borders and identities are threatened, anxieties about risk and uncertainties in social relations and social movements tend to be projected on to a concern with the body and the way in which it is schooled. It is therefore not surprising that Conservative governments in the UK and elsewhere, have sought to restore and reassert the certainties of a 'traditional' social and moral order and images of the body compatible with this; and to create a context in which any endeavour to promote (egalitarian) principles and practices that jeopardize that 'order' can be even more easily controlled and inhibited.

In the UK, Ministers of State have routinely traded in sepia images of a lost golden age. It is time, so their argument goes, 'to return to "our" roots, to lead the country back, "across the board", to "core values", to the old ways of teaching traditional subjects' (Jenkins, 1993). From this perspective, we need more competition, more punishment, 'more basics, more self-discipline, old commonsense British values' (Jenkins, 1993, quoting John Major). Others may claim that there is no 'crisis', only a lack of imagination on the part of politicians and educationalists to deal with the challenges of new and changing times. In our view, recent education policies relating to teaching and teacher education have to be understood within this context – as both an expression of these changes and a response to them. They endeavour simultaneously to both curb and control the drift towards 'social disintegration' while giving expression to the flexibilities required of the 'new' modern age. Policy on education can as a result often seem 'confused, containing mixed messages' (Hartley, 1993). On the one hand, there is a consistency running throughout recent education policy that serves to limit that 'flexibility' (Penney and Evans, 1994a). For example, the National Curriculum attempts to homogenize the educational experiences that children receive in the state schools; it sets out to make individuals 'more the same'. On the other hand, local management of schools (LMS) and open enrolment (OE) celebrate 'choice and diversity' in the system and create conditions that set schools and the individuals within them distinctly apart. In this respect, recent legislation seems to express the very confusions of the age, or 'should we say, the very ages which seem contemporaneously to be both upon us (post modernity) and behind us (modernity)' (Hartley, 1993, p. 83). How are physical educationalists to respond when asked to 'deliver' a National Curriculum for Physical Education (NCPE) in very different contexts? Whether recent legislation will press teachers to reconstruct their pedagogies and curricula in a direction needed in a social democracy to help children to come to terms with the identities, opportunities and challenges of new and changing times, is the matter to which we return later.

BACK TO THE FUTURE?

Simon Jenkins reminds us that John Stuart Mill once glumly observed that his fellow citizens seemed to carry their eyes in the backs of their heads. Golden age theory, he stresses, is fine for platitudes but makes poor history and dreadful policy (*The Times*, 13 October 1993, p. 20). He is right. Nostalgia is a dreadful guide to policy, yet this is exactly the stuff that has driven government reforms of schooling and teacher education in the UK in recent years.

By contrast, the stance we take here is that now, more than ever, we need in PE well-trained, highly skilled, *forward looking* professionals, able to deliver what Denis Lawton (1989) calls a 'reconstructionist curriculum': a curriculum that (in the context of PE) lays as much stress upon physical development as it does upon social values, and provides experiences appropriate for developing citizenship and social co-operation in sport, PE, leisure and health, as in other walks of life; a curriculum in which knowledge for its own sake is not ignored, but is questioned, and in which knowledge is justified in terms of social needs, not in terms of custom, tradition, nor cultural heritage *per se* (Lawton, 1989). This, as Lawton emphasizes, is not to imply that there is no value in other models but that, 'given a democratic society which values certain kinds of freedom, a version of social reconstruction is the most appropriate planning model' (Lawton, 1989, pp. 47–8). Unfortunately, this is not the kind of curriculum that government policy on education is pressing teachers to achieve.

Government reforms of schools and teacher education in the UK have to be viewed as tied into a broader package of legislative measures on education, which together represent an attempt at radical and thorough-going reform of the whole education system in England and Wales. In passing, we might also note that the 'new agenda' in education is not peculiar to Britain. Education in many countries throughout the world is now moving through landscapes that defined the education environment in the UK throughout the early 1980s and 1990s (Gilroy and Smith, 1993). We have strong suspicions that many others, beyond our UK shores, will be experiencing 'changes' that resonate with those described in this chapter and, like readers in Britain, may find themselves questioning what in reality is the extent and purpose of 'reform' and how much really is 'new' and 'progressive' in what they are being asked to teach and know.

PHYSICAL EDUCATION AFTER ERA: PLAYING BY MARKET RULES

The Education Reform Act (ERA) (1988) was a unique and complex package of legislation that addressed the content and structure of state education in England and Wales. In this section, we highlight the inseparable nature of these two issues and illustrate how, despite the rhetoric of 'freedom' and 'choice' in 'the market', the ERA signalled the establishment of 'new', more centralized, control over both the content and form of the schools curriculum. Specifically, we describe how the ERA, along with other policy initiatives concerned with both education and the wider provision and resourcing of sport, have increasingly restricted the capacity of PE teachers to develop innovative and progressive approaches to teaching and learning in PE. We point to the text of the NCPE, recent legislation on initial teacher training (ITT) and the context in which education provision is occurring 'post-ERA', as unlikely to foster the development of either equity or quality in PE in schools.

MANAGING THE CRISIS

The ERA (1988) was putatively a 'radical' educational solution which privileged 'the market' as the natural saviour of the economy's and the nation's moral welfare. Over the last fifteen years, Conservative governments in the UK have propounded the view that there is a crisis in state schools and the wider world of education; they have cited inefficiency and wastage in the system due to too much centralization and the progressivism (egalitarianism) of radical experts (teachers and teacher educators) preventing parent consumers enjoying access to the 'educational goods'. The cry has been 'give power back to parents', 'make schools more responsive to the market', 'only decentralization will raise standards and change the form and content of education in accordance with that of market demands' (Evans and Davies, 1990). Two of the policy initiatives incorporated within the ERA – local management of schools (LMS) and open enrolment (OE) – in particular, together presaged decentralization and established the 'market rules' by which schools now operate and conditions in which they have no choice but to compete with one another. No state school in England and Wales can ignore that the reality of these policies is that the provision of 'quality' education (and specifically their capacity to employ new staff, replace those leaving, to fund and undertake curriculum development) now centres on their ability to maintain a 'healthy' intake of pupils against the pull of influences created by 'competitor schools'. While inside schools, under the conditions created by LMS and OE, financial concerns and 'efficiency' have been privileged in decisions concerning how the institution is to operate, how resources are to be allocated to different subject areas and what curriculum the school will offer. What is affordable and what will further the 'marketability' of the institution has seemingly become more important than what will serve the varied needs and interests of pupils, at least in some schools (Bowe *et al.*, 1992; Penney, 1994; Penney and Evans, 1994b). Certainly, in the course of our research[1] we have witnessed the 'language of the market', sponsored by LMS and OE, becoming firmly embedded in the institutional structures and practices of schools. Not only head teachers, but also heads of departments now have budgets allocated at least in part on the basis of the pupils they are able to attract. Subjects as well as schools are in open competition. Of course, neither of these phenomena is 'new'. Post-ERA competition is simply more out in the open, but it also has added edge, status and significance. No one can afford not to play 'the competitive game' (Penney, 1994; Penney and Evans, 1994b). As Ball (1993a) has noted, the circumstances are such that 'resistance' (on the part of schools or individual teachers) does not challenge the policies. Rather, it places in jeopardy teachers' and schools' own futures. This is the context in which PE is being provided, and the conditions under which teachers have had to prepare for and deliver a quality 'NCPE for all'.

PLAYING BY MARKET RULES

Historically, PE has struggled for recognition and status as a subject within the curriculum of state schools, often despite the high profile that school sport sometimes receives in wider public debates. Consequently, PE has often been low on the list of priorities for resource allocations. The hegemony of the 'academic subjects' has also ensured that from this lowly position, in 'market conditions' (when in competition with other subjects), PE may be regarded as a subject that can readily accommodate cuts or compromises in resource allocation, for example, in staffing. Our research has revealed that, post-ERA, many secondary schools have had to place increased reliance on non-specialist input for PE, as they strive to minimize expenditure on their largest budget item (Penney, 1994; Penney and Evans, 1994b). For example, in the schools surveyed in one LEA, 24 (41 per cent) schools reported the use of at least one male non-PE specialist, while 12 (20 per cent) of schools reported using at least one female non-PE specialist, to deliver the PE curriculum (Penney and Evans, with Hennink, 1994). In these circumstances, the prospects of ensuring continuity and progression in teaching and learning in PE and of providing a 'broad and balanced' curriculum are certainly not good. The 'PE' expertise and knowledge that non-specialists are able to offer is invariably no more than a personal interest in a specific sport, often a competitive team game. Although this represents a potentially valuable support for specialist teaching, it is hardly (as we have seen in some schools[1]) a substitute. Non-specialist teachers are rarely familiar with the range of other activities, or the kind of innovatory approaches to teaching and learning in PE, that can benefit all children. Furthermore, with so little timetabled time available to teach PE, the use of off-site facilities has become a luxury all too few pupils may enjoy. Again, the breadth and balance in PE to which all pupils are entitled is threatened and, post-ERA, is certainly something that not all pupils experience or receive.

Putatively, LMS offered new opportunities for the development of PE and sport provision in schools in England and Wales. The ERA enabled schools to keep any monies they generated from 'external' (community) use of facilities. The Sports Council, one of the main sponsors of sport in the UK, along with other sports agencies and a good many educationalists, understandably saw ERA legislation as offering a clear incentive for the development of 'partnerships' in provision between community and schools (Penney, 1994). However, the 'opportunity' to generate income and to foster partnerships has not been experienced uniformly by all schools. Not for the first time, the gap between rhetoric and reality, in this case of 'partnerships' between community and schools, has proven very difficult to bridge. What the rhetoric overlooks is that state schools are not homogeneous either in form or resource. Not all schools have facilities that lend themselves to such developments, nor the expertise and support within and beyond the institution to develop these initiatives; nor are all schools located in highly 'marketable' locations. Making no concession to such differences in the education system, the ERA conveniently overlooked some basic inequalities and 'arrived' without resourcing to either support or sustain 'across the board' developments of this kind. As other contributors in this volume note, 'partnership' schemes remain essentially reliant on individual initiative and, invariably, goodwill. A political climate that has derided and undervalued PE teachers, and legislation that has left many feeling overworked, has not been a sound basis for promoting either goodwill or progress of this kind. The longer-term picture may continue to reflect both the inadequacies in planning and resourcing inherent in this initiative and recent government policies concerning the provision of sport for young people have effectively dismantled all Sports Council responsibilities for developing policies and practices of 'sport for all' (*Guardian*, 29 September 1994, p. 24).

Furthermore, even for those taking up these 'opportunities', the benefits are questionable. Some PE teachers are already concerned about the overuse of facilities and the problems in upkeep that arise in conditions of 'dual' or 'community' use. In addition, some head teachers and heads of PE have serious doubts over where, post-ERA, funding for the repair and replacement of both major items of equipment and facilities, is to come from (Penney, 1994). The devolution of funding from local education authorities (LEAs) to individual schools has called into question not only the long-term security of school sports facilities but also the possibilities of achieving anything approximating comparability of provision across the state system. In effect, although LMS and OE are couched in a language of opportunity rather than constraint – and celebrate the spirit of the 'free market', individual involvement and control of resource – the signs are that these policies may have resulted in more differentiation and a more socially and educationally divided school and wider school system. The rhetoric of popular choice, of 'partnership' and higher standards for all may have obfuscated the reality of a divided, quality differentiated, unequal and rigged market (Wragg, 1988; Evans and Davies, 1990).

Ironically, there was at least the promise within the ERA of an apparently secure and exciting future for PE. In principle, the introduction of a National Curriculum offered a small step towards greater equity and the development of quality in provision in the sense that NC texts articulated the entitlement of all pupils in England and

Wales to a 'broad and balanced' curriculum. The inclusion of PE as a compulsory subject throughout the 5–16 curriculum was viewed, by many, as a major achievement for the subject. The future of PE, underpinned by principles of equity, seemed secure. The procedures for making the National Curriculum for Physical Education (NCPE) seemed to provide an opportunity for physical educationalists to build on emerging developments, such as new approaches to games teaching and the introduction of health-related exercise initiatives, to establish a curriculum that would ensure breadth and balance in the context of PE and signal a commitment to raising standards of its teaching and learning in all schools.

However, for a variety of reasons (Penney, 1994; Evans and Penney, 1994b), not least of which was government interference in the 'making' of the NCPE texts, many of these opportunities were 'lost', either removed from the texts by Ministers of State or by government agencies like Schools Curriculum and Assessment Authority (SCAA), fearful either of the costs of the recommendations or their ideological intent. The remaining text of the NCPE now reinforces a very narrow and 'traditional' definition of PE as comprising a set of separate and distinct areas of activity and openly accords the highest status to that area that has long dominated the PE curriculum in state schools, namely, competitive team games. Nowhere does the text prompt teachers to reflect on present provision, or consider how or why they teach. Rather, with the underlying concern resting with the resource implications of recommendations, the emphasis has been placed on 'flexibility' in the requirements; the stress has been on accommodating within the NCPE the vast differences in PE provision in different schools, particularly with respect to the range of activities enjoyed by pupils. Although this appears to 'liberate' teachers and schools, it also effectively means that achieving breadth and balance in the NCPE rests with the 'accident' of a teacher's interests and predisposition and the level of support and resources schools can offer in the implementation of the NCPE. Consequently, although some children in some schools will clearly benefit and see the promises of the NC fulfilled, others will not. As scarce resources and competition commingle, innovative approaches in pedagogy, curriculum design and delivery, may be very hard to find and teachers may be 'encouraged' to either 'accommodate' NC demands or regress to staid and familiar practices that are both cheap and easy pedagogically to deliver.

Having been largely excluded from its development, few PE teachers viewed the arrival of the NCPE very positively. Arriving without resources, time and money to accompany it or to nurture and sustain its development in schools let alone foster the development of 'alternative' approaches to implementation, PE prospects of 'progress' seem pretty remote. Furthermore, in the context of LMS and OE, 'progressive' or 'alternative' approaches to curriculum design and delivery may not be attractive. Schools cannot ignore the criteria laid down by central government upon which the delivery of the NC will be publicly judged. National tests are becoming the 'obvious' criteria by which schools' performance in 'the market' are judged – expressed in 'league tables' from which 'value added' are excluded. The fact is that the game is not being played on an even surface, that teams vary in their composition and the resources they have to draw on. To make matters worse, the focus on 'results' may further reinforce subject divisions and emphasize the status differential of academic and practical subjects as well as the 'product' rather than 'processes' of education. This may further reinforce the low status of PE and make investment in its curriculum development even less likely. It may also force PE teachers who, like their academic counterparts, are experiencing pressures towards 'marketability' and public account-ability, towards the adoption of a questionable and limited criteria of 'success'. Already we are finding that in some schools performance in extra-curricular PE, invariably in team games, has been emphasized above all else that comprises the content and purposes of PE (Penney, 1994; Penney and Evans, 1994b). We do not have to deny either the importance of this aspect of PE provision or the needs of the elite performer. But if this one aspect of PE is exaggerated at the expense of all else in PE, it will cater for the needs of all too few children. Sadly, a well-established bias in the PE curriculum has been reinforced rather than challenged by ERA's demands. Post-ERA schools may have neither the inclination nor the resource to develop an 'active school' (see Chapter 8 in this volume) or adopt any other innovatory approach to the teaching of PE. At worst, 'market rules' threaten to put an end to the many positive developments that have emerged in PE in the past decade, sanctified by assumptions about the universal goodness of the properties of competitive team games.

Devolution of the funding *and* management of education has also threatened the development of PE in other respects. The quality of a subject and the sophistication of its pedagogy is, we would argue, largely determined by the quality of its personnel, its teachers, and the knowledge and expertise that they bring to the subject via ITT and later programmes of further professional development. However, in recent years, moneys for in-service training (INSET) have become yet another area of pronounced competition within schools. Support for attendance at INSET activities is no longer guaranteed and neither is the provision of a quality ITT. LEAs like schools are playing by 'new' market rules, post-ERA. Their concerns are also for 'survival' and 'cost efficiency'. INSET courses are provided only if there are enough customers to cover costs and thus warrant provision of the service. Planning is driven more by economic expediency than educational need. LEAs can no longer afford subsidization; the generation of profit is the central driving concern. PE advisers and inspectors are themselves a 'luxury' not all LEAs have been able to afford (Evans and Penney, 1994a).

INVESTMENT IN THE MARKET?[2]

In the context of uncertainty surrounding the availability of any INSET for PE, it would not be unreasonable to suppose that ITT post-ERA would emerge as a critical area for investment, to ensure that the ERA and the National Curriculum in particular fulfil their promise of 'raising standards in education'. Yet this has not been the case. A whole range of legislation has ensured that the knowledge base of ITT has been systematically eroded as the input of higher education to teacher training has been severely restricted and controlled, and moves towards a clearer identification of teachers as technicians rather than professionals have occurred.

Redefining the meaning of teacher education has been a fundamental part of this process, as has been greater centralization of the curriculum of teacher education. (In the mid-1980s, the Council for the Accreditation of Teacher Education (CATE) was created. Also there have been various attempts to 'open up' (de-regulate) routes into teaching, e.g. in the late 1980s, the Licensed and Articled Teachers schemes; and the

'Mums army', 1993. Thereby, we proceed with the process of de-professionalizing teacher education in the early 1990s (Maguire and Ball, 1993). The detail of how we reached where we are now in terms of policy prescriptions for ITT in England and Wales has been provided elsewhere (Maguire and Ball, 1993; Evans, 1995b). Quite spectacular changes have beset those institutions involved with initial teacher education over the last decade. A series of steps (e.g. in 1983 *The Content of Initial Training*, followed by the White Paper on *Teaching Quality*, then *Circular 3/84*, the *Green Paper 1988* advocating the Licensed and Articled Teacher schemes; see Gilroy, 1992) effectively began a process of reconstructing the structure of teacher education, defining course content and concomitantly the conception of what it is to be a teacher educator. These changes peaked when Kenneth Clarke, then Secretary of State for Education, stated in a speech to the annual North of England Education Conference on 4 January 1992 that he proposed that the vast majority of initial teacher education courses would be shortened to nine months and be located in schools and away from colleges, polytechnics and universities. It was announced that he planned to make mainstream post-graduate courses 80 per cent school-based (subsequently reduced to 60 per cent) (DFE, 1992). The move to three-year BEds is also gathering momentum everywhere. These proposals were subsequently developed into a *Consultation Document* issued on 28 January 1992 (DFE, 1992). As Gilroy (1992) points out, the proposals contained in that document represented a dramatic and abrupt reversal of the direction taken by developments in the policy for teacher education over the last 100 years. It had taken teacher education 150 years to develop from a rejection of a school-based pupil–teacher apprenticeship scheme to one whereby students were inducted into the profession of teaching through structured combination of training and education in both school classrooms and institutions of higher education (Gilroy, 1992). A situation had been achieved in which virtually all new entrants to the teaching profession were graduates who had experienced professional training in education. This was clearly a situation that the government was very anxious to now change.

Stuart Maclure (TES, 1993), the former editor of *The Times Educational Supplement*, reminds us that the thing to remember about government plans for teacher training is that there is a plot and a sub-plot. The plot, he says, is straightforward. Get more teacher education into schools. Give practising teachers a bigger part to play in the professional preparation of their future colleagues. There are many reasons why this could be good news. Certainly many teachers would testify to the merits and benefits of developing closer relationships, a 'partnership' with teachers in schools as part of the enterprise of developing a quality PE. However, the sub-plot is more sinister. It is, as far as is possible, to take teacher training out of higher education and ultimately to sever the connections between the study of education in higher education and its practice in school. This we contend is a deeply damaging idea. John Patten's *Proposals* (DFE/Welsh Office, 1993), most of them now embedded in the Education Act (1994), were a further advance on Kenneth Clarke's proposals, recommending not just a 'school-based' teacher education but a 'school-centred training', a form of practice in which relationships between schools and higher education are not just further weakened but potentially dismantled. The initial composition of the English Teacher Training Agency (TTA), announced in September 1994, with Baroness Cox and Professor O'Hear as their research and scholarly vanguard, should alert us to the fact that the 'common sense' represented by Gillian Shephard (the Conservative

Minister for Education) in this matter, is still in perilous equilibrium with these forces which see college-based training as the enemy. How has this come about?

BACK TO BASICS

Government policy in a liberal democracy derives from a whole variety of influences, opportunities and constraints, and it would be a mistake to see new right influences on the ERA as entirely driven by clearly articulated ideological positions. However, under the Thatcher government, various new right think tanks – notably the Centre for Policy Studies and the Hillgate Group (Maguire and Ball, 1993) – expressing either neo-liberal or neo-conservative ideals (Ball, 1990), have had a considerable influence on policy in ITT. Among their various arguments are that ITT courses place too little emphasis on the learning of subject knowledge, too much emphasis on educational theory, are obsessed with race, gender and inequality, produce students who have no respect for traditional values, are too expensive and are ineffective (Whitty, 1993, p. 265). These views have been expressed alongside and complementary to the emerging proposal for new routes into teaching of the 1980s and 1990s. These unrepresentative, unelected cabals have had a powerful impact on government policy on education with views such as these:

> Teachers with Cert.Ed. after their names have studied nonsense for three years. Those with BEd for three or four years. Those with PGCE have had a rest for one year studying nonsense after doing a proper subject and those with MEd or Adv Dip Ed have returned for super nonsense. (Anderson, 1982, p. 11)

To these individuals, teacher education is a waste of time. Teachers are over-trained and badly trained. Disturbingly, such views were neither contested nor refined by those given political authority and responsibility for the welfare of teachers and the education system as a whole. Take this view for example:

> Barmy theory has led teachers into dangerous paths of pedagogical untruth. As is well known, teachers do not need training, they just need to be able to walk into a school and read the instructions delivered from the centre. It may help to know a 'subject' but having any ideas about how children learn, or develop, or feel, should be seen as subversive activity. Teacher educators who have peddled their subversions should be hunted down and hanged by the entrails of the last educational sociologists. (Stones, 1992, p. 111)

This is Kenneth Clarke the British Secretary of State for Education, delivering a speech to teacher educators with the rubric *Check on Delivery* in January 1992. As Gilroy (1992) points out, the rubric says it all. In this view, teaching is delivery of a commodity, a process which does not need theory or professionals of any standing. It needs effective managers, educational technicians. In this discourse of derision, theoretically informed professional teachers and teacher educators, are defined as either mad or bad.

Given statements of intent such as this, teacher educators in the UK have had every right to be worried for their professional well-being. Of course, to be paranoid does not preclude the possibility that someone is out to get you! Physical educationalists have needed to look over their shoulders given 'leadership' of this kind. As Gilroy (1992) points out, virtually all the shibboleths of the cabal who had Kenneth Clarke's ear can be identified in that January speech, the material of which was then re-presented in a *Consultation Document* (DES, 1992). The whole process of teacher training was to 'be based on a more equal partnership between school teachers and tutors . . . with the schools themselves playing a much bigger part' (DES, 1992, p. 7). The 'partnership' was defined as 'one in which the schools and its teachers are in the lead in the whole of the training process, from the initial design of a course through to the assessment of the performance of the individual student' (DES, 1992, p. 8). Of the secondary postgraduate Certificate in Education (PGCE), 80 per cent (later 60 per cent) was to be school-based (i.e. four days a week). Resources for teacher training would move from higher education to schools identified by certain criteria (academic results, staying-on rates, truancy figures and so on) and would include private schools. These changes were to take place with effect from September 1992 with all secondary PGCE courses meeting their requirements by September 1994. The length of the BEd/BA was to be reduced and these courses subjected to the 80 per cent ruling for the school-based elements of their work.

John Patten's *Proposals for the Reform of Initial Teacher Training* continued the job began by Kenneth Clarke in 1992, but the pace of change increased, the pressure intensified and the stakes raised even higher (Maguire and Ball, 1993). Patten's proposals marked another stage in the redefinition and reconstruction of the work of teacher educators and the professional standing of teachers. Again, we have to look beneath the surface rhetorical justification of these proposals to see what ends they are intended to serve. At a glance, the proposals reflected:

- a concern to raise educational standards and levels of skill, and to equip people to cope with change;
- a growing emphasis on the competencies necessary for effective practice;
- the importance of training being closely linked to its practical application;
- the need for continuing training and development through working life; and
- increasing the effectiveness of expenditure on training (DFE, 1993)

Few, we guess, would disagree with these as statements of intent. The claim is that 'higher standards' will be achieved through reforms which ensure that 'teachers have the key classroom skills to maintain discipline, introduce pupils to the National Curriculum; and use testing and assessment to improve their own teaching as well as keep pupils and their parents informed about progress' (DFE, 1993, p. 1). They imply a transfer of power from higher education to schools and a transferred location for much of the learning involved in ITT. The implication is that by moving students from universities into schools, they automatically receive a more relevant training in the practice of teaching. What model of the student is implicit in this locational shift? What assumptions are being made about the nature of what is to be learned? (McCulloch, 1993, p. 295).

It is also worth noting what support there was in 'the market' for these changes. There is little evidence to suggest that either the 'consumers' (parents) or the 'producers' of education (teachers and teacher educators) wanted these reforms. However, such was the government's commitment to these policies that, in October 1994, the Teacher Training Agency (TTA) was established to 'encourage' school-centred initial teacher training (SCITT), with a statutory responsibility not only for the central funding of all courses of ITT in England but also for research. The TTA, which will run all teacher education under regulations made by the Secretary of State, will have to assume, in the face of HMI advice on previous schemes, that a wholly school-based system of initial teacher education will prove successful and that less time can be spent on the ITT of teachers. No educational justification has been thought necessary for this initiative. Not for the first time in recent years, neither 'fact' (in the form of research evidence or informed opinion) nor reason has been allowed to stand in the way of central government's ideologically driven judgements on teaching and ITT (Simon, 1988).

Again we need to read recent education legislation, and John Patten's *Proposals for the Reform of Initial Teacher Training* in particular, in context. Like earlier attempts to discipline teacher education (see, for example, DFE, 1992, *Circular 9/92*) the proposals sought to amplify and extend specific elements of the conservative project. 'It tightens up the regimes of control in and around teacher education and furthermore attempts to shut down any gaps or spaces for accommodations or subversions' (Maguire and Ball, 1993, p. 11). It is therefore not surprising that they met with stern resistance from many quarters. For example, in a scathing attack on the proposals the *TES* (1993) (not noted for its radical positioning) commented that 'even by the standards to which we have unhappily grown accustomed lately, the government's *Proposals for the Reform of Teacher Training* is a singularly dishonest document'. It goes on, '[T]he need' we are told 'to raise the professional skill of new teachers has been pointed up [*sic*] by recent evidence from the Office of Standards in Education (OFSTED) that around a [*sic*] third of lessons taken by new entrants were unsatisfactory.' The *TES* pointed out that HMI 'pointed up' no such thing. The opening words of HMI's own summary *The New Teacher In School* are: 'In 1992, over 90 per cent of head teachers considered their new teachers to have been adequately prepared for their first teaching post and over 70 per cent of lessons taught by new teachers were considered by HMI as satisfactory or better.' In the body of their report HMI say that this proportion closely matches that of teachers in general 'For any training system to match the attainments of an established profession is an indication of its competence not the reverse' (*TES*, 1993, 17 September).

The proposals also offered the prospect of a new style restricted 'QTS' for nursery and infants. In Maclure's view (*TES*, 1993), this was the thin end of a thick wedge to separate primary from secondary training, and to introduce three-year BEd courses including a six-subject BEd to prepare teachers for work across the primary curriculum, both creating considerable stir within universities.

Will such changes mean that PE teachers will be taught what to teach, but not what they need to know to be able to teach? Will they lead to the preparation of teachers sophisticated in their understanding of children and young people, knowledgeable of the relationships between their physical, social and cultural development, able to innovate as well as manage and sustain order and control?

CONTROL IN THE MARKET: THE 'KNOWLEDGE BASE' OF PHYSICAL EDUCATION

The conception of knowledge implicit in John Patten's *Proposals for the Reform of Initial Teacher Training* also deserves serious consideration in our appraisal of the future of PE. The document (DFE, 1993, p. 4) states that courses will be required to:

equip students with essential 'competencies', including the subject knowledge and professional and personal skills which new teachers need to manage, maintain order and teach effectively in their classrooms. The development of complete profiles of new teachers' competencies will help ease the transition from initial training to induction.

Arguably, no one would contest the view that teachers need to be competent. But again we have to be clear about what this term really means. As McNamara (1992) points out, it has been a fundamental and dominant assumption within government education policy on the curriculum in recent years that the 'outcomes' of teacher education courses can be articulated in and as a set of competencies. Teachers have been encouraged to conceptualize teaching as a shopping list of constituent components which relate to composite skills and knowledge. None of this would be objectionable to most teacher educators so long as they are regarded as a simple minimum rather than an adequate conceptualization of what it means to be a teacher (Maguire and Ball, 1993). However, as McNamara points out, these competencies are now assumed to be measurable and amenable to expression as profiles which map out student teachers' abilities at the completion of their initial training. In his proposals, for example, the Secretary of State says:

> all teachers should start their careers with profiles of competencies, which set out their professional capabilities and give a picture of relative strengths and weaknesses. Such developments will help those recruiting newly qualified teachers to plan induction and development programmes, and can form the basis for a permanent record of the teacher's professional development throughout his or her career. (DFE, 1993, p. 16)

Again, we have to see this proposal not simply as an attempt to state the knowledge base of teaching but as a means of further deregulating entry to the teaching profession. McNamara (1992) points out, the switch of emphasis from the process of teacher training to a focus upon competencies has a number of advantages for policy makers and politicians, but few, we suggest for teachers.

> First, it provides a means of (superficially) demonstrating to the lay public that teacher training courses are being made 'relevant' to the needs of children and the schools. Second, by shifting the emphasis from course process to course outcomes it may be possible to persuade some teacher trainers that they have more autonomy and control over the training process, so long as their students manifest the appropriate competencies at the completion of their course. (McNamara, 1992, p. 16)

McNamara cautions us against this because, embedded in this view, is a more fundamental challenge to teacher education. He goes on, once the emphasis is placed upon 'outcomes' the training process itself is called into question and is 'up for grabs'.

> There is no longer any difficulty in reconciling criteria so that they relate to different routes into teaching be they conventional or non-conventional modes of training. In this way, the institutional context and form of teacher training ceases to be important; what matters are the competencies students can demonstrate after the completion of a variety of training experiences. Moreover, any form of training becomes problematic; a prospective teacher who has worked in industry, the services, or other walks of life may be presumed to already possess many of the required competencies and, so it may be argued, training may need to offer little more than provide the requisite extra competencies. (McNamara, 1992, p. 273)

This view is not far fetched. It undergirds the *Proposals for the Reform of Initial Teacher Training*. Prescribing teacher education in terms of competency outcomes not only determines the structure and content of teacher education, it also ensures that teacher trainers are no longer free to decide how to train teachers as they judge professionally appropriate. McNamara reminds us that the *Consultation Document* (DES, 1992) statements removed reference to gender and multicultural issues, dimensions of teacher education which many teacher educators consider it essential for their courses to address (ibid, p. 274). However, achieving competence is not the same as being an effective teacher. Personally, we share McNamara's view that teacher education:

> involves assisting individual students, whatever their particular repertoires of dispositions and aptitudes, to develop the all-round competence which will enable them to teach effectively in the variety of contexts they will encounter during their careers.

This requires more than:

> instilling in students units of competence, made up of a number of elements of competence (with associated performance criteria) (Employment department group, 1989). (McNamara, 1992, p. 283)

Instead, it warrants practices informed by knowledge and understanding and suitable amounts of appropriate theory. Like Whitty (1993, p. 269) we would argue that:

> we should neither abandon conventional routes nor oppose the development of new ones. While we do not need homogeneity of provision, we do need a comprehensive structure for teacher education, so that questions of resourcing and quality assurance can be tackled on a coherent and consistent basis.

BACK TO THE FUTURE 2

So again we must consider what recent ITT legislation is designed to achieve. Will the 'de-theorizing of teacher education, the privileging of the practical over the critical and through this the de-skilling of teachers' (Maguire and Ball, 1993, p. 19) raise standards in education? Or, will it simply break the connection between higher education and the training of teachers? Will it curb the move towards an all-graduate profession, undermine the professionalism of teachers and reduce teacher education to a functional and instrumental set of concerns 'emphasizing only what will be professionally useful to teachers',

> a form of instrumental knowledge which is typically portrayed as neutral and value free, where education is simply a means to given ends and all that is needed is a check list of competencies which need to be achieved. (Maguire and Ball, 1993)

Sadly, ERA legislation (and the National Curriculum in particular) may have facilitated this process. On the surface, the knowledge base for early years teaching, for PE and some other subjects, as listed in National Curriculum documentation looks relatively simple. It is all too easy to infer from a cursory glance at the ring-binders that contain the National Curriculum subject specifications, that teachers can make do with a brisk year or two (three at most) on-the-job training provided they have had some previous experience of children, or involvement in sport. Is this the quality of teacher, teaching and training that we want to see?

CONCLUSION

Even if we disagree profoundly with some or all of the above analysis, we cannot ignore the questions being asked. Will the types of training proposed by recent legislation on ITT attract good candidates? Will it produce better educated and more competent teachers? Will those teachers have been given a sound basis for continued career-long professional development? Will the 'school-centred training' that the reforms are intended to promote, build on and extend a widely accepted commitment to partnership between tutors and teachers? Will shortened training courses send clear messages to potential recruits about the status and attractiveness of PE teaching? Will they take account of the modest educational performance of many candidates for such courses and the need for adequate time to be available in which to equip them with the necessary confidence and skills to work in difficult conditions, and provide support for them during periods of school-based study? Both ITT and the programmes of continuing professional education, mainly higher degree work, provided by universities and colleges are invaluable opportunities for teachers to examine, analyse and criticize both their own actions as well as official policies and actions. This may not always be convenient or pleasant for schools, politicians and administrators, but it is a proper aspect of higher education's responsibilities (Edwards, 1993) and a safeguard for democracy. Will such opportunities continue to feature in the experience of teachers of PE? In the eyes of some, the ERA and more recent education legislation has already seriously damaged the opportunities for teachers to develop pedagogies that are reflective and innovative. As Stones points out:

> The deprecation of pedagogy is continued in the way practical experience is held forth as the means by which teaching quality is to be enhanced. Coming through loud and clear is that it is practical teaching experience that counts and the best way to keep teacher trainers up to scratch is to return them to the real world of the classroom. There is absolutely no recognition of the need to develop a rigorous, theory based practically oriented pedagogy. It clearly is not necessary. All that is needed is to know the subject and have enough exposure to classrooms. Is this to be the ignorant outcome of the wealth of research finding on the need for a deep understanding of the way children think and learn (and don't learn) before one can teach them the academic discipline one is privy to? Any practice that arises from the fiats enunciated here [reference to legislation on ITT] could set back the development of pedagogy and teacher training for years to come. (Stones, quoted in Smith, 1993, p. 55)

There may be places in the future where the narrow instrumentalism of the new right is kept at bay and where space for reflective teaching and teacher education remains. Like Hartley (1993, p. 87), we would maintain that much here will depend on the strength of local and national economies. If difficulties with public expenditure persist or deepen, then the percentage of Gross National Product (GNP) to be spent on education, including teacher education, will be prone to further inspection. The principles of relevance, certainty, cheapness and choice, rather than educational opportunity and need will drive practice in ITT and schools (Smith, 1993, p. 87). This is not what we need.

Given the reality of cultural diversity in the UK, a number of options are available to teachers and teacher educators. They can ignore diversity and continue to prepare teachers for some mythical homogeneous society where everyone shares the characteristics and sporting interests of the dominant culture group. Alternatively, they can, as Tabachnick and Zeichner (1993, p. 116) contend, develop teachers' cultural sensitivities and prepare them to teach cross-culturally. In this pluralist response, issues related to cultural diversity – including the idea that there are 'localized' conceptions and expectations of 'the body', physical activity and sport – have to be infused into the entire curriculum of teacher education and schools, and teachers have to be taught how to incorporate the cultural resources that their students bring to the school into their instructional programmes. We share Hagele's (1994, p. 8) view that traditional (sport) activities, 'with their orientation towards performance, competition, youth, men, fairness, and team spirit' have, in recent years, been relativized by women, older people, marginal social groups, and people involved with fitness and therapeutic sport. Children and young people, like many adults, are now driven by concepts of self-realization, participation and co-operation, as well as the individualization of lifestyle. They also desire more sensuality in everyday sport and physical activity, as well as greater co-operation, and variety in games and physical activities, as exemplified in dance. Can these changes be expressed through the centralized prescriptions of a NCPE and a rhetoric that looks *back* to 'basics' rather than *forward* to progressive ideals? We think not. If physical educationalists (teachers and teacher educators) are to empower children and young people with feelings of confidence and control over their own bodies (irrespective of their ability, size or shape) and provide them with a knowledge of their and others' potential for fitness, health and involvement in physical activity and sport, then they will certainly have to 're-discover' the equity principles that have been lost from the text of the NCPE (DES, 1991) and find the space in ITT, INSET and school timetables, to reflect the needs and expectations of the individuals in their care and the communities from which they derive. This will not only require pedagogies that are theoretically sophisticated, sensitive, flexible and capable of innovation. A precondition of their existence is a commitment from central government to levels of resourcing that are sufficient to ensure that all children irrespective of their culture, class location or 'market rules', receive the PE that they need and deserve.

NOTES

1. This paper draws on data from research, directed by John Evans and Dawn Penney, investigating 'The Impact of the Education Reform Act on the Provision of Sport and PE in Schools'. The project is funded by the Economic and Social Research Council and the Leverhulme Trust. We are grateful for their support.
2. This section of the paper draws on and develops text first published in Evans (1995a) Reconstructing teacher education, in the *European Journal of Physical Education Review* (in press). We are grateful to the editor for his permission to use material from that article in this paper.

REFERENCES

Anderson, D. (1982) *Detecting Bad Schools: A Guide for Normal Parents*. London: The Social Affairs Unit.

Apple, M. (1993) *Official Knowledge. Democratic Education in a Conservative Age*. New York: Routledge.

Ball, S. (1990) *Politics and Policy Making in Education*. London: Routledge.

Ball, S. (1993a) 'Education policy, power relations and teachers' work', *British Journal of Educational Studies*, **41**, 106–21.

Ball, S. (1993b) 'Education markets, choice and social class: the market as a class strategy in the UK and the USA', *British Journal of Sociology of Education*, **14**, 3–19.

Bowe, R., Ball, S. and Gold, A. (1992) *Reforming Education and Changing Schools*. London: Routledge.

DES (1991) *Physical Education for Ages 5 to 16*, Department of Education and Science/Welsh Office.

DES (1992) *The Reform of Initial Teacher Training (Consultation Document)*, 40, London: Department of Education and Science.

DFE (1992) *Initial Teacher Training (Secondary Phase)*, Circular 9/92, London: Department for Education.

DFE (1993) *The Government's Proposals for the Reform of Initial Teacher Training*, Department for Education/Welsh Office.

Edwards, A. (1993) 'Change for the worse', *Times Educational Supplement*, 29 October, p. 5.

Evans, J. (1995a) 'Reconstructing teacher education', *European Journal of Physical Education Review*, in press.

Evans, J. (1995b) 'Schooling in the fast lane', *British Journal of Sociology of Education*, in press.

Evans, J. and Davies, B. (1990) 'Power to the people? The great Education Reform Act and tomorrow's schools: A critical and comparative perspective', in Lauder, H. and Wylie, C. (eds), *Towards Successful Schooling*. London: Falmer Press, pp. 53–71.

Evans, J. and Davies, B. (1992) 'Physical education post ERA in a postmodern society', in Evans, J. (ed.), *Equality, Education and Physical Education*. London: Falmer Press, pp. 239–42.

Evans, J. and Penney, D. (1994a) 'What ever happened to good advice?', *British Educational Research Journal*, **20**, 519–33.

Evans, J. and Penney, D. (1994b) 'The politics of pedagogy. Making a National Curriculum PE', *Journal of Education Policy*, **10**, 27–44.

Evans, J. and Penney, D. (1995) 'Physical education, restoration and the politics of sport', *Curriculum Studies*, **3**, 183–96.

Featherstone, M. (1988) 'In pursuit of the postmodern', *Theory, Culture and Society*, **5**, 195–217.

Giddens, A. (1991) *Modernity and Self Identity*. Oxford: Basil Blackwell.

Gilroy, D. (1992) 'The political rape of initial teacher education in England and Wales, a JET rebuttal', *Journal of Education for Teaching*, **18**, 5–23.

Gilroy, D. and Smith, M. (eds) (1993) *International Analyses of Teacher Education, Journal of Education for Teaching*. London: Cassell.

Guardian (1994) 'Sport for the best, not all', 29 September, p. 18.

Hargreaves, A. (1994) *Changing Teachers, Changing Schools*. London: Cassell.

Hagele, W. (1994) 'The crisis in sport', *International Journal of Physical Education*, **31**(2), 7–14.

Hartley, D. (1993) 'Confusions in teacher education: a postmodern condition?', in Gilroy, P. and Smith, M. (eds), *International Analyses of Teacher Education, Journal of Education for Teaching*, **19**, 83–95.

Jenkins, S. (1993) 'It's yesterday once more', *The Times*, October 13, p. 20.

Kellner, D. (1988) 'Postmodernism as social theory', *Theory, Culture and Society*, **5**, 2–3, 239–71.

Lawton, D. (1989) *Culture and the Curriculum*. London: Hodder and Stoughton.

McCulloch, M. (1993) 'Democratisation of teacher education: new forms of partnership for school based teacher education', in Gilroy, P. and Smith, M. (eds), *International Analyses of Teacher Education, Journal of Education for Teaching*, **19**, 293–305.

Machine, S. (1993) 'Fight this tooth and nail', *Times Educational Supplement*, June 18, p. 16.

McNamara, D. (1992) 'The Reform of Teacher Education in England and Wales: Teacher Competence, Panacea or Rhetoric?', *Journal of Education for Teaching*, **18**(3), 273–85.

McRae, S. (1993) *Cohabiting Mothers*. London: Policy Studies Institute.

Maguire, M. and Ball, S. (1993) Teacher Education and Education Policy in England. Unpublished paper, King's College, London.

Penney, D. (1994) 'No Change in a New ERA?' The Impact of the Education Reform Act on the Provision of PE and Sport in State Schools. PhD thesis, University of Southampton.

Penney, D. and Evans, J. (1994a) 'Changing Structures; Changing Rules: Implications for Curriculum Planning in Schools'. Paper presented at the *CEDAR International Conference 'Changing Educational Structures: Policy and Practice'*, University of Warwick, April.

Penney, D. and Evans, J. (1994b) 'Controlling management and managing control: autonomy and control in an imperfect market'. Paper presented at the *BERA Annual Conference*, September, Oxford.

Penney, D. and Evans, J., with Hennink, M. (1994) *Implementation of the NCPE: Report of Findings of Questionnaire Survey of State Secondary Schools*, ESRC Project Report, University of Loughborough.

Shilling, C. (1993) 'The Body, Class and Social Inequalities', in Evans, J. (ed.), *Equality, Education and Physical Education*. London: Falmer Press, pp. 55–74.

Simon, B. (1988) *Bending the Rules*. London: Lawrence and Wishart.

Smith, M. (1993) 'Ed Stones and JET: a retrospective', in Gilroy, P. and Smith, M. (eds), *International Analyses of Teacher Education, Journal of Education for Teaching*, **19**, 49–59.

Stones, E. (1992) Editorial, *Journal of Education for Teaching*, **18**, 111–13.

Tabachnick, B.R. and Zeichner, K.M. (1993) 'Preparing teachers for cultural diversity', in Gilroy, P. and Smith, M. (eds), *International Analyses of Teacher Education, Journal of Education for Teaching*, **19**, 113–25.

The Times Educational Supplement (1993) 'A quango too far', 17 September, p. 18.

Wragg, T. (1988) *Education in the Market Place: The Ideology Behind the 1988 Education Bill*, London: Jason Press for the NUT.

Whitty, G. (1993) 'Education reform and teacher education in England in the 1990s', in Gilroy, P. and Smith, M. (eds), *International Analyses of Teacher Education, Journal of Education for Teaching*, **19**, 263–77.

Chapter 2

Growth, Maturation and Physical Education

Neil Armstrong and Alison McManus

INTRODUCTION

Children are not mini-adults. They are growing and maturing and their physical needs and capabilities are changing as they progress through the four Key Stages of the National Curriculum. With a prescribed curriculum, it is vital that teachers understand and recognize individual differences in rate of growth and maturation if they are to deliver the high quality PE programme to which young people are entitled. This chapter aims to provide an overview of children's and adolescents' growth and maturation with reference to their physical performance, motor performance and physical activity. It is envisaged that it will inform subsequent contributions focusing specifically on PE in each of the four Key Stages.

GROWTH AND MATURATION

The terms growth and maturation are often used synonymously but despite being closely related they describe different processes. Growth refers to an increase in the size of the body or any of its parts. Maturation refers to the tempo and timing of progress toward the mature biological state. Growth does not cease when maturity is attained but continues throughout adult life as in nearly every tissue and organ there is a recurring cycle of growth, death and replacement. All parts of the human body do not grow at the same rate and therefore the relative size and weights of tissues and organs change.

The most obvious change from birth to adulthood occurs in stature (height). Figure 2.1 describes the rate of gain (or velocity of growth) in stature; the figure illustrates that although both sexes follow the same pattern of growth there are significant differences in both timing and magnitude of change.

Height increases rapidly during the first two years of life and by the age of 2 the child has attained about 50 per cent of adult stature. The rate of increase in height, however, falls continuously from birth onwards and reaches its lowest point just before

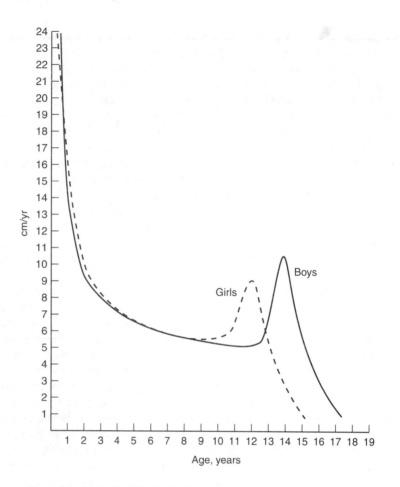

Figure 2.1   *Typical individual velocity curves for stature in boys and girls. Curves reprinted from Tanner et al. (1966) with permission.*

the initiation of the adolescent growth spurt. The timing of the initiation of the spurt is subject to wide individual variations. It may occur as early as 7.7 years or as late as 10.0 years of age in girls. The normal range for boys is 8.6 to 12.4 years of age. On average, the growth spurt occurs almost two years earlier in girls (9.0 years) than in boys (10.7 years). In the year preceding his spurt, the average boy grows about 5.0 cm in height and then increases in stature by about 7.0 cm in the first year of his spurt, by about 9.0 cm in the second year and by about 7.0 cm in the final year. After this, the rate of growth rapidly decreases to approximately 3.0 cm in the year following the spurt and to around 2.0 cm in subsequent years until adult height is attained at about 18 years of age. In girls, the velocity of growth is somewhat lower, at about 6.0, 8.0 and 6.0 cm per year during the three-year period of the spurt. Girls attain adult height about two years earlier than boys. The peak rate of growth in height – peak height velocity (PHV) – occurs at approximately 11.9 years in girls and 14.2 years in boys, but the time of PHV may range from 10.3 to 13.2 years in girls and 11.9 to 16.2 years in boys.

The sex difference in young adult stature of about 13.0 cm is not primarily due to the adolescent growth spurt as boys only gain an extra 3.0 cm or so during this period. Boys, however, have the advantage of two years extra pre-adolescent growth at a rate of 5.0 cm per year and this accounts for most of the adult differences in stature.

In the first year of life, trunk length is the fastest growing component of stature, whereas from then until puberty the legs account for 66 per cent of the total increase in height. Growth in leg length ceases earlier than growth in trunk length; trunk growth therefore makes a greater contribution to increase in stature during the spurt. During early adolescence, youngsters have relatively long legs but the appearance of long-leggedness disappears with the subsequent increase in trunk length (or sitting height). The leg length of girls is, on average, slightly longer than that of boys for a short period in early adolescence. Boys normally surpass girls in leg length by age 12 years but they do not catch up with girls in sitting height until about 14 years of age. At adolescence some youngsters have relatively large hands and feet, but by the time the spurt has ended, hands and feet are a little smaller in proportion to arms, legs and overall height.

At puberty, differences in body shape become apparent between the sexes and one of the most marked changes concerns the shoulders and hips. Girls experience a large adolescent spurt in hip width whereas boys have a particularly marked spurt in shoulder width. As the pelvis broadens, girls' hips move further apart and away from the mid-line. This is one of the reasons why older girls tend to throw out their heels when they run, as their thighs have to create a greater angle to bring their knees together. After the growth spurt, boys have significantly broader shoulders than girls. As even small differences in shoulder breadth can result in large differences in upper trunk muscle mass, this partially explains why strength differences between older boys and girls are much greater in the upper body than in the legs. When greater upper body muscle mass is combined with the greater leverage of longer arms, one of the reasons for boys' generally better performance in throwing, rowing and racquet sports becomes apparent. On the other hand, the broadening of the hips in girls lowers their centre of gravity. This provides greater stability and is perhaps the primary reason why girls generally have better balance than boys.

Growth in body mass differs from that of height during the pre-adolescent period; from about the age of 2 years there is a slight, but constantly accelerating, rate of increase prior to the adolescent growth spurt. The spurt in mass is similar to that in stature but normally occurs a few months later (Figure 2.2). The spurt in boys' body mass is primarily due to gains in skeletal tissue and muscle mass with fat mass remaining relatively stable. Girls experience less dramatic rises in skeletal tissue and muscle mass but a continuous rise in fat mass. Girls gain on average 33.5 kg between the ages of 7 and 18 years while boys experience an increase in mass of about 43.8 kg over the same time period.

Muscle mass comprises about 25 per cent of body mass at birth. It increases with age and marked sexual differences become apparent during and after the adolescent growth spurt. The peak muscle growth velocity occurs later than the PHV and is often coincidental with the peak velocity of shoulder width. Although girls do have an adolescent spurt in muscle mass, it is much less dramatic than that of boys. Nevertheless, as girls' spurt occurs earlier than that of boys, they often have more muscle mass than boys for a short period. It has been estimated that relative muscle

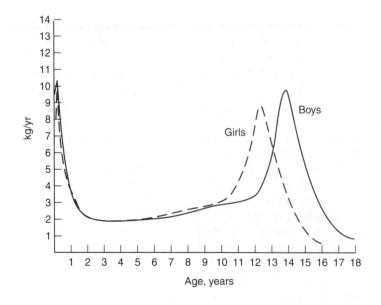

Figure 2.2 *Typical individual velocity curves for body mass in boys and girls. Curves reprinted from Tanner et al. (1966) with permission.*

mass increases from 42 per cent to 54 per cent of body mass in boys between 5 and 17 years. It increases from 40 per cent to 45 per cent of body mass in girls between 5 and 13 years and then, in relative terms, declines after 13 years of age. This is due to an increase in fat accumulation during female adolescence.

At birth, 10–12 per cent of total body mass is fat. During childhood girls have only slightly more body fat than boys, perhaps 18 per cent and 16 per cent of body mass respectively at the age of about 8 years. During the adolescent growth spurt, girls' body fat increases to about 25 per cent of body mass while boys decline to about 12–14 per cent body fat. This extra fat may be advantageous to girls in some situations. It aids buoyancy, it helps to maintain body temperature and provides a significant energy store. However, in activities which require moving body mass on land girls are generally penalized for carrying excess fat mass. The fat increase at puberty is largely responsible for the changing shape of the female adolescent and subsequent alterations in centre of gravity. These changes may adversely affect performance in activities such as gymnastics which may have been taken up several years earlier with a very different body shape and size.

At puberty, both boys and girls undergo changes in their secondary sex characteristics. Boys' penises and testicles enlarge and hair grows in the pubic region. The spurt in height begins about a year after the first testicular enlargement and PHV occurs after about a further year, when the penis is growing maximally and pubic hair is well advanced. Facial hair appears later and the breaking of the voice also happens relatively late in puberty. In girls, usually the first event to be noticed is the advent of the breast bud at about 11 years of age but there are wide individual variations. Pubic hair usually appears later but in a significant number of girls pubic hair appears before the breast bud.

No single means of assessment provides a complete description of maturity during adolescence but Tanner's (1962) five-point scale, based upon the development of secondary sex characteristics, is valuable and widely used. The extent of breast development in girls, genital development in boys and pubic hair growth in both sexes are visually assessed and rated. At stage 1, there is no evidence of development and the child is classified pre-pubertal. Stages 2, 3 and 4 depict specific changes in secondary sex characteristics during adolescence and Tanner (1962) provides appropriate photographs and precise descriptions of each stage for classification purposes. Stage 5 denotes the attainment of full sexual maturity. Progression through the stages, however, may range from two to five years and there is no consistent relationship between the age at which a child enters puberty and the rate of progression to full maturity.

Menarche, the age at which menstruation commences, occurs relatively late in puberty at about 13 years. Menarche is closely related to the height spurt although the hormonal significance is unknown. All girls start to menstruate when the height velocity is falling and, on average, menarche occurs at the time of maximum deceleration of growth in stature. Menarche may be delayed by intensive training but from a physiological perspective this should not in itself be harmful. However, if an intensively training youngster has a significantly delayed puberty together with amenorrhea, medical and nutritional advice may be necessary.

GROWTH, MATURATION AND PHYSICAL PERFORMANCE

In this section, we will focus upon some of the physiological factors which influence physical performance: aerobic fitness, anaerobic fitness, muscular strength and flexibility.

Aerobic fitness

Physical activity requires energy and the energy to support muscular contraction can be provided either aerobically (using oxygen) or anaerobically (without oxygen). Aerobic exercise is, of course, dependent upon pulmonary, cardiovascular and haematological components of oxygen delivery as well as the oxidative mechanisms of the exercising muscles. As maximal aerobic exercise is limited by peak oxygen consumption (peak $\dot{V}O_2$) this parameter is widely recognized as the best single index of aerobic fitness. The measurement of peak $\dot{V}O_2$ requires the child to exercise almost to exhaustion while his/her oxygen consumption is monitored, normally in a laboratory. Reliable data on children under the age of about 8 years are difficult to obtain and we will therefore limit our discussion to the more secure database of children and adolescents aged 8 to 16 years; see Armstrong and Welsman (1994) for a detailed analysis.

Boys' aerobic fitness (peak $\dot{V}O_2$) increases progressively in relation to chronological age, body size and maturation whereas girls' data show a similar but less consistent trend. At the beginning of Key Stage 3, boys' peak $\dot{V}O_2$ is about 18 per cent higher than that of girls. By the end of Key Stage 4, the difference between the sexes will have increased to about 37 per cent.

As most physical activity involves moving body mass from one place to another, to compare the peak $\dot{V}O_2$ of individuals who differ in body mass peak $\dot{V}O_2$ is usually expressed in relation to mass as mL/min.kg. Mass-related peak $\dot{V}O_2$ is the conventional method of expressing children's and adolescents' aerobic fitness but, recently, its validity has been challenged. Armstrong and Welsman (1994) suggest that the use of ratio standards (e.g. mass-related peak $\dot{V}O_2$) may have clouded our understanding of growth and maturational changes in peak $\dot{V}O_2$, and alternative statistical methods may be more appropriate to model and interpret functional changes in aerobic fitness during growth. However, for the purpose of this chapter, and to interpret the extant literature, we will confine discussion to conventional ratio standards.

When peak $\dot{V}O_2$ is expressed relative to body mass a different picture emerges from that apparent when absolute values are used. Boys' mass-related peak $\dot{V}O_2$ remains stable from pre-puberty through to post-puberty (about 49 mL/min.kg). In girls, however, from about the beginning of Key Stage 3, a gradual deterioration in aerobic fitness can be observed (about 45–39 mL/min.kg). This decline in girls' mass-related aerobic fitness is related to the accumulation of subcutaneous fat during maturity and for some early maturers it may be apparent during Key Stage 2.

The well-publicized belief that British children's and adolescents' aerobic fitness is low, and has deteriorated over time, stems from a misunderstanding of the concept of aerobic fitness and its assessment and interpretation. The peak $\dot{V}O_2$ values of British children and adolescents compare favourably with those of children and adolescents from elsewhere. Comparisons of recent data with earlier studies of similar groups of youngsters suggest that the peak $\dot{V}O_2$ of British children and adolescents has not deteriorated over the last fifty years; see Krahenbuhl *et al.* (1985) and Armstrong and Welsman (1994) for comparative data. The European Pediatric Work Physiology Group have expressed the view that a low mass-related peak $\dot{V}O_2$, in the absence of other health-related problems, may contribute to health risk. Risk levels of 35 mL/min.kg for boys and 30 mL/min.kg for girls were proposed. Less than 2 per cent of the children and adolescents tested in our laboratory during the last ten years could be classified as 'at risk' using these criteria. This is not to say that efforts should not be made to enhance further the aerobic fitness of children and adolescents, but there is little evidence to suggest that they are unfit.

Children are probably the fittest section of the population but, although their mass-related peak $\dot{V}O_2$ is at least as good as that of adults, their movements are less efficient, they have a lower metabolic scope (ratio of peak to resting oxygen consumption) and smaller stores of muscle glycogen. During prolonged aerobic exercise, children are therefore at a disadvantage when compared to adolescents and adults. A further consideration when comparing the potential of children to sustain aerobic exercise is the environmental conditions. Children have immature temperature regulatory systems which limit their ability to sweat and they also have large body surface areas compared to their muscle mass, which makes them particularly vulnerable at extremes of temperature.

Anaerobic fitness

Much less attention has been paid to the measurement and interpretation of children's and adolescents' anaerobic fitness than to their aerobic fitness despite the primacy of anaerobic energy during activities of high intensity and short duration. There are actually two anaerobic energy systems, both of which contribute to anaerobic performance. Very short, but intensive, exertion relies predominantly upon the high energy phosphate stores (adenosine triphosphate and creatine phosphate) in the muscles. These stores are, however, limited and able to support maximal exercise for only about five seconds. Longer high-intensity activity relies upon the breakdown within the muscles of glycogen (from carbohydrate in the diet) to pyruvic acid. This series of reactions, known as glycogenolysis, generates energy to support muscular contraction. It is most important near the beginning of exercise, when oxygen consumption is low, and during very intensive exercise, when the anaerobic production of pyruvic acid exceeds the capacity of the aerobic system to oxidize it. A build-up of pyruvic acid results in the formation of lactic acid which accumulates in the muscle and eventually brings muscular contraction to a halt.

Anaerobic performance is difficult to assess but the available evidence is unequivocal. Boys' anaerobic performance increases with age from childhood through to adulthood. Even when analysed in relation to body mass the anaerobic performance of 8-year-old boys is only about 70 per cent of 11-year-old boys. There is, however, little evidence to support an adolescent spurt in anaerobic performance. Girls' anaerobic performance also increases from childhood to adolescence, but appears to attain a maximal value during the teen years and then stabilizes with a few minor variations. Sex-related differences in anaerobic performance are minimal during the pre-pubertal period, but during adolescence boys become significantly better anaerobic performers than girls and they retain this advantage into adult life.

Pre-pubertal children are sometimes regarded as 'metabolic non-specialists' since those who score highly on anaerobic tests also tend to have a high peak VO_2. In other words, the child who excels in sprint-type activities during Key Stages 1 and 2 is often also above average in longer-duration activities and successful in a variety of team games. As youngsters progress through adolescence, it becomes apparent that those who are capable of high anaerobic performance may not have a similar aerobic potential. This is the typical adult model.

When peak anaerobic performance and peak aerobic performance are expressed as a ratio, the value increases from 2 at 8 years of age to around 3 in late adolescence, and then it remains stable through the late teenage period. This indicates that anaerobic performance (fitness) improves relatively more than aerobic fitness, with age. Although pre-pubertal children are adequately equipped to handle activities which require very short but intensive exertion (i.e. those supported by the muscle stores of high-energy phosphates) they are more 'aerobic' than adolescents and well-suited to relatively long periods of moderate to vigorous physical activity. With young children, however, one has to remember that distances which seem short to adults may seem a very long way. A 50–80 m run may be an aerobic activity to a child in Key Stage 1.

Muscular strength

Muscular strength is the ability of a muscle group to exert force against a resistance in one maximal effort. Strength, and strength measurement, have received considerable attention in adults, but secure data from children and adolescents are sparse and predominantly derived from cross-sectional rather than longitudinal analyses. Most studies have focused upon grip strength which may not be representative of general (or composite) strength development. Nevertheless, the extant literature is consistent despite the nuances of testing procedures and variation in the nature of strength measures.

Muscular strength, whether expressed in terms of isolated muscle groups (e.g. grip strength) or as a composite (total of strength scores from several different muscle groups), increases linearly with advancing age until the onset of puberty. Although sex-related differences in strength have been reported in children as early as 3 years of age, gender differences are small prior to puberty and there is considerable overlap of male and female strength scores. Boys experience a marked increase in strength during the pubertal years and it continues to increase, albeit at a slower rate, during the late teenage period. In contrast to boys, there is no clear evidence of an adolescent spurt in girls' muscular strength which continues to increase at a rate similar to that seen during the pre-pubertal period.

The small pre-pubertal strength difference between boys and girls is greatly magnified during the adolescent spurt and whereas the absolute strength of a 7-year-old girl may be about 92 per cent of that of a similar aged boy it will be, on average, only 60 per cent of a similar aged boy by the age of 18 years. However, because of the timing of the pubertal spurt, some girls may be stronger than some boys towards the end of Key Stage 2 and the beginning of Key Stage 3. The sex-related difference in strength is more marked in the upper extremity and the trunk than in the lower extremity, even after adjusting for size differences between boys and girls. Although there are clear physiological reasons for the sex-associated differences in strength – see Blimkie (1989) for a comprehensive review – the contention that the augmented difference in upper extremity strength may be influenced by socio-cultural factors cannot easily be dismissed.

Composite strength increases only slightly faster than body mass during the pre-pubertal period for both sexes. There is little change in mass-related composite strength for girls following the onset of puberty, but males benefit from an acceleration of mass-related composite strength through puberty and into the late teenage period. By Key Stage 3, these sex-related changes in strength–mass ratio give boys an advantage over girls in activities involving the support of body mass, e.g. gymnastics. Girls are further disadvantaged by the increase in body fat which, generally, is deposited around the hips. The smaller upper body muscle mass and greater total lower body mass leads to a further imbalance of relative upper and lower body strength. This can have the effect of making adolescent girls 'bottom heavy', making lifting and manoeuvring their body mass more difficult.

Flexibility

Flexibility, which has been defined as the range of possible movement available in a joint or groups of joints, is an important, though frequently neglected aspect of performance. Very little is known about the flexibility of non-athletic children and adolescents since much of the research has focused on specific, elite groups such as ballet dancers and gymnasts. Furthermore, the available data from children and adolescents have been confounded by the use of inadequate methods of assessing flexibility and the specific nature of flexibility, which can be both joint and body side specific.

There is little scientific evidence to support the popular beliefs that flexibility declines with increasing age or that there exists a critical period during which flexibility is maximal. In general, flexibility has been found to increase between the ages of 7 and 11 years and recent evidence from children engaged in formal sports training supports the view that the flexibility of older children can be increased with training.

Although it appears that girls are more flexible than boys, the evidence is equivocal. However, the anatomical design of the female pelvic area, specifically adapted for childbirth, allows for a greater range in hip and lower limb flexibility. As girls reach puberty, the broadening of their hips further increases the range of movement in this area. The concomitant lowering of the centre of gravity and shorter leg length enhances trunk flexion. The difference in the type of activities commonly engaged in by boys and girls may also help to explain the often observed greater flexibility of girls, since girls tend to be involved in more activities requiring greater general joint movement, such as gymnastics.

A number of long-term problems associated with hypermobility of joints through excessive training programmes during childhood have been identified. Flexibility training should be conducted cautiously with children, because of the asynchronomous growth of bone and musculo-tendinous units. During periods of rapid growth (Key Stage 3), joints become progressively taut; as a consequence, a loss of flexibility may occur and, at this time, the risk of injury is greatly increased. Repetitive movements such as those encountered using ballistic stretching techniques are not recommended, since the uniqueness of the growing musculo-skeletal system makes the child extremely vulnerable to soft tissue and skeletal injury.

Exercise training and fitness testing

It appears that training regimes introduced at the appropriate time in the child's development will induce favourable changes in aerobic fitness, anaerobic fitness, muscular strength and flexibility. Armstrong and Welsman (1993) have provided guidelines for developing exercise training programmes for children and adolescents.

Any activity which is rhythmical, uses large muscle groups and can be sustained continuously for a reasonable length of time can be used to improve aerobic fitness. Suitable activities include swimming, cycling, running, skipping and some types of dancing. Even pre-pubertal children can improve their aerobic fitness with an appropriate training programme. A typical exercise training prescription for children and adolescents would involve maintaining their heart rate above 80 per cent of maximum (160 beats/min) for at least twenty minutes for not less than three times per week.

Anaerobic (glycogenolytic) training involves repetitions of near-maximal effort for perhaps thirty seconds and is very strenuous. The available evidence suggests that this type of training is probably of little value until late adolescence. Similarly, due to the possible damage which could occur to the growth zones of the skeleton, it is probably best to be cautious about maximal resistance training (e.g. weight training) until the growth spurt is virtually over. Pre-pubescent children are quite capable of increasing their muscular strength in response to resistance training but they should be encouraged to use submaximal resistances, perhaps their own body mass (e.g. situps, pullups).

It has been suggested that training for increased joint mobility should start before puberty as long as it is carried out with a concern to avoid damage to the joints and vertebral column. However, older children and adolescents can enhance their flexibility with a regular programme of static stretching exercises. Static stretching involves slowly stretching a muscle longer than its normal length and holding the stretch for 6–10 seconds. There is much less chance of tearing the soft tissue and causing muscular soreness with this type of stretch than with other techniques such as ballistic stretching.

It is unrealistic to expect a significant increase in children's and adolescents' fitness within the limited time available for curricular PE. In our view, the emphasis should be placed on helping young people to understand the principles underlying health-related physical activity and teaching them how to develop their own exercise training programmes which can be periodically reappraised and modified as they grow older and their aspirations change. There is no convincing evidence to support the view that training must be started early in life in order to experience sporting success as an adult, and early specialization is often counter-productive. Sporting success during childhood is linked to rate of maturation. Early maturing boys have an advantage in many sports whereas it is often late maturing girls who are successful, e.g. in gymnastics.

A recent survey (Harris, 1994) demonstrated that most secondary schools include compulsory fitness testing within their PE curriculum. We have severe reservations about the value of fitness testing because of the lack of tests suitable for use in the school environment that provide valid and objective measures of fitness. However, in the context of the present chapter, it is readily apparent that fitness test scores must be strongly related to the maturity of the child. The use of norm tables confounds the issue of interpreting fitness scores because tables constructed on the basis of chronological age cannot logically be used to classify children at different levels of maturity. Furthermore, having different norms for boys and girls results in different expectations. Norms are based on performances rather than capabilities and if teachers accept lower norms for girls as reflecting acceptable performances, girls may tend to meet these lower expectations.

GROWTH, MATURATION AND MOTOR PERFORMANCE

The more complex movements involved in sport and dance are dependent upon fundamental motor tasks such as running, skipping, hopping, jumping, catching, throwing, kicking and balancing. The initial learning of fundamental motor tasks occurs during the pre-school years but it is during Key Stages 1 and 2 that most children learn and refine their movement patterns so that they resemble those of skilled adults. Performance of several motor tasks continues to improve through Key Stages 3 and 4.

In Key Stage 1, the overall running pattern of the child appears similar to that of the adult but, of course, speed of running is considerably slower than that of older children and young adults. Basic refinements in running pattern occur during the early school years as the child grows bigger and becomes stronger. Stride length increases and the ability to exert muscular power improves. These changes result in a linear increase in speed in both sexes at least from 5 to 11 or 12 years of age. Sex differences in speed are not very large from 5 to 8 years but, by the age of 9 years, boys tend to be faster runners than girls. During adolescence, the difference in speed of running between boys and girls is magnified as boys' running speed continues to increase with age up to about 17 years, although there is no indication of a clear adolescent spurt in performance. Girls exhibit only a slight increase in running speed from 12 through to 17 years of age. Shuttle running, which is also to some extent a measure of agility, also improves with age. There is a marked improvement in both boys' and girls' performance from 5 to 8 years and then improvement at a lesser rate in boys to 18 years and in girls to 14 years. The sex difference in shuttle run performance is negligible from 5 through 7 years of age and small from 8 to 14 years of age.

Girls appear to acquire control of foot movements at an earlier age than boys. Most children can gallop, skip and hop before they leave Key Stage 1, but girls learn sooner than boys, and DeOreo and Keogh (1980, p. 80) have suggested that girls hop 'more gracefully in contrast to boys who seem more forceful and flat-footed'.

From the age of 5 to 11 years the ability to jump for distance (standing long jump) increases linearly with age at a rate of about 7.5–12.5 cm per year. Throughout this period, the average boy can jump 7.0–12.0 cm further than the average girl but there is some overlap and it is not unusual for some girls to jump further than similarly aged boys. From about 11 years of age, girls' performance levels out and may even decline in late adolescence. Boys experience an adolescent spurt in standing long jump performance and sex differences in performance during adolescence are marked. For example, from age 7 to 11 years, both boys and girls increase the distance jumped by about 30 per cent. Comparable figures from age 7 to 15 years are 78 per cent for boys and 47 per cent for girls. Age trends and sex differences in the vertical jump are similar to those for standing long jump, although boys do not appear to experience such a marked adolescent spurt in performance.

The basic patterns of catching and throwing are usually mastered by the end of Key Stage 1. However, it is usually Key Stage 2 or even Key Stage 3 before a mature level of catching ability is attained. Too few data on sex differences are available to be certain, but it appears that boys reach the most mature level of catching development before girls. Boys also throw much further than girls at all ages from 5 years onwards. The sex difference in throwing performance during childhood is greater than for other basic skills and does not accurately reflect the difference in arm strength between boys and girls in Key Stages 1 and 2. The difference in throwing performance is magnified during adolescence when boys are often able to throw a ball twice as far as girls. Unlike other basic motor skills, there is little overlap between the performance of similarly aged boys and girls, and boys are generally able to throw as far as girls who are 2 or 3 years older. The potential influence of socio-cultural factors cannot be ignored as they probably reinforce boys' underlying physiological advantages.

During Key Stage 1, most children mature to the point that they can kick both a stationary and moving ball. The ability to kick with accuracy and force increases through Key Stage 2 and into Key Stage 3. Kicking distance and accuracy increase with advancing age and boys outperform girls at all ages. Much of the sex differences in kicking may, of course, be socio-cultural.

Although balance is essential to the performance of many motor tasks, it is difficult to isolate it, define it and measure it. Balance performance improves with age, at least until adolescence, and it appears that girls perform better than boys throughout childhood.

Some, predominantly cross-sectional, data suggest a period of 'adolescent awkwardness' which may have adverse effects on balance, particularly in boys. Available longitudinal data relating boys' motor performance to the growth spurt do not, however, suggest a period of adolescent awkwardness (Malina and Bouchard, 1991). Beunen and Malina (1988) acknowledge the complexity of the concept of adolescent awkwardness, but point out that any decline in performance does not occur in all motor tasks and is temporary. They emphasize (1988, p. 535): 'The individuality of adolescent changes in growth and performance must be recognized and appreciated.'

HEALTH-RELATED PHYSICAL ACTIVITY

There is convincing evidence that appropriate physical activity during adult life confers some protection from coronary heart disease, counters obesity, reduces high blood pressure, retards osteoporosis, improves mental well-being, and even reduces the incidence of some cancers (Fentem *et al.*, 1988). It appears that adults' physical activity patterns have their origins in childhood (Activity and Health Research, 1992); therefore, encouraging children to adopt and sustain physically active lifestyles may have significant long-term health benefits.

Data describing the current physical activity patterns of British children and adolescents are sparse but remarkably consistent. Sleap and Warburton (1994) have provided valuable insights into the physical activity patterns of children aged 5 to 11 years. Studies in our laboratory have documented the levels of physical activity of 11- to 16-year-olds (Armstrong *et al.*, 1990). The findings are disturbing and clearly demonstrate that many children in each Key Stage of the National Curriculum have low levels of physical activity. Boys appear to be more active than girls from an early age and there is a marked decrease in girls' habitual physical activity as they progress through Key Stages 3 and 4. Sleap and Warburton commented that, sustained moderate-to-vigorous physical activity was 'particularly low' during PE lessons. On examination of 12-hour heart rate records, taken during a normal school day, we found that PE sessions were rarely perceptible with some children and adolescents.

In the light of these findings, we believe that all children and adolescents should be encouraged to adopt active lifestyles, but perhaps girls should be specifically targeted for support. Gender stereotypical behaviour is apparent even in Key Stages 1 and 2 and the school has been identified as one of the primary conveyors of gender-related behaviour and attitudes within the physical activity domain. Within school sport, girls' games such as hockey and netball appear to carry less prestige than boys' games such as football and rugby. This may reinforce the relative unimportance of physical activity in the lives of female children and adolescents, whereas the dominance of boys' games in the social life of the school may reinforce the ideology of domination of women by men.

Females tend to lack confidence in the domain of physical activity and one of the important benefits of participation in physical activity is the psychological changes that accompany enhanced well-being. For many girls, PE can develop a feeling of alienation from their bodies, as many adolescent girls do not conform to the 'desired' physique they believe society values. Developing a physically athletic body is seen as abnormal and peculiar to many girls, as it is in direct conflict with the ideology of femininity advocated by society. Increasing the activity levels of girls has tremendous potential to enhance their sense of competence in the physical domain. In our view, physical educators need to reflect on the organization, presentation and content of their programmes at each Key Stage in order to challenge the gender ideologies reflected in many PE curricula.

The provision of a high activity content should be an important component of most PE lessons but a regimented style of PE is not the answer. Children's resistance to participation in compulsory exercise programmes is well-documented. The emphasis, in this context, should be placed upon providing a range of enjoyable experiences of physical activity and upon developing a repertoire of motor skills in relation to growth and maturation. This sort of approach may be more likely to enable children to experience success in physical activities, to develop confidence in their own ability, and to encourage them to pursue more active lifestyles.

SUMMARY

The revised National Curriculum in Physical Education (NCPE) retained the end of Key Stage statements because they 'describe the types and range of performance which most pupils should characteristically demonstrate at the end of each key stage' (NCPE, p. i). This chapter has shown, however, that from an early age performance varies with growth and maturation within a given age group and between the sexes. This has significant ramifications for the implementation of the NCPE. For example, mixed sex contact sports become potentially dangerous once boys reach mid- to late adolescence. Standards need to be adjusted appropriately for boys and girls as the difference in their ability to perform many athletic and gymnastic tasks widens. These standards, however, must be demanding for both sexes and not encourage under-achievement from girls.

British children's current level of physical activity is a cause for concern. Girls appear to be less active than boys in all Key Stages of the curriculum but the gender difference widens as they progress through Key Stages 3 and 4. PE teachers are well-placed to foster more active lifestyles. The National Curriculum suggests that the promotion of health-related physical activity 'should permeate the areas of activity and need not be taught in isolation' (p. ii). However, it may be necessary to place physical activity experiences into a theoretical framework to help young people to develop an understanding of the beneficial effects of physical activity and the way these benefits can be achieved and sustained through adult life.

Research has suggested that girls will develop a lower self-confidence than boys if they begin to fail in competitive tasks. Very often, the tasks expected of children – such as throwing and kicking a ball – are 'masculine' tasks. Lirgg (1991) suggests that the more masculine the task, the more the confidence of boys will grow while the confidence of girls lessens. This may be reflected by the ability of prepubertal boys to throw further than prepubertal girls of the same age. More attention needs to be directed towards why gender differences exist among prepubertal children when no physiological explanations are apparent. Perhaps inadequate or inappropriate instructions and feedback, fewer opportunities to practise and less encouragement to participate, result in slower motor development in skills such as throwing. It is also possible that experiences of failure by many girls may lead to the development of negative self-efficacy resulting in less effort to become successful.

Children grow and mature at their own pace and their performance in all aspects of PE will vary as they progress through early childhood and adolescence into young adulthood. In the interpretation and implementation of the National Curriculum, physical educators must recognize the individual differences in the rate of growth and maturation of young people and the influence of these changes on their capabilities and aspirations.

REFERENCES

Activity and Health Research (1992) *Allied Dunbar National Fitness Survey*. London: Sports Council and Health Education Authority.

Armstrong, N., Balding, J., Gentle, P. and Kirby, B. (1990) 'Patterns of physical activity among 11 to 16 year old British children', *British Medical Journal*, **301**, 203–5.

Armstrong, N. and Welsman, J. (1993) 'Training young athletes', in Lee, M. (ed.), *Coaching Children in Sport*. London: Spon, pp. 191–203.

Armstrong, N. and Welsman, J. (1994) 'Assessment and interpretation of aerobic fitness in children and adolescents', *Exercise and Sport Sciences Reviews*, **22**, 435–76.

Beunen, G. and Malina, R.M. (1988) 'Growth and physical performance relative to the timing of the adolescent spurt', *Exercise and Sport Sciences Reviews*, **16**, 503–40.

Blimkie, C.J.R. (1989) 'Age and sex-associated variation in strength during childhood: anthropometric, morphological, neurologic, biomechanical, endocrinologic, genetic and physical activity correlates', in Gisolfi, C.V. and Lamb, D.R. (eds), *Youth, Exercise and Sport*. Indianapolis: Benchmark Press, pp. 99–164.

DeOreo, K. and Keogh, J. (1980) 'Performance of fundamental motor tasks', in Corbin, C.B. (ed.), *A Textbook of Motor Development*. Dubuque, Iowa: Brown, pp. 76–91.

Fentem, P.H., Bassey, E.J. and Turnbull, N.B. (1988) *The New Case for Exercise*. London: Sports Council and Health Education Authority.

Harris, J. (1994) 'Health-related exercise in the National Curriculum: results of a pilot study in secondary schools', *British Journal of Physical Education Research Supplement*, **14**, 6–11.

Krahenbuhl, G.S., Skinner, J.S. and Kohrt, W.M. (1985) 'Developmental aspects of maximal aerobic power in children', *Exercise and Sport Science Reviews*, **13**, 503–38.

Lirgg, C.D. (1991) 'Gender differences in self-confidence in physical activity. A meta-analysis of recent studies', *Journal of Sport and Exercise Psychology*, **8**, 294–310.

Malina, R.M. and Bouchard, C. (1991) *Growth, Maturation and Physical Activity*. Champaign, Ill.: Human Kinetics.

Sleap, M. and Warburton, P. (1994) 'Physical activity levels of preadolescent children in England', *British Journal of Physical Education Research Supplement*, **14**, 2–6.

Tanner, J.M. (1962) *Growth at Adolescence* (2nd edn). Oxford: Blackwell Scientific Publications.

Tanner, J.M., Whitehouse, R.J. and Takaishi, M. (1966) 'Standards from birth to maturity for height, weight, height velocity and weight velocity: British children, 1965 – I', *Archives of Disease in Childhood*, **41**, 454–71.

Chapter 3

Psycho-social Development from 5 to 16 years

Martin Lee

INTRODUCTION

When we deal with children, we sometimes forget that they perceive and respond to the world in a rather different light than we do. This is one manifestation of important differences between children and adults. The process of changing from one to the other is rather drawn out and takes in the region of twenty years; indeed some parents may feel that their children never reach that state of independence which appears to be a major element of adulthood! The metamorphosis incorporates, for example, changes in physique and physical function, psycho-physical function, psychological function, and the ability to function appropriately in society. Not only are the changes in these functions interrelated but individuals experience them at different times and different rates. While some mature earlier than others, and with different characteristics and abilities, there is a considerable degree of consistency about the sequences involved. The differences which exist between children and adults challenge the assumptions which underlie our interactions as adults; these assumptions should, consequently, be abandoned in favour of recognizing the limitations and uniqueness of childhood.

Significance of psycho-social development

Associated with the rather visible physical changes in body size and shape, development of the body to function more effectively, and the development of ability to move and control the body and external objects, is the rather less visible progress towards taking one's place in a society. This may be a major characteristic of becoming a human being; it requires individuals to be able to differentiate themselves from others, yet to be able to take the position of others, and understand the world from a collective perspective. Without the psycho-social advances which occur during childhood and adolescence, human societies would not be able to exist as we know them. Hence, the patterns of change which occur are of utmost importance to an understanding of both individual development and social continuity. The changes which accompany the transition from childhood to adolescence and adulthood are not only of interest to parents and teachers but are a major field of academic enquiry. Study has been directed not only to the rapid biological upheavals which occur during adolescence, but also to the cognitive and social changes which young people experience, upon which they are increasingly able to reflect, and to the multitude of social events and changes to which young people are currently exposed (Brooks-Gunn and Paikoff, 1992).

In this chapter I will address some of the ways in which children differ psychologically from adults and describe some patterns of psycho-social development which have been identified. In essence, there is a cognitive-developmental thread which runs through the different issues which are addressed, and a central construct is that of self-concept. Hence I shall begin by describing recent perspectives and developmental trends in self-concept, which will provide the basis for a discussion of both children's interpretations of ability and of their moral reasoning. I shall finish with a short section on patterns of play, paying attention to children's initiation into the world of games with rules.

SELF-CONCEPT

The notion of self-concept has been a significant element in psychology since the days of Wundt and James at the turn of the century and, despite being overshadowed by the behaviourist school for a significant period, it has been in evidence since then in the writings of Allport, Maslow and Mead all of whom have advocated the importance of self-image as a major determinant of human behaviour (Glick and Zigler, 1985). It has also become a most important concept in the world of education (Burns, 1979) and PE (Hellison, 1973). Indeed few self-respecting contemporary physical educators would prepare a curriculum without reference to the benefits which it could have for self-development; it is also implicit in the objectives of the National Curriculum. We believe that the experiences we provide in the gymnasium, on the playing field and in the outdoors, give opportunities for young people to reveal, and become aware of, new aspects of themselves. Of course, the possession of a particular quality does not necessarily imply that the individual recognizes it; the fact of self and the knowledge of it are not synonymous. Hence the role of education may not be simply to develop self but also to act as an agent for the revelation of those qualities, positive or negative, which the individual already possesses.

What is self-concept?

The term self-concept is only one of a family of terms which are used in connection with one's perceptions of who and what one is. Others which occur frequently in the literature are self-image, body-image, self-esteem, self-worth, self-feelings, self-beliefs, etc. Indeed there appears to be plethora of constructs which include 'self' as a prefix, and until relatively recently few of them have been the subject of developmental investigation or have been utilized with children younger than about 10 years of age (Harter, 1983; Marsh *et al.*, 1991). Given that childhood is widely considered to be a critical period in the development of self-knowledge and positive self-feelings, the lack of research is to be regretted. However, more recent research has taken young populations as its focus and has promoted a more careful examination of the construct from both theoretical and methodological points of view.

A major impetus was provided by Shavelson *et al.* (1976) who defined self-concept as 'an individual's perception of self, formed through experience with the environment, interactions with significant others, and attributions of his/her own behaviour'. This self-concept is perceived as being multifaceted and hierarchical, such that specific behaviours and perceptions contribute to the construction of more general domains. Among other writers, there appears to be a consensus that self-concept may best be considered to be a hypothetical construct organized into components and sub-components describing one's competencies and characteristics, their relative importance and a general sense of self-worth (Eccles *et al.*, 1989).

The importance of self-concept

Self-concept has been considered an important element in recent explanations of human behaviour. Interest in the topic resulted from the growth of phenomenological psychology which gave a central role to the perception and interpretation of the outside world in determining behaviour. From this perspective, perceptions of self are accorded considerable importance since they affect the way in which the external world is interpreted. In this way, self-concept may be viewed as a set of attitudes about a particular attitude object – the self (Burns, 1979). This approach suggests that not only is self a product of interaction but it also defines appropriate interactions in the same way that attitudes act as filters of experience. Hence, early definitions of self may become self-perpetuating and determine future behaviour and patterns of social interaction.

Models of self-concept

The concept of self, advanced above, is the product of an evolving research field which has revealed rather more complex structures than initially envisaged. Thus different models have been proposed to describe the structure of self.

Uni-dimensional

The early stages of the recent growth in self-concept research commonly assumed that all components of self-esteem could be combined to provide a single, all inclusive measure. This approach invited criticism on the grounds that items included in the instruments are accorded equal weighting in a manner which ignores the complexity of the dynamics of the relationships between them. As a result, descriptions using this approach gloss over the possibility that people may have different degrees of differentiation of self, and experience feelings of high self-esteem in some areas but not in others.

Multidimensional

Consequently, considerable research has been devoted to examining the structure of self as multidimensional and the degree to which it is differentiated into separate components. If the self is viewed as a collection of selves, each of which can be separately identified and evaluated, it is possible to explain more carefully the perceptions and behaviour of individuals in different settings. Thus it has been proposed that not all self-representations can be available at any one time and, hence, a particular element may be selected as appropriate at a given moment. This has been referred to as the 'working self'. Such an interpretation has a number of advantages; it accommodates:

(a) research which indicates that current evaluations and perceptions are influenced by current beliefs,
(b) the view that self is not static but dynamic, and
(c) a view that the self can be both stable and malleable (Markus and Wurf, 1987).

Hierarchical

Hierarchical models propose that not only is the self comprised of a variety of self-representations but also that they are organized into systems in which specific perceptions contribute to increasingly general perceptions at successively higher levels. Thus, for example, the ability to perform a specific sport skill may contribute to the perception of competence in that sport. If it is supported by a range of skills in the sport, the belief of competence is strengthened. A child might then say: 'I am a good football player.' Similarly, competence in a wide range of sports permits the child to say: 'I am good at sport.' Competence in a variety of fields may lead to an overall judgement of competence and feelings of high esteem of a global nature.

A proposition derived from hierarchical models is that individuals attach more importance to particular domains than to others and that the resultant emphases provide better indicators of self-concept ratings. While there is an appealing logic that domains of competence which are important to individuals will have greater affect on self-evaluations, the evidence is not yet clear. In an extensive study of relationships between the global and specific dimensions of self-concept, Marsh (1993) showed that while weightings based upon the relative importance of domains predicted well for groups of adolescents, those based on individual perceptions of importance were not good predictors. Marsh comments that while the concept of a hierarchical structure is demonstrable, the hierarchy is weak and its relationship to global self-esteem is limited.

The evidence for a hierarchical structure of self, and of the role of salience in it, needs further clarification but Marsh's (1993) conclusions imply that the claims to develop perceptions of positive global self-esteem among adolescents through the medium of PE and sport participation may be misplaced. Rather, teachers should be aware of the dynamic nature of self, of the domain specific effects of the opportunities they provide, and of young people's working self-concept (Markus and Wurf, 1987).

Developmental patterns

Some rather clear patterns have been noted in the development of self-concept. First, children demonstrate the capacity to identify different facets of self by 5 years of age (Marsh *et al.*, 1991). Second, increasing differentiation is associated with age (Marsh *et al.*, 1984). Third, young people's self-representations become increasingly abstract and less concrete with increasing age (Harter, 1983). Fourth, self-esteem which is high in early and mid-childhood decreases in late childhood and adolescence before increasing again in late adolescence (Eccles *et al.*, 1989; Marsh, 1989).

The proposition that the self-concepts of children become increasingly differentiated with age and cognitive development has been carefully investigated in recent years. The multifaceted model of self-concept has been clearly described with children and adolescents (Harter, 1983). In an extensive research programme, Marsh has shown that children between 5 and 10 years of age can identify self-concepts of physical abilities, physical appearance, relations with peers, relations with parents, reading, mathematics, school subjects and a general self-concept (Marsh *et al.*, 1984, 1991). He also found evidence for increasingly clear differentiation of those facets with age. Thus it appears that children, even at an early age, have rather more sophisticated views of self than had hitherto been considered. If facets become more differentiated with age, then it can be suggested that teachers, parents, peers and others play important roles in providing the information by which children come to see themselves more clearly.

In an extensive review of the literature to date, Harter (1983) concluded that children progress from self-description based on concrete observable characteristics to trait descriptors and finally to self-representations based on psychological processes such as attitudes, emotions and motives. Broadly, this seems to be congruent with the cognitive developmental model of Piaget. The use of concrete characteristics as descriptors (e.g. 'I have blue eyes') is evidence of a less abstract form of thinking than is possible in the formal operations period when children can more easily understand the meaning of qualities – such as friendly, shy and kind – still less than descriptors which invoke the analysis of their own psychological interior (Rosenberg, cited in Harter, 1983).

Given that it occurs during the school years, educators may find themselves burdened with responsibility for the decline in self-concept in pre-adolescent years. This, however, would be facile. Marsh (1989) points out that young children frequently show evidence of unrealistically high self-concepts. They may claim levels of achievement and expectation which are unwarranted and it would be unfortunate if their self-concepts did not become more realistic on the basis of further experience. On the basis of his research, Marsh suggests that the egocentric nature of young children and their high, less clearly differentiated self-concepts, are relatively independent of external criteria. As they age, they incorporate more external information such that the self-concept becomes more closely aligned with external criteria.

If this is so, then the sources of information which children and adults use to assess their competence and, hence, self-esteem become most important. It is a premise of symbolic interactionism (Mead, 1934) that self is a result of interaction with significant others. Since the significance of particular others may be considered to differ for individuals and that, as people progress through life, they are exposed to many others, then it follows that not all significant others have the same influence during different stages of development or in specific settings. Hence, teachers may be expected to have more influence than parents or peers at certain times and vice versa. The sources of information which young athletes use to assess their competence has been shown to vary according to their age, perceptions of competence and beliefs about personal control.

In a study of young athletes between 8 and 14, Horn and Hasbrook (1987) found that in the 10–14 age group, children with high perceived competence and internal perceptions of control used significantly more internal standards of self-evaluation. This was not the case for younger children. However, in a study of elite junior swimmers Lee and Christensen (1993) found that high self-esteem athletes used more of both internal and external sources of information than did those of lower self-esteem; they were more hungry for information about their performance.

PERCEPTIONS OF DIFFICULTY AND ABILITY

An area of cognitive development, that has become of great interest in recent years, addresses the question of how children interpret success and ability; there is evidence that children's interpretations differ from adults. First, the distinction between difficulty and ability is not made immediately by young children and, second, they cannot readily distinguish the relative importance of ability and effort in accounting for their success or lack of it. Children pass through a series of stages before they are able to understand that the ability to do something is a capacity which differs among individuals and which is exploited to the extent that one makes an effort (Nicholls, 1990). The identification of such a pattern has led to the observation that Nicholls' approach may provide an explanation for the phenomenon of 'drop-out' from children's sport (Roberts, 1984; Duda, 1987).

What difficulty means to children

Nicholls explored children's understanding of the difficulty of a task by asking them to recognize that a puzzle which could be solved by a small proportion of peers was harder than one which could be solved by a greater proportion. As a result of this investigation, Nicholls found that the concept of 'difficulty' differs for children than for adults and that development appears to occur in three stages: egocentric, objective and normative.

At the egocentric level, at about 5 years of age, difficulty is self-referenced and children answered questions about difficulty in terms of their own success expectations. Thus 'hard' is 'hard for me', and the task difficulty is judged by one's own performance. At the second, objective, level children recognized that puzzles with more pieces were harder and, hence, difficulty is independent of expectations of success and can be seen as a concrete property of the task. However, 'hard' may still mean 'it's too hard for me', because ability and difficulty are still not differentiated. At the normative level, difficulty is comparative. The understanding that difficulty can be expressed in terms of the proportion of others who can achieve success is a mature view: 'hard' now

Table 3.1 *Stages in attaining the distinction between ability and effort*

Level	Age range	Characteristics
Level 1	5–6	Effort or outcome is ability. These are not differentiated as cause and effect.
Level 2	7–9	Effort is the cause of outcomes. Equal efforts are expected to lead to equal outcomes.
Level 3	7–11	Effort and ability are partially differentiated. Explanations of different outcomes following equal effort imply different ability but are not systematically pursued.
Level 4	12–13	Ability and effort are fully differentiated. Ability is a capacity which limits the effect of effort.

(Adapted from Nicholls, 1978)

means that not many others can do it. Now, difficulty and ability are differentiated (Nicholls, 1990; Nicholls *et al.*, 1986). The attainment of this distinction may be a condition of the increase in children's use of social comparison to assess their abilities at about 7 years of age (Nicholls, 1990).

Understanding ability

The attainment of a differentiation between ability and effort also appears to take place in a series of stages. Nicholls (1978) showed that children have not developed the adult understanding that ability is the capacity to perform a task. In a study, in which children were shown films of two other children doing mathematics tests, one appeared to be working diligently throughout while the other spent more than half the time in non-work activities. Subjects were asked to account for the outcomes of the test after being told that the lazier child scored better. Analysis of the answers revealed a series of four stages of thinking (Table 3.1).

The stages, as in all stage descriptions of developmental phenomena, are subject to a degree of overlap, some children achieve a stage earlier than others and vice versa, but there is good reason to believe that the clear recognition of ability as a capacity which limits performance outcomes is not generally attained until about 12 years of age, in both academic and sport domains (Nicholls and Miller, 1984; Smith and Whitehead, 1994).

The attainment of the final stage may be important in affecting persistence and future participation because, if ability is low, effort cannot compensate and there is no point in trying. As children move from the simple PE environment to that of competitive sport, and this may occur at quite early ages, there is an expectation that they understand a competitive structure which has been designed for adults by adults. Thus, the limitations that face children as they assimilate new experiences may result in their drawing inaccurate conclusions about the reasons for their success or failure and for future expectations. Not only may they make inaccurate attributions but, more importantly, they construct different meanings for those attributions. Thus, the equivalence of ability and effort is an expression of a confusion of concepts which nevertheless has real meaning for them.

It is important for teachers and coaches to recognize these patterns of thinking because it may have implications for the way in which children respond during early adolescence. If pre-adolescents are successful and attribute their success to effort, which for them is the same as ability, it may be difficult for them to come to terms with relative lack of success in mid-adolescence because they simply do not have the ability (capacity) to succeed. Conversely, for those with genuinely high levels of ability, the interpretation of success as being due to effort when they have, in fact, had to expend little effort may result in their being unable to make the greater levels of effort needed to succeed at a later date.

INTERPERSONAL RELATIONS AND MORALITY

A very important part of psycho-social development is that of developing a sense of morally acceptable behaviour. It has long been a basic tenet of PE that it has a major role to play in the development of 'character', though 'character' has not often been clearly defined in this context. Despite the lack of conceptual clarity, and perhaps aided by apparent increase in the violation of moral principles in sport, the development of sportsmanship remains an important topic in children's sport (Lee and James, 1986). Questions of character and sportsmanship imply a consideration of moral reasoning and how it develops in children; in particular, it provokes consideration of how children think about moral decisions in sports situations. This necessarily leads to a consideration of moral development: Does the way in which people resolve moral dilemmas change with age?

Moral development

The major theoretical explanation of moral development considers that it follows the pattern of cognitive development. Thus, as children become more capable of abstract thought, the more sophisticated they become in making moral decisions. Using Piagetian theory of cognitive development as a springboard Kohlberg (1976) and Haan (1978) have outlined theories in which children pass through different stages of moral reasoning before attaining maturity.

Kohlberg

Kohlberg (1976) proposed that people pass through three levels of moral reasoning: egocentric morality, social responsibility and independent morality. In each level, he proposed two substages characterized by slightly different orientations to moral problems. In the first individuals take normative or consequence stances to the resolution of moral dilemmas. Normative decisions are based on rules and roles; consequential decisions are based on judgements of the effects of actions on self or others. In the second substage, decisions are made on the basis of higher level principles of justice. These include consideration of liberty, equality and contract, in combination with the recognition of conscience and the presentation of an ideal image.

Egocentric morality

At this level, the two stages are: punishment and reward; and individual instrumental purpose. Children do not understand how social norms and rules work, nor how they affect moral responsibility; consequently, moral decisions are made on the basis of self-interest.

Social responsibility

This is the conventional level of morality which recognizes the predominance of the needs of the group or society as a whole. Thus individuals are motivated to live up to the expectations of others and to adopt the principle of the 'golden rule'. There is an emphasis on conformity, adherence to rules and social maintenance. The key to moral decision making lies in meeting normative expectations rather than in making independent judgements.

Independent morality

Decision making, at this level, is characterized by independence from the normative demands of the group. It emphasizes individual rights and universal ethical principles which lead to the development of a personal code of behaviour.

Three criticisms of the theory have been made which are pertinent to this discussion. First, a central proposition of stage theories is that the attainment of a stage of development precludes regression to an earlier stage of thought. While this might not be significant in the case of the attainment of the ability–effort distinction, in the case of morality it suggests that the attainment of, for example, conventional levels of moral reasoning prevents reasoning at the pre-conventional level. A second criticism is that each stage is characterized by a structural wholeness which prevents people from making differential judgements in different situations. Third, since moral development depends upon cognitive development only clever people can make mature moral decisions. However, Lind (1985) has argued persuasively that such criticisms can be refuted on grounds of interpretation and method.

Evidence for the validity of the proposed stages has demonstrated that egocentric morality dominates during childhood. Initially, it is based on compliance to authority. During mid-childhood, moral decisions are made on the basis of self-interest and fair exchange. During late childhood, egocentric reasoning is still predominant but, from about 10 years of age, it declines in favour of social responsibility. By the age of 14, the latter becomes the most commonly exhibited mode of moral reasoning and increases in importance throughout adolescence and adulthood. During secondary school years, the principle of the 'golden rule' is the most common basis for making moral decisions. The incidence of independently principled judgements begins to appear in young adulthood but is limited even among mature samples (Colby and Kohlberg, 1987; Walker, 1989).

Haan

A student of Kohlberg, Norma Haan, has proposed an alternative model to explain how we resolve moral dilemmas which draws upon the nature of daily negotiations. It incorporates two principles: the need for moral balance; and the need for moral dialogue.

Moral balance

The principle of moral balance suggests that interpersonal negotiations include agreements and obligations between the parties which are demonstrated in the dialogue between them. Agreement is reached when both parties accept the existence of a moral balance between their respective needs and obligations. In sport, there is a set of formal laws which govern the activity, but the players also agree to abide by a set of accepted norms of behaviour. Violations of this set of agreements may well lead to cries of 'Unfair!'

Moral dialogue

If the balance in a particular setting is tipped one way or another, then a moral dialogue is initiated which may result in behavioural changes to restore the moral balance. This does not mean that the parties necessarily sit down and discuss the problem, though indeed this may be part of the process. The negotiation may take the form of retaliation with a possible decline into a downward spiral of negative behaviour.

Haan proposed a framework of five stages of moral development which are characterized by three processes: assimilation, accommodation and equilibration (Table 3.2).

In the assimilation phase, self-interest is paramount; it is difficult for children to accommodate the needs of others. The second phase, accommodation, involves a seeking of balance on the basis of good faith such that one party will not take advantage of the other. This approximates to the conventional morality of Kohlberg and the application of the 'golden rule'. The final phase, equilibration, requires individuals to revert once again to a dialogue in which individual interests are served within a specific situation such that both partners can benefit.

Games and sport provide situations in which the principles of moral dialogue and moral judgement are frequently activated. While operating within a set of constitutive rules, participants are called upon to agree, if only tacitly, to those rules, not only as written but also in the spirit which they represent. Violations of the rules, or the spirit, destroy the balance which must then be restored. If this can be done positively then the game can continue amicably, if not then it will deteriorate as opponents seek to establish an advantage.

The extent to which PE and sport can contribute to the development of moral judgement, often regarded as sportsmanship, has come under critical review in recent years. For example, it has been shown that, among adult athletes, there appears to be

Table 3.2 *An interactional model of moral development*

Level	Stage	Features
Assimilation	Power balancing	Now moral view; demands are self-interested.
	Egocentric	Individual accepts compromises to sustain self-interest.
	balancing	Expectations of others are based on the belief of the similarity of others. Violations lead to 'tit for tat' dialogue.
Accommodation	Harmony balancing	Moral balance based on good faith; giving to others in order to maintain the social order.
	Common interest balancing	Moral balance based on group harmony with a belief in common rights and duties. Rules protect against bad faith and are accepted to preserve group interests.
Equilibration	Mutual interest balancing	Dialo gue to establish harmony between the parties as the situation and personal interests require. Acceptance of delicate moral balances which require flexibility.

(Adapted from Haan, 1978)

a regression to lower levels of moral reasoning when taking part in sport (Bredemeier and Shields, 1984). The observant reader will notice that this provides some evidence to support the first two criticisms of Kohlberg's theory which have been reported above. Bredemeier and her co-workers have also reported age group differences in moral reasoning in line with Haan's model (Bredemeier, 1994) but regression of moral reasoning in a contrast of life and sport settings has not been clearly demonstrated with youth populations.

One important study informs the process of moral education in a PE context. Working with young children, aged 5 to 7, in a summer sports camp, Bredemeier showed that a PE environment can be used to promote levels of moral reasoning, but that it is necessary to have a deliberate strategy to do so. Improvements were achieved by methods in which children either (a) discussed the nature of the moral conflicts which they faced in the course of their activities or (b) were exposed to teachers who modelled prosocial behaviour (Bredemeier *et al.*, 1986). While the results were encouraging, it must be recognized that (a) in order to be effective, the social benefits sought were a specific objective of the teaching programme with strategies designed to bring it about and (b) this was a very young sample. Although the key conditions of the programme may be accepted in the PE environment this may not be so in club-based competitive sports, especially for adolescents.

DEVELOPMENTAL IMPLICATIONS OF PLAY AND GAMES

Finally, I would like to turn briefly to developmental aspects of play as they inform the conduct of PE and sport. It has been widely observed that children's play changes with age, i.e. it is developmental in nature (Smith and Cowie, 1988). Hence, it may be proposed that changes in the nature of play are associated with the developmental needs of the child. Careful observers of play indicate that children progress from a world of play which is typically egocentric to one in which a major element is the interaction with others. Piaget, for example, describes a progression from practice play, in which infants learn sensorimotor skills, through symbolic play, to games with rules.

The last stage takes the form of entering into games with a rule structure which is agreed prior to participation and is typically reached after 7 years of age (Smith and Cowie, 1988). This is significant for PE programmes since it suggests that, until that time, children are not sufficiently mature to play in a formal game with rules. In the earlier stage, children learn to adopt roles through fantasy or make-believe play. But here the roles may change at a whim as children act out one role before changing to another. Rule-governed play, however, represents a transition to an adult world of games where there is a commitment to publicly agreed constraints and less flexibility.

To return to the notion of self-concept development, let us consider an analysis of games by Mead (1934). Mead assumes that human society is based upon a consensus developed through shared meanings. Rule-governed games, which include formally constituted sports, demand that the participants share a collective symbolism and can assume roles which are enacted according to the expectations of other participants. To play a game effectively, the participants must, therefore, not only understand their own role but also that of all the other players. They must know both what others are likely to do and also how others will respond to their own actions. Playing team games, therefore, poses complex social problems for children. For adolescents, the group culture is dominant and they become critically aware of role expectations. At this point, games may have their greatest impact.

This perspective indicates a number of conclusions. The first is that it is unreasonable to expect young children to be able to play team games involving a large number of players because they cannot understand the complexity of team play. Teachers will recognize the 'beehive' games of football in which the players all cluster around a ball which moves slowly around the playing area and which arise when there are many children and little equipment. It follows that it is better to introduce games with small groups each with adequate equipment. The second is that as games are introduced each child should be given the opportunity to play in all the positions on the team so as to learn the expectations of the different roles of the playing positions. In this way, they will better understand the structure of the game as it becomes more complex.

This shift from fantasy to games with rules also signals children's ability to play for longer in larger groups to regulate their own behaviour according to agreed rules (Cole and Cole, 1989). I was presented with an excellent example of this a few years ago. A colleague described the control of break-time soccer in a middle-school playground. The children found that with several games being played simultaneously, they frequently interfered with each other. Two boys decide to organize a league without staff assistance. By working with the others, they determined selection procedures, fixed playing times, points and sanctions for rule violations. Teams were selected to be equally balanced and controls for foul play were determined by opposing captains. A particularly interesting feature was that the playground was on a slight slope and, in the interests of fairness, the stronger team always played uphill. This provides a good example of children in mid- and late childhood demonstrating understanding of the demands of rule-governed games and being able to enter into a moral dialogue to achieve moral balances. It should also provoke consideration of how rules are introduced to children in games. Typically, rules in games are imposed by adults. However, by allowing children to develop rules themselves in order to allow the objectives of the game to be achieved more readily, they are given the opportunity to understand the bases upon which the rules which govern social behaviour are devised. This is itself a most important part of psycho-social development.

SUMMARY

This description of psycho-social changes which occur during childhood has highlighted some of the processes which may affect children's participation in physical activity, both in the school environment and outside it. It also informs the implementation of the National Curriculum by alerting teachers to what they may expect of children at each stage.

There are consistent threads running through the processes I have described. The first is that children initially learn about themselves before learning about the world outside; the second is that early understanding is based on concrete thinking prior to the attainment of more abstract patterns of thought. This is evident in the research on self-concept, assessment of the difficulty of tasks and of ability, and of the structure of moral reasoning. The period of mid-childhood (Key Stage 2) appears to be significant in that the foundations for an understanding of life in the social world begin to make their presence felt more strongly. Social comparison processes become more evident, games with rules and groups become more common, and children begin to see the need for negotiating agreements with others as a result of their social experience. However, Key Stage 3 appears to represent the period when children begin to demonstrate a clear understanding of sophisticated concepts required by mature self-evaluation and the growing influence of social responsibility in moral decision making. Teachers can use these trends to further their understanding of children's behaviour in PE and, more importantly, to structure PE experiences in ways which recognize children's limitations.

REFERENCES

Bredemeier, B.J.L. (1994) 'Children's moral reasoning and their assertive, aggressive, and submissive tendencies in sport and daily life', *Journal of Sport and Exercise Psychology*, **16**, 1–14.

Bredemeier, B.J. and Shields, D.L. (1984) 'Divergence of moral reasoning about sport and everyday life', *Sociology of Sport Journal*, **1**, 348–57.

Bredemeier, B.J., Weiss, M.R., Shields, D.L. and Schewchuk, R.M. (1986) 'Promoting moral growth in a summer sports camp', *Journal of Moral Education*, **15**(3), 212–20.

Brooks-Gunn, J. and Paikoff, R.L. (1992) 'Changes in self-feelings during the transition towards adolescence', in McGurk, H. (ed.), *Childhood Social Development*. Hove: Lawrence Erlbaum Associates, pp. 63–97.

Burns, R.B. (1979) *The Self-concept: Theory, Measurement, Development and Behaviour*. London: Longman.

Colby, A. and Kohlberg, L. (1987) *The Measurement of Moral Judgement: Vol. 1: Theoretical Foundations and Research Validation*. Cambridge: Cambridge University Press.

Cole, M. and Cole, S.R. (1989) *The Development of Children*. New York: Scientific American Books.

Duda, J.L. (1987) 'Toward a developmental theory of children's motivation in sport', *Journal of Sport Psychology*, **9**, 130–45.

Eccles, J., Wigfield, A., Flanagan, C.A., Miller, C., Reuman, D.A. and Yee, D. (1989) 'Self-concepts, domain values, and self-esteem: Relations and changes at early adolescence', *Journal of Personality*, **57**(2), 283–310.

Glick, M. and Zigler, E. (1985) 'Self-image: a cognitive-developmental approach', in Leahy, R.L. (ed.), *The Development of Self*. Orlando, FL: Academic Press, pp. 1–54.

Haan, N. (1978) 'Two moralities in action contexts: Relationships to thought, ego relations, and development', *Journal of Personality and Social Psychology*, **36**, 286–305.

Harter, S. (1983) 'Developmental perspectives on the self-system', in Hetherington, C.H. (ed.), *Handbook of Child Psychology, Vol. 4: Socialization, Personality, and Social Development*. New York: Wiley (4th edn), pp. 275–386.

Hellison, D. (1973) *Humanistic Physical Education*. Englewood Cliffs, NJ: Prentice-Hall.

Horn, T.S. and Hasbrook, C.A. (1987) 'Psychological characteristics and the criteria children use for self-evaluation', *Journal of Sport Psychology*, **9**, 208–21.

Kohlberg, L. (1976) 'Moral stages and moralisation: The structural-developmental approach', in Lickona, T. (ed.), *Moral Development and Behaviour*. New York: Holt, Rinehart, and Winston, pp. 31–53.

Lee, M.J. and Christensen, N. (1993) Self-esteem and selection of sources of evaluative information among young competitive swimmers. Paper presented at the European Congress of Sport Psychology, Lisbon, Portugal, July.

Lee, M.J. and James, R. (1986) Issues in children's sport. Paper presented at the Annual Conference of the British Association of Sports Sciences, Birmingham, September.

Lind, G. (1985) 'The theory of moral-cognitive development: A socio-psychological assessment', in Lind, G., Hartmann, H.A. and Wakenhut, R. (eds), *Moral Development and the Social Environment: Studies in the Psychology and Philosophy of Moral Judgement and Education*. Chicago: Precedent, pp. 21–53.

Markus, H. and Wurf, E. (1987) 'The dynamic self-concept: A social psychological perspective', *Annual Review of Psychology*, **38**, 299–337. (Reprinted in Halberstadt, A.G. and Ellyson, S.L. (eds) (1990) *Social Psychology Readings: A Century of Research*. New York: McGraw-Hill, pp. 79–88.)

Marsh, H.W. (1989) 'Age and sex effects in multiple dimensions of self-concept', *Journal of Educational Psychology*, **81**(3), 417–30.

Marsh, H.W. (1993) 'Relations among global and specific domains of self: The importance of individual importance, certainty and ideals', *Journal of Personality and Social Psychology*, **65**(5), 975–92.

Marsh, H.W., Barnes, J., Cairns, L. and Tidman, M. (1984) 'Self-description questionnaire: Age and sex effects in the structure and level of self-concept for preadolescent children', *Journal of Educational Psychology*, **76**(5), 940–56.

Marsh, H.W., Craven, R.G. and Debus, R. (1991) 'Self-concepts of young children 5 to 8 years of age: Measurement and multidimensional structure', *Journal of Educational Psychology*, **83**(3), 377–92.

Mead, G.H. (1934) *Mind, Self, and Society*. (Morris, C.W. ed.) Chicago: University of Chicago Press.

Nicholls, J.G. (1978) 'The development of the concepts of ability, perception of academic attainment, and the understanding that difficult tasks require more ability', *Child Development*, **49**, 800–14.

Nicholls, J.G. (1990) 'What is ability and why are we mindful of it? A developmental perspective', in Sternberg, R.J. and Kolligan, J. (eds), *Competence considered*. New Haven: Yale University Press, pp. 11–40.

Nicholls, J.G. and Miller, A.T. (1984) 'Reasoning about the ability of self and others: Developmental study', *Child Development*, **55**, 1990–9.

Nicholls, J.G., Jagacinski, C.M. and Miller, A.T. (1986) 'Conceptions of ability in children and adults', in Schwarzer, R. (ed.), *Self-related Cognitions in Anxiety and Motivation*. Hillsdale, NJ: Erlbaum, pp. 265–84.

Roberts, G.C. (1984) 'Toward a new theory of motivation in sport: The role of perceived ability', in Silva, J.M. and Weinberg, R.S. (eds), *Psychological Foundations of Sport*. Champaign, Ill.: Human Kinetics, pp. 214–28.

Shavelson, R.J., Hubner, J.J. and Stanton, G.C. (1976) 'Self-concept: Validation of construct interpretations', *Review of Educational Research*, **46**(3), 407–11.

Smith, A.G. and Whitehead, J. (1994) Toward the evaluation of children's development in reasoning about ability and effort in sport. Paper presented at the Annual Conference of the North American Society of the Psychology of Sport and Physical Activity, Clearwater, Florida, USA, June.

Smith, P.K. and Cowie, H. (1988) *Understanding Children's Development*. Oxford: Blackwell.

Walker, L.J. (1989) 'A longitudinal study of moral reasoning', *Child Development*, **60**, 157–66.

Chapter 4

Physical Education at Key Stage 1

Carolyn Jones

In this analysis of PE at Key Stage 1 it will be necessary, within the context of pre-school and infant PE, to:

1 identify the nature of PE in the infant and pre-school years;
2 from this context, review the National Curriculum for Physical Education (NCPE) at Key Stage 1; and
3 discuss possible ways forward.

Since the post-war years, the hallmark of pre-school and infant education, in state schools, has been the provision of a play-based child-centred, differentiated and developmental curriculum with a 'learning by doing' emphasis (Blenkin and Kelly, 1987). Knowledge is perceived as integrative and the curriculum has been organized into areas of experience: the human and social; linguistic and literacy; mathematical; moral; physical; scientific, spiritual, and technological (DES, 1985). This frame also corresponds to an HMI (1992) view of areas of human giftedness which includes 'general intellectual ability, specific aptitude in one or more subjects, creative or productive thinking, leadership qualities, ability in creative or performing arts and psycho-motor ability' (DES, 1992a, p. 1). Thus PE, from foundation through to excellence, has become a recognized area of human achievement and of knowledge, of a procedural or of a practical kind (Carr, 1978; Arnold, 1979). Clearly, each area of experience is quite distinctive with its own unique structures, concepts and skills (Hirst, 1989; DES, 1985, 1989a; Arnold, 1979). However, there is also subject-matter overlap with common areas of study. These may be presented as 'educational encounters' in a topic or issue form (Stenhouse, 1975; Kelly, 1982).

Contingently, more flexible organizational structures developed in support of this more open learning approach such as the integrated day, team teaching, mixed ability grouping and the rotational use of activities (where groups investigate a topic through a subject focus). This often took place within an open-plan resource-based environment which could be indoors and/or outdoors (the former being the choice of most infant schools and the latter being favoured by nursery schools).

These pedagogical developments were mirrored in the changing PE programme of the infant school. Movement education gradually replaced the prescriptive physical training programme of the 1933 syllabus (Bray, 1992). The principles of movement, as developed by Rudolph Laban, applied a more generalized approach to content with an expectation of a wide variety of creative responses rather than a standardized outcome. The focus was on the child rather than on the activity (Cameron and Cameron, 1969).

Educational gymnastics and dance were activities particularly associated with movement education (DES, 1967). The application of Laban's movement principle (of weight, space, time and flow) allowed content to be organized into thematic (and topic) form which could then be presented, within a lesson, as developmental tasks (with problems to be solved) or as individual explorations and experimentations so that each child could produce their own movement solutions, findings and responses.

The DES publication (1972) confirmed the movement curriculum (of educational gymnastics and dance) and the accompanying more democratic teaching styles and strategies (Bilborough and Jones, 1973). However, the term 'physical education' was also employed to denote an extended range of activities (to include games, athletics, swimming and outdoor pursuits) to be used to promote the development of the whole child. Later HMI publications (DES, 1985; 1989a; 1989b; 1991) confirmed this infant-led developmental play-based movement approach to teaching and learning in PE as being important throughout primary education and beyond.

The value of movement-based PE lay in its accommodation of whole-child development, in its focus on child-centred learning and in its structural provision for differentiation. The research of Tanner (1978) revealed the wide variation in the growth patterns of each child (to the extent of up to four years difference developmentally in a class of 10-year-olds). The uniqueness of each child was confirmed as a central tenet in the teaching of PE. Stage theorists, for example, Piaget, identified sequential landmarks to guide teaching and learning in all areas of experience. Following on from this, it became important to present subject matter within the frame of a permissive environment (Blenkin and Kelly, 1987) which was seen to take account of individual differences (inherited and environmental) and which would cater for early and late developers (Tanner, 1978). The movement-based PE was, above all else, an enabling and facilitating system which was achievement-based.

Movement-based PE also offered, theoretically, the promise of cross-curricular work and curriculum integration (emphasizing the whole curriculum). Thus, movement-based PE has rightly found favour in the pre-school and in the infant curriculum because of its developmental, child-centred and creative focus.

Concurrent with the changing PE curriculum ran significant developments in the organization of sport (through the Sports Council, the CCPR and the local authorities) and dance (through the Arts Council and local authorities). The PE of the young child focused on the provision of a generalized motor programme to meet their needs (and interests). The worlds of sport and dance, however, were concerned to provide for foundation, participation, performance and excellence in selected activity forms. Even accepting the significant strides forward in the current coaching methods of activity specialists, provided by the training programmes of the National Coaching Foundation, the emphasis remains on the activity form (with the accompanying focus on the early identification of talent and activity specialization) rather than on the children (and their need for a broad and balanced curriculum). Thus, a gap has now emerged between what is taught in curriculum PE by phase specialists at Key Stage 1 and the aspirations of sport and dance agencies. This divergence has been the subject of scrutiny over the last decade, following concerns relating to the quality of the teaching of PE at Key Stage 1 (PEA, 1987; Sports Council, 1993; Arts Council of Great Britain, 1993).

Recent educational change (i.e. the introduction of the National Curriculum in 1988) has structurally imposed a ceiling on the amount of PE which can be taught at Key Stage 1, given the new nine-subject-based National Curriculum with its overriding emphasis on the 'core' subjects; it has served to throw into sharp relief what is possible, and desirable, in curriculum PE, and what is required for activity developments in sport and dance. Thus, the question of the role of PE at Key Stage 1 needs to be examined before arriving at any judgements on the future direction of PE and sport and dance.

THE ROLE OF PHYSICAL EDUCATION AT KEY STAGE 1

Intellectual development

While the links established between physical activity and intellectual development (forms of thinking and of abstraction) may be strongest in the pre-school years (Curl, 1990), it is, nevertheless, advisable to ensure that provision is made for the 'late' developer and the slow learner at Key Stage 1. It is, therefore, important to indicate the potential links between movement and cognitive development.

Recent research on brain development (Gregory, 1989; Brierley, 1990; Tanner, 1978), suggests that by the age of 5 years, the brain of the child has reached approximately 90 per cent of its adult weight and that over half of the mental mapping, used to structure thinking, may, by this time, be laid. From the work of Tanner (1978), it is clear that the sensory-motor and perceptual areas of the brain are ahead of the rest. The work of Piaget confirms the importance of the sensory-motor phase in cognitive development and in learning *per se*. Athey (1990) has progressed the work of Piaget on schema theory (those generalizable, repeatable patterns of behaviour which lay the foundation for concept development and abstract thinking). Athey has identified different types of schemas – action, graphic and symbolic. The action schema are identified as:

- horizontal and vertical orientations;
- diagonals;
- positioning;
- trajectory;
- transporting;
- enclosure;
- rotation and swinging.

These may be recognized by a child moving equipment (reconstructing the environment) or travelling with equipment in a purposeful way (moving a friend on a push-along vehicle in transport play). The child's understanding of, for example, transporting may be further revealed in graphic form (in their drawings or in constructions) or in symbolic form (as they become garage mechanics). These action schema provide the templates for thinking in movement (enactive mode) as well as having the potential to be used in other forms of representations (graphic and symbolic).

Moveover, thinking in movement can promote the early use of skills important to intellectual development such as problem-solving, exploration and experimentation, testing, hypothesizing, predicting, detecting, recognizing and analysing. Additionally, physical activity, especially outdoors, can encourage the child to secure information about themselves and their environment. Sitting on top of a climbing frame, climbing a tree, jumping off a piece of apparatus, hanging upside down, climbing in and out of a wooden box, moving inside a tunnel or rolling inside a barrel, kicking or throwing a ball and catching it, and playing with small apparatus (hoops, quoits, bean-bags and bats and balls) – these activities all help a child to develop motor control sufficient to enable them to secure an understanding of the topological property of objects (Athey, 1990), and to appreciate the shape, form and movement of entities. This spatial understanding and an appreciation of the texture and form of objects can provide the foundations of learning of a logico-mathematical, scientific and artistic kind. More-over, McCall (in Oates, 1979) details the link between movement and language development while Matthews (in Blenkin and Kelly, 1987) indicates its close links with drawing (and, of course, with writing).

According to Bruce (1987), following on the work of Bruner, there are also different modes of learning: the enactive (action); the iconic (graphic or visual) and the symbolic (or abstract). The enactive mode which precedes the rest, may be the most developed learning mode, and, therefore, should be the most accessible vehicle for learning in the early years. However, each mode also interacts with the other which is supportive of early learning. Additionally, there may be a preferred mode of learning (e.g. practical learning or visual learning) and of achievement (and psycho-motor giftedness confirms this). Finally, cognition also involves the process of imaging. According to Roberts (1981), imaging (the ability to recall by way of mental pictures, past events, or experiences) is important to representation (schematic development) and, very significantly, it may stay with the individual for life. Thus, the stronger the sensory impressions (from multi-sensory forms of which the kinaesthetic is a lead agent in the early years), the stronger the likely memory traces which are created. This has implications for memory training and successive formal learning (since memory is an important mechanism for academic achievement).

It would appear, from the current range of research, that the pioneers of early childhood education, such as MacMillan (1930) and Isaacs (1932), still offer sound advice in the programme which they promoted for pre-school education. Certainly, movement or physical play featured quite prominently within this approach to learning because of its perceived values to the intellectual and overall development of the child.

More recently, however, corresponding to the development of nursery and reception classes in schools which, in 1993, amounted to some 630,000 children (DFE, 1993), we have seen the introduction into the country of the USA High Scope programme. This is a cognitively based curriculum; it is highly structured and prescriptive, and promotes activities which have a claimed high cognitive yield (Silva *et al.*, 1986). PE is not given a high priority and the PE syllabus used resembles the very formal work of the 1933 syllabus. It is important, if children are not to be disaffected from schooling by the age of 7 years (the age when many European children have only just started school!) that all the needs of children are met, and that intellectual development is promoted in the most accessible and achievement-based way, namely through an emphasis on play-based PE, art, drama and language (in a resource-based outdoor as well as an indoor environment). The plight of the 4-year-old in school needs to be remembered (Education, Science and Arts First Report, 1988; DES, 1989b, 1990; Bennett and Kell, 1989).

Psycho-social development

This aspect of development has been detailed by Martin Lee (1996). Of significance, at Key Stage 1, is the use of the inherited basic motor patterns (Gallaghue, 1989) to ensure the relative success in PE of every young child. Confidence in the self, and a display of motor competency to one's peers, is of significance to the feelings of self-worth of the child during this egocentric phase. Moreover, a movement-based PE programme should ensure that 'hard for me' is not interpreted as failure, but rather as a result of understood difference. In this way, assistance may be given to children to survive the 'drop out' phenomenon of early adolescence. Most particularly, the principle of relative success, and a broadly based programme, should be used to motivate girls (Armstrong and McManus, 1996).

According to Tanner (1978), 'children are a collection of their skills', and achievable personal motor competency should help most children to feel at ease with their own bodies, to relate to others and to decentre (to put themselves into another person's shoes). Psycho-social development rests upon the planned use of the PE curriculum at Key Stage 1. This is also the case in respect of moral development as outlined in Lee's (1996) adapted interactions and model of moral development (Table 3.2). Deliberate training through, in particular, games and gymnastics situations needs to be planned to move children appropriately through from power balancing to egocentric balancing to harmony balancing levels during this age phase. This may then, perhaps, bring some credibility to the claims of those who consider games to be important for character training (Sproat, cited in the *Guardian*, 1 March 1994; in *The Times*, 8 and 9 April 1994; Hansard, 1994; Department of National Heritage (DNH), 1995).

Physical and psycho-motor development

This area focuses on the unique contribution of PE to the early years' curriculum. Armstrong and McManus (in Chapter 2), detail the physiological development of children from pre-school to Key Stage 4. Of particular significance to children from 2 to 7 years is that the activity patterns for active health are laid during this period. It is, therefore, important that whole body activity is fostered (routinized exercise regimes are inappropriate), that sufficient time is allocated to ensure access of children to a broad range of activities and that opportunities for physical activity (with small apparatus, adventure and/or soft play), extend into playtimes, after school, weekends and in vacation times. A positive experience and enjoyment of physical activity, and an emphasis on 'pleasurable performance', are essential prerequisites to a future active lifestyle and for preventive medicine. Finally, girls should be given as much encouragement as is possible to develop a broad repertoire of skills in order to promote future interest and enjoyment in physical activity.

The period around 2 to 7 years of age is also important for the development of the basic motor skills or patterns (Gallaghue, 1989). These are inherited to a rudimentary level and, if developed to mechanical efficiency (at 6 or 7 years of age), can be the key to the relative success of each child in PE. Thus, additional to the provision of a resource-based stimulating environment, which can be explored through movement, must be the learning of these actions, for 'skills are taught not caught' (Arnold, 1968). The different range of motor patterns, categorized by Gallaghue (1989) uniquely provide the content of the syllabus in the core activities (gymnastics, dance and games) of PE at Key Stage 1 (and in the pre-school). The different contexts in which they are used confirms these motor patterns and encourages their modification, refinement and diversification. According to Sugden (1990), there is a strong argument for stating that, by the age of 7 years, children will develop all the fundamental skills they will ever possess.

In teaching these skills (which also form the foundation for activity skills) it is important, in the early years, to make reference to children's maturity of vision (hand–foot–eye co-ordination), balance, body awareness and gross, and later, fine motor control. The young child moves more easily from the more closed skill context of gymnastics, dance, athletics and swimming to the more complex open context of games playing (especially team games). Clearly, it is important to progress the work by providing relevant contexts for action

- when both the body and the environment are stable;
- when the body is moving but the environment is stable;
- when the body is stable but the environment is changing, and finally;
- when the body is moving and the environment is changing.

In order to facilitate skill competency (and success), it is also important to develop a broad repertoire of individual skills, performed well, first, on the spot, then in the general space (with different levels, directions and speeds) and, finally, in individual movement pattern games (with rules, territory and techniques selected by the children). Co-operative skills can then be successfully developed, and both individual and co-operative skills can then be used at Key Stage 2 competently in the competitive contexts of small-sided games (invasion, net and striking/wall). It is counter-productive to focus on small-sided games before individual skills are mastered (as confirmed by the 'drop out' phenomenon). Young children also enjoy expressing feelings and communicating through movement. Dance forms (especially the creative) allow for the use of these basic motor patterns in a range of rhythmic contexts, which also encourage motor pattern diversification and innovation. For survival, health and safety reasons (and for later access to water sports and outdoor activities) opportunities should also be provided for swimming and outdoor and adventurous activities. All the activities of PE are, therefore, important for psycho-motor development and learning. It is the range of experiences which will enable children to exercise their right to choose an activity for life and which will motivate them to be active for life. A more narrow ability-based sports or dance curriculum could undermine these aims.

To summarize, PE in the pre-school and at Key Stage 1 is important for its contribution to the whole curriculum, to whole-child (intellectual, psycho-social and physical and psycho-motor) development and in laying the foundations of the basic motor skills which are essential to the development of the activities of PE at Key Stage 2 (and to the specialized activities of sport and dance).

THE NATIONAL CURRICULUM FOR PHYSICAL EDUCATION (NCPE) AT KEY STAGE 1

In 1992, PE was introduced as a statutory subject within the National Curriculum – a legal requirement of the Education Act (1988). The National Curriculum legalized the entitlement of children in state schools – including those with special educational needs (SEN) – to a balanced, relevant and differentiated curriculum. PE had some status in that it was the only subject, outside the 'core', to be compulsory for all children from 5 to 16 years of age. The NCPE was very much the formalization of past practice, i.e. a movement-based programme which used the six activities to promote whole-child development and learning. The standardization of practice was effected through a process design of planning to ensure that teachers (Blenkin and Kelly, 1987, p. 118):

> instead of concentrating on particular areas of subject content they concern themselves rather with the creation of a structure for the learning processes which they are concerned to encourage.

The concern was, therefore, to use physical activity to develop the cognitive and physical processes. The psycho-social processes were informally included in the General Requirements of the Order and these aspects have been more fully defined in the Physical Education Non-Statutory Guidance produced by the National Curriculum Council (NCC) in June 1992 (pp. B1, D5, G1, 2, 5 and 6).

The key concern of the NCPE was to promote the development of the sub-processes of planning, performing and describing alongside active health and safety. This was to be achieved in a way that was morally acceptable. Equality of opportunity, and individual differences, were to be respected. Moreover, for the first time, not only was content defined (in the Programmes of Study), but an attainment target was introduced in the form of four end of Key Stage statements (EKSS). Assessment was, therefore, introduced as an essential to the teaching–learning cycle, to be used diagnostically (to identify a pupil's needs, to provide landmarks of achievement and to provide some kind of curriculum audit) albeit in a very modest way.

At Key Stage 1, the NCPE which was introduced in August 1992 and reviewed during 1994 was, according to the newly established Schools Curriculum and Assessment Authority, well received by a range of respondents, but most particularly by teachers (SCAA, 1994b). It was deemed to be credible, manageable and flexible – a good match to the child and teacher adjustable. However, teacher discontent with educational change (Blackburn, 1994; Skidelsky, 1993), particularly with the implementation of the National Curriculum and especially at Key Stage 1 (Hofkins, 1994), led to pressure being placed upon government to review the National Curriculum. On 7 April 1993, John Patten, the then Secretary of State for Education, invited Sir Ron Dearing to conduct a review of the National Curriculum and of the framework for assessing pupils' progress. Following extensive consultations, Dearing produced an Interim Report for ministers (SCAA, 1994a), which was accepted by government, as was the final report submitted in December 1993 and published by SCAA (1994b). Teacher reservations centred upon the assessment burden and with the curriculum overload produced at Key Stage 1. The nine subject curriculum (and R.E.) was for the most part detailed, prescriptive and unwieldy (TES, 1994a, 1994b; Sweetman, 1994; Young, 1994). The Physical Education order, which was one of the last to be introduced (DES, 1992b), was already essentialist and trim (with no statutory assessment requirement). Nevertheless it, along with the other Foundation Subjects was trimmed by the Dearing pruning shears (Spencer, 1994; SCAA, 1994b). Content cutback in the new order (DFE, 1995) is of significance. The physical education curriculum is no longer broad and balanced at Key Stage 1 (since athletics and outdoor and adventurous activities have now been deferred until Key Stage 2). Moreover, the incomplete gymnastics (there is no work on space and shape) and dance content (all the dynamics are not covered and music is the only stimulus for composition work) suggest that even the foundations of the 'core' knowledge is no longer statutory.

The common requirements of infant practice such as equality of opportunity, a focus on how children learn and cross-curricular work is not stated though it is, perhaps, assumed. Performance is now the focus since it expresses simultaneously the other aspects of planning and describing. At Key Stage 1, this is to be encouraged. A standard of achievement has now been reinstated, normally equivalent to level two of the ten-level scale (DES, 1991, p. 20) in relation to performance in games, gymnastics and dance, in the four end of Key Stage descriptors (a new designation). This minimal assessment requirement is recorded and reported at the end of each year. Thus, teachers at Key Stage 1 work towards ensuring, through the 'core' physical activities, that (DFE, 1995, p. 11):

> Pupils plan and perform simple skills safely and show control in linking actions together. They improve their performance through practising their skills, working alone and with a partner. They talk about what they and others have done and are able to make simple judgements. They recognise and describe the changes that happen to their bodies during exercise.

Thus, the new NCPE still remains relatively faithful to traditionalist infant and pre-school practice, for it is still designed around a process model. It is, therefore, very much concerned with the education of the young child but with a clearer definition of the importance of physical development (active health) and psycho-motor learning (with the stress on performance). The 'core' activities remain so that the foundations of physical learning (as defined by the basic motor patterns) are virtually covered. However, access is now deferred for some activities, which are important to health and to our culture (outdoor and adventurous activities, athletic activities and possibly swimming) There is also the issue of a structural bias towards competitive games, even at Key Stage 1 (DFE, 1995). This may affect the provision of a broad and balanced physical education curriculum, which is important for the young child where a broad repertoire of skills is needed for optimum development (Sugden, 1990).

Despite these reservations, the NCPE at Key Stage 1 has been well-received by teachers who appear to feel competent to teach it (SCAA, 1994b). Of course there is room for improvement, (OFSTED, 1993, 1995). Potentially, there is also, through the flexible curriculum process design the opportunity to produce a good match between process (with its child-centred, movement-based approach) and product (with a more skill-based, activity approach). Certainly the final form of the revised NCPE was the result of a considerable amount of consultation between the different interest groups from education, sport, dance, health and politics (SCAA, 1994b).

However, although the NCPE is based upon an educational rationale which takes account of the wider societal perspectives, its potential effectiveness has been undermined by the overriding priority given at Key Stage 1 to the 'core' subjects and to an academic curriculum.

This academic bias, effected by government through the assessment requirements of the National Curriculum, the publication of results and by the teacher training and school inspection systems, has marginalized the NCPE (and sport). In turn, this has impacted upon children's health (Sleap and Warburton, 1994; McManus and Armstrong, 1995) and upon their sporting prowess (Wood, 1994; Hymans and Grice, 1994).

However, the tension in schooling between satisfying educational priorities and provision for sport has now been resolved by a Policy Statement, sponsored by the Prime Minister (DNH, 1995). According to the Prime Minister, his intention is,

> To put sport back at the heart of weekly life in *every* school. To re-establish sport as one
> of the great pillars of education alongside the academic, the vocational and the moral.
> (John Major's introduction to DNH, 1995)

In this document, the government has set out a detailed blueprint for the development of sport in schools, and particularly in respect of the promotion of the traditional sports such as cricket, hockey, swimming, athletics, football, netball, rugby and tennis (DNH, 1995).

The impact of this policy will be significant. It will raise physical education to a curriculum subject with both a high status and profile. However, it is also essential to discuss the effect of this initiative on the implementation of the new NCPE at Key Stage 1.

THE FUTURE DIRECTION OF THE NCPE AT KEY STAGE 1

The key elements of this government initiative in relation to the education of young children may be summarized as follows;

1 There will be a greater concentration in the revised NCPE on traditional team games and competitive sport as these are applicable to young children.
2 All 5–7-year-olds will be taught the skills of competitive games and how to play them (in relation to their stage of development).
3 The focus is deliberately on sport (especially games), but the broader base remains since the NCPE is further confirmed by government in the document.
4 All schools should offer two hours per week of physical education and sport in formal lessons (with the possibility of a further four hours per week for those schools wishing to achieve a gold star award for quality and innovation).
5 All schools should seek to extend sporting opportunities at lunch-times, in the evenings and at weekends (using on-site and off-site facilities).

6   OFSTED will inspect the quality and range of games offered as part of the physical education curriculum and report on this.

7   OFSTED will report on provision outside the formal curriculum and they will be required to identify good practice in school sport.

8   OFSTED will monitor and report on teacher training institutions and Her Majesty's Chief Inspector of Schools will be required to report annually on the state of physical education and sport in schools (to ensure the effecting of policy).

9   New teacher training courses must meet the revised National Curriculum (to ensure that infant teachers can deliver a quality NCPE).

10   In order to improve the achievements in sport (and particularly games), all trainee and serving teachers will have the opportunity to acquire coaching qualifications, and schools will be encouraged to use volunteers (from higher education and elsewhere) to enhance activity performance in both curriculum and non-curriculum time.

11   The Sports Council will review the appropriateness of existing coaching schemes offered by National Governing Bodies and they will ensure the effective use of resources (e.g. the dual use of school facilities).

12   Regional Sports Councils will have a key role to play in developing school–club links and governing bodies of sport will be required to develop plans for school sport projects).

13   Lottery money will be used (to be distributed by the Regional Sports Councils) to improve facilities, to preserve playing fields and to provide enhanced coaching and competitive opportunities so that by the year 2000 all young people will have access to quality provision.

This new policy throws up a range of new issues. These relate to the control of physical education and sport in schools. Responsibility now appears to be in the hands of the DNH (with the DFE responding to designated areas of policy). Policy coordination and implementation now seem to be within the brief of the Minister for Sport, with enhanced powers being given to national and regional sports councils. Thus, the education service, even given the autonomy of each school, may be involved, less in policy making and more in its implementation.

Further, the infant and pre-school teacher may now be only one of a range of personnel who could teach the NCPE and provide sporting experiences in non-curriculum and after-school time. Clearly, it is envisaged that activity teaching will be delivered by those with a 'games assistant' or 'coaching' qualification (National Coaching Foundation, 1995). This will provide a particular challenge to the continuance of the early years movement-based education, which has thrived on its whole-child, cross curricular and play-based emphasis. It will also create some practical problems relating to the screening, coordination and monitoring of personnel who work with young children (there are rigorous requirements relating to the suitability of trainee teachers in respect of intellectual and personal qualities).

The implementation of the NCPE is assured but its success will be determined by the quality management of the government's new policy for sport in schools. Those involved in the delivery of the early years curriculum (to include the expanding pre-school area), will also have to find ways of incorporating yet another set of complex government directives into their school development plans.

THE IMPLICATIONS FOR NCPE AT KEY STAGE 1

Initial impressions are that the teaching of the NCPE at Key Stage 1 should be greatly improved by this government initiative. Certainly, the Prime Minister's claim that the new plans are the most important set of proposals ever published for the encouragement and promotion of sport is difficult to dispute (DNH, 1995):

> Government policy is unashamedly ideological as competition is promoted through the reinstatement of sport (especially team games) back into the heart of the curriculum. Indeed, the change in emphasis in physical education at Key Stage 1 is reflected in the government's use of the term, 'P.E. and Sport' in schools. Thus, whilst sport may form part of the NCPE at Key Stage 1 (through the gymnastic activities, the games and the optional swimming components) further provision must now be made for an identifiable sports programme which will extend into non-curriculum and after-school time.

Thus the new policy should meet many of the reservations which were documented relating to the quality of the teaching of physical education in primary schools and in the decline of school sport (PEA, 1987; School Sport Forum, 1988; Hymans and Grice, 1994; Spencer, 1994; Wood, 1994). Certainly there is no reason now why the delivery of the NCPE should be minimalist rather than essentialist. The structural measures to be taken in terms of funding, facilities and resource improvements, a credible time allocation and better professional training, monitoring, inspection and reporting systems should systematically improve the quality of NCPE as well as enhancing the sporting experience of children.

In terms of the implementation of this new policy there are already plans that are in place to support this initiative. The Sports Council launched its National Junior Sports Programme at the RECMAN conference in March 1995. A major component of this strategy is to be implemented by the new charity 'Youth Sport Trust'. It has been established to work in partnership with the Sports Council, supported by some private sector funding, to develop the 'Top Programme'. This is made up of four sections which parallel the Sports Council's 'Sports Continuum'. The emphasis for pre-school and Key Stage 1 children will be on the development of 'Top Play' schemes. These focus on the promotion of core skills and fun sport mostly of a games type (Youth Sport Trust, 1995). Additionally, activity development officers funded in part or in total by the regional Arts and Sports councils, local authorities and the governing bodies of sport have already established a support service within a number of schools. This has included work with infant teachers and classes during both curriculum and extra-curriculum time.

CONCLUSION

These are exciting times offering tremendous opportunities to provide quality physical education and, in the future, sport as well. However, 3–8 years is also a vulnerable period in the growth and development of young children. If the intention is to realize the maxim, 'Physical activity for life', then the young child must always have a central place in the implementation of any physical education and sport programme. In the NCPE at Key Stage 1, it is the child that counts, not just the activity. If this principle is respected in future policy then schools may be the institutions which safeguard children's cultural and physical rights. Thus, in the future, it may well be said once again, 'To feel one's life in every limb, that is the life of early childhood'. (MacMillan, 1930).

REFERENCES

Armstrong, N. and McManus, A. (1996) 'Growth, maturation and physical education', in Armstrong, N. (ed.), *New Directions in Physical Education: Change and Innovation.* London: Cassell, pp. 19–32.
Arnold, P. (1968) *Education, PE and Personality Development.* London: Heinemann.
Arnold, P. (1979) *Meaning in Movement, Sport and Physical Education.* London: Heinemann.
Arts Council of Great Britain (1993) *Education, Dance in Schools.* London: Arts Council.
Athey, C. (1990) *Extending Thought in Young Children.* London: Paul Chapman.
Bennett, W. and Kell, J. (1989) *A Good Start. Four Year Olds in Infant Schools.* London: Blackwell.
Bilborough, A. and Jones, P. (1973) *Developing Patterns in Physical Education.* London: London University Press.
Blackburn, L. (1994) 'Dearing seeks end to test boycott', *Times Educational Supplement,* 21 January.
Blenkin, G. and Kelly, A.V. (1987) *Early Childhood Education. A Developmental Curriculum.* London: Paul Chapman.
Bray, S. (1992) 'Towards the National Curriculum – A review of developments in PE in primary schools in England and Wales during the twentieth century', *Bulletin of Physical Education,* **28**, 7–25.
Brierley, J. (1976) *The Growing Brain.* Windsor: National Foundation for Educational Research.
Brierley, J. (1990) *Growth in Children – Mirror of Society.* Unpublished text – by permission.
Bruce, T. (1987) *Early Childhood Education.* London: Hodder and Stoughton.
Cameron, W.McD and Cameron, M. (1969) *Education in Movement in the Infant School.* London: Basil Blackwell.
Carr, D. (1978) 'Practical pursuits and the curriculum', *Journal of Philosophy of Education,* **12**, 69–80.
Curl, G. (1990) A critique of the B.C.P.E. interim working group progress report. Article presented and submitted to the *IWG*, Bournemouth, March.
DES (1967) Children and their primary schools. A Report of the Central Advisory Council for Education. England. Vols 1 and 2, London: HMSO.
DES (1972) *Movement – Physical Education in the Primary Years.* London: HMSO.
DES (1985) *The Curriculum from 5–16.* London: HMSO.
DES (1989a) *Physical Education from 5–16. Curriculum Matters 16.* London: HMSO.
DES (1989b) *Aspects of Primary Education. The Education of Children Under Five.* London: HMSO.
DES (1990) *Starting with Quality.* The Report of the Committee of Enquiry into the Quality of Educational Experience offered to 3–4-year-olds. London: HMSO.
DES (1991) *The Teaching and Learning of PE. Aspects of Primary Education.* London: HMSO.
DES (1992a) *The Education of Very Able Children in Maintained Schools. A Review by H.M.I.* London: HMSO.
DES (1992b) *Physical Education in the National Curriculum.* London: HMSO.
DFE (1993) *Pupils Under Five Years of Age in Schools in England, January 1992.* Prepared by the Government Statistical Service, May.
DFE (1995) *Physical Education in the National Curriculum.* London: HMSO.
Department of National Heritage (DNH) (1995) *Sport. Raising the Game.* London: DNH.
Education, Science and Arts First Report (1988) *Education Provision for the Under Fives.* London: HMSO.
Gallagahue, D. (1989) *Motor Development.* Indianapolis: Benchmark Press Ltd.

Gilliver, K. (1995) 'Physical education in the National Curriculum', *British Journal of Physical Education*, **26**, 7–9.

Gregory, R. (1989) *The Oxford Companion to the Mind*. Oxford: Oxford University Press, pp. 541–3.

Hansard (1994) *The Queen's Speech to the Commonwealth*.

HMI (1992) *The Education of Very Able Children in Maintained Schools*. London: HMSO.

Hirst, P.H. (1979) 'Human movement, knowledge and education', *Journal of Philosophy of Education*, **13**, 101–8.

Hirst, P.H. (1989) 'The concepts of physical education and dance', *Collected Conference Papers in Dance*. London: NATFHE Dance Section.

Hofkins, D. (1994) 'Curriculum has damaged morale', *TES*, 24 June.

Hohhman, M., Bennet, B. and Weikart, D. (1979) *Young Children in Action*. Ipsilante, Michigan: High Scope Press.

Howard, R. (1987) *Concepts and Schematas*. London: Cassell Education.

Hymans, C. and Grice, A. (1994) 'Athletes to be groomed at schools for sport', *Guardian*, 13 September.

Isaacs, S. (1932) *The Nursery Years*. London: Routledge, Kegan and Paul.

Kelly, A.V. (1982) *The Curriculum*. London: Harper & Row.

Lee, M. (1996) 'Psycho-social development from 5–6 years', in Armstrong, N. (ed.), *New Directions in Physical Education Volume 3: Change and Innovation*. London: Cassell, pp. 33–47.

McManus, A. and Armstrong, N. (1995) 'Patterns of physical activity among primary schoolchildren', in Ring, F.J. (ed.), *Children in Sport*. Bath: Bath University Press, pp. 17–23.

MacMillan, M. (1930) *The Nursery School*. London and Toronto: JM Dent and Sons Ltd.

National Coaching Foundation (1995) 'Great boost for coaching', *Supercoach*, **7**, 1.

National Curriculum Council (1992) *PE in the National Curriculum. Non Statutory Guidelines*. York: NCC.

Oates, J. (1979) *Early Cognitive Development*. London: Croom Helm in Association with the Open University Press.

OSE (1993) *Physical Education. Key Stages 1, 2 and 3. First Year*. London: HMSO.

OFSTED (1995) *Physical Education. A Review of Inspection Findings 1993–94*. London: HMSO.

Physical Education Association of Great Britain and Northern Ireland (1987) *Physical Education in Schools. Report of a Commission of Enquiry*. London: Ling Publishers.

Roberts, M. (1981) 'The unity of the child as expressed in his play life', in Roberts, M. and Tamburrini, J. (eds) Edinburgh: Holmes McDougall, pp. 121–3.

SCAA (1994a) *Physical Education. Revised Draft Proposals*. London: Schools Curriculum and Assessment Authority.

SCAA (1994b) *The Review of the National Curriculum – A Report on the 1994 Consultation*. London: Schools Curriculum Assessment Authority.

School Sport Forum (1988) *Sport and Young People: Partnerships and Action*. London: The Sports Council.

Silva, K., Roy, C. and Painter, H. (1986) *Childwatching at Playgroup and Nursery School*. London: Basil Blackwell.

Skidelsky, Lord (1993) 'Test knowledge but not values', *TES*, 30 July.

Sleap, M. and Warburton, P. (1994) 'Physical activity levels of pre-adolescent children in England', *British Journal of Physical Education Research Supplement*, **14**, 2–6.

Spencer, D. (1994) 'No winners in the P.E. order', *TES*, 18 November.

Sports Council (1993) *Young People and Sport*. London: Sports Council.

Stenhouse, L. (1975) *An Introduction to Curriculum Research and Development*. London: Heinemann.

Sugden, D. (1990) 'Development of physical education for all', *British Journal of Physical Education*, **21**, 247–51.

Sweetman, J. (1994) 'Unwrapping Sir Ron's Christmas parcel', *Guardian*, 11 January.

Tanner, J.M. (1978) *Education and Physical Growth*. London: Hodder & Stoughton.

Times Educational Supplement (1994a) 'Only teachers can improve standards', *TES*, 7 January.
Times Educational Supplement (1994b) 'Advantage Patten', *TES*, 14 January.
Wood, N. (1994) 'Blueprint for the revival of school sport', *The Times*, 8 April.
Young, S. (1994) 'The oldest new policy of them all', *TES*, 21 January.
Youth Sport Trust (1995) *Bringing Sport to the Life of Young People. The Top Programmes.*
    London: Youth Sport Trust.

Chapter 5

Physical Education at Key Stage 2

Anne Williams

CONTEXT

The Education Act (1988) was formulated on the premise that all children are entitled to a broad, balanced, relevant and differentiated curriculum. For PE, breadth was defined in terms of six activity areas: games, gymnastics, dance, athletics, swimming and outdoor/adventurous activities. The PE Order (DES, 1992) required primary school teachers to include all six areas within the curriculum, although there was some flexibility in that swimming could be included at either Key Stage 1 or at Key Stage 2. The Dearing review demanded that all subjects 'slim down' their area of the curriculum to solve some of the difficulties created by a clearly overloaded programme. The latest proposals, however, continue to include all six activity areas at Key Stage 2, thereby presenting a considerable challenge to schools. PE continues to be taught largely by non-specialist teachers and is just one of ten required subject areas at Key Stage 2, all of which now demand a level of subject knowledge which is problematic for many Key Stage 2 teachers. The size and staffing structures of many primary schools do not always allow for specialization at present and it is difficult to imagine significant change in the short term. It thus seems likely that the expectation that all Key Stage 2 teachers will cover PE alongside other National Curriculum subject areas will continue. There is therefore a considerable challenge facing the PE profession if National Curriculum targets are to be achieved.

The end of Key Stage statements (EKSS) for Key Stage 2 published in the original PE Order (DES, 1992) are as follows:

By the end of Key Stage 2, pupils should be able to:
a) plan, practise, improve and remember more complex sequences of movement;
b) perform effectively in activities requiring quick decision-making;
c) respond safely, alone and with others, to challenging tasks, taking account of levels of skill and understanding;
d) swim unaided at least 25 metres and demonstrate an understanding of water safety;
e) evaluate how well they and others perform and behave against criteria suggested by the teacher and suggest ways of improving performance;

f) sustain energetic activity over appropriate periods of time in a range of physical activities and understand the effects of exercise on the body.

The draft proposals for the revision of the National Curriculum present new EKSS in prose form as follows (SCAA, 1994):

Pupils make appropriate decisions quickly and plan their responses in different environments. They develop their skill by exploring and making up activities and by expressing themselves imaginatively. They practise, adapt, improve and repeat longer and increasingly complex sequences of movement. They measure and compare results of their own performance. They begin to show an awareness of the importance of taking account of different levels of skill and understanding in order to work safely alone and with others. They make judgements of performance and suggest means of improvement in simple technical language. They sustain energetic activity over appropriate periods of time and show an understanding of what is happening to their bodies while they are exercising.

Comparison of the two reveals that little has changed. The requirement to swim 25 metres has been removed, but it remains in the Programme of Study (PoS) for Key Stage 2 swimming which is a requirement if not completed at Key Stage 1 and is thus statutory. Scrutiny of the activity-specific PoS does reveal that some statements have been taken out; however, closer inspection shows that several of the statements which have been removed could in fact be subsumed under others. For example, 'be guided to perform in a controlled manner and to understand that the ending of one action can become the beginning of the next' (DES, 1992) does not feature in the SCAA proposals. If could be argued that the requirement that pupils practise and refine actions and make increasingly complex movement sequences (SCAA, 1994, p. 3) implies both controlled performance and the ability to perform so that the ending of one action becomes the beginning of another. However the new order is interpreted, the Key Stage 2 teacher still faces a considerable challenge. He or she has not only to offer a curriculum which is accessible to all pupils but, if equal opportunity is to be approached, the curriculum should be designed to enable pupils of different abilities, cultural backgrounds and gender to benefit.

THE CHILD AT KEY STAGE 2

PE at Key Stage 2 is challenging, not only because of the subject knowledge demanded of the teacher, but also because of the developmental stages through which pupils pass during this time, as described in Chapter 2 of this volume. The years from about 8 to 12 are often characterized as the 'skill-hungry' years, or the optimum time for the learning of physical skills. It has been suggested that failure to capitalize upon this optimum period for learning, the precise age of which will vary from child to child, can lead to long-term under-performance or even to alienation from physical activity. The latter has been noted particularly with respect to girls.

The Key Stage 2 years are, for many children, a period of rapid growth and physical development, although the pattern will vary, not only from one individual to another, but also between boys and girls. While regular vigorous activity is important at times of rapid physical growth, there are potential dangers in inappropriate or excessive physical demands being placed upon the body at this time, and these need to be understood by the teacher. The trend towards lower activity levels among children has been well documented, particularly through the work of Armstrong (Armstrong and McManus, 1996) who has demonstrated that relatively few children at Key Stage 2 reach activity levels which would be seen as sufficient to be beneficial in terms of health-related fitness. This places a major responsibility upon the school which, for most children, will be an important provider of activity opportunities and a significant influence on disposition to undertake additional exercise.

At the other extreme is a concern about an increase in over-use injuries among pupils of this age group as a result of either too heavy or inappropriate training, or of too much match play. While the school is unlikely to be the direct cause of such problems, teachers are potentially well placed to educate parents in this respect. In activities such as swimming or gymnastics, where high performance levels at an early age are the norm, the teacher can sound a timely warning if over-ambitious parents are tempted to push children unacceptably hard. In games such as soccer, where the talented young player can be called upon by the school, the area and the local club, the school can monitor the level of match play and advise if it appears to be becoming excessive.

A major challenge for the teacher at Key Stage 2 is the wide range of physical development among the typical class. The average age of puberty is two years younger for girls than for boys, but there is also considerable individual variation within each sex group. Furthermore, when the typical developmental range of four years within one age cohort is added to the chronological range of one year, it is obvious that, within one Key Stage 2 class, the range, in terms of physical development will be up to five years. When one considers that this is equivalent to asking a 5-year-old to compete against a 10-year-old, the implications of performance comparisons within the Key Stage 2 class begin to become apparent.

One potential effect of this is to give the early maturing child a clear advantage if only because of the positive effect on performance and learning of success and achievement. Given the public nature of the child's achievements in PE, compared with other subjects where one's shortcomings can be concealed more easily, it is all too easy for the child who is less mature physically to be discouraged by relative failure when compared with more mature peers. A PE curriculum which over-emphasizes competition against others, rather than against one's own previous personal best will not meet the needs of all pupils.

The second factor which needs understanding by the teacher is the way in which developments at puberty can affect boys and girls in different ways. It is well known that high-level performers tend to be early maturing boys but late maturing girls. Boys gain in strength and in physical efficiency post puberty. Girls, in contrast, may become less mechanically efficient because of the physical factors outlined in Chapter 2. Thus some girls will reach their personal physical peak prior to puberty. Given the large number of girls, compared with boys, who will reach puberty during Key Stage 2, this factor is important for the teacher who is interested in encouraging optimal achievement by all pupils.

These developmental factors have implications for lesson content and for teaching styles. In particular, the range of physical differences to be found within the typical Key Stage 2 class demands effective differentiation if all are to achieve. In addition to physical differences, the teacher requires an understanding of the way in which factors such as gender, race and special needs affect pupil progress in PE.

In addition to the physical differences identified above, many other factors will affect the response of the child to the curriculum offered. Previous or ongoing out-of-school experience of physical activity, dispositions towards activity in general or towards specific activity areas are affected significantly by social circumstances. Socialization remains differentiated by class, race and gender. Many practices remain, both in school and outside, which while appearing trivial, contribute to the formation of the child's identity. Sexual division of labour within the family remains, to a large extent, both overt and sharply defined. It is therefore important that the school avoids perpetuating this through, for example, expecting 'strong boys' to move equipment. This is particularly inappropriate in a class of pre-puberty pupils where the strong pupils may well be girls. Physical and play activity has little significance for families from some cultures, particularly some Asian communities. The previous experience of pupils from such families may have been very restricted compared to that of some of their peers. Moreover, their attitude towards PE may be affected by family perceptions of its lack of importance.

Opportunities for informal physical play outside school can be limited by physical circumstances, by concern for children's safety or by changing social behaviour patterns. In contrast, opportunities for participation in a whole range of organized physical activities through various mini-sport sessions, gymnastics clubs, swimming sessions and so on, have probably never been greater for those with the means to both travel to them and to pay for participation. What has previously been a difference in the kind of outside-school physical activity experiences available to those from different social backgrounds has now become, for many, a difference in activity level. Many parents are, understandably in the light of recent events, reluctant to allow children to play at any distance from home. Girls are more likely to be restricted than boys although, in many areas, both sexes may be affected. The result is that the kind of informal play activity and street play which typified the childhood activities of previous generations are no longer available.

By the time the child reaches Key Stage 2, the effect of these variables will be to produce marked differences in confidence and performance. Lack of experience compared to peers may reduce confidence while socialization into a culture which sees physical activity as unimportant or inappropriate for a particular group may affect both previous experience and disposition to learn.

By Key Stage 2, pupils will have had three years experience of school PE and will have more clearly formed concepts of success and failure, winning and losing, than the reception class child for whom the notion that everyone can be a winner is still a part of his or her personal reality. This means that success and failure within the PE context is likely to have a significant effect upon individual self-esteem although the processes involved in the development of self-esteem are not yet well understood (Fox, 1992).

What does seem to be clear is that the development of a sense of perceived physical competence and success in all pupils is crucial if lifelong involvement in physical activity is seen as a significant outcome of a successful PE programme. Those for whom school PE results in low perceptions of physical competence are likely to seek feelings of self-worth in contexts other than the physical and to reject future involvement in physical activity whether within the school curriculum or outside.

DIFFERENTIATION

It will be clear from the above that, without differentiation, many pupils will be unable to reach their potential in PE. Effective differentiation requires both organizational and teaching strategies which will support the learning of all pupils. Good practice in differentiation, whatever the subject, should result in the presence of a variety of learning activities, the maintenance of a high level of productive work, busy motivated pupils and the preservation of order and discipline (Simpson, 1989).

The way in which pupils are grouped can facilitate differentiation. Although the motivation afforded by opportunities to practise and perform with friends should not be discounted, friendship groups may not equate to ability groups. Ability groups will facilitate the setting of differentiated tasks or the provision of extensions for those who find the tasks too easy. For example, where small-sided games are being played, different rule modifications can be imposed on different games depending upon the ability of those playing. Apparatus arrangements in gymnastics can be organized so that, for example, different heights or sizes of supporting surface are available, to be used by pupils as appropriate. Here, pupils can select their own group by choosing, with guidance if necessary, the apparatus which is within their capability.

The availability of a range of equipment and resources can also help. In fielding games, for example, giving pupils choice of different sizes of bat can enable all to contact the ball and to score runs or rounders, while enabling the more able, or the more physically mature to have the challenge of using more demanding equipment. Gymnastics apparatus placed at different heights will accommodate differences in size, confidence and ability.

The way in which pupils are given different roles and responsibilities within the lesson can also offer provision which is differentiated as well as a broader range of opportunities to achieve. Involvement of pupils in planning and evaluating their work, noted by Her Majesty's Inspectorate (DES, 1991) as a feature of good practice in primary school PE, can enable some, who find physical performance difficult, to display high levels of understanding, knowledge and analysis. In games, for example, pupils whose achievement in the skills of the game are limited by ability, lack of experience or physical immaturity, may well be able to analyse play and discuss tactics in a way which is well beyond their physical performance. In gymnastics and dance, pupils' compositional skills may be more fully developed than their physical abilities.

Some pupils, in some activities, will need challenges beyond those which the school can provide if they are to achieve their full potential. For these pupils, extra-curricular provision, or club links, can be an important aspect of differentiated provision. It should, however, be remembered that while the talented pupil's level of physical skill may be far in advance of his or her peers, levels of understanding, especially in activities where training can be ritualized and routine, for example swimming, may well be similar. Neither should it be assumed that the talented performer has necessarily acquired the skills of analysis needed for planning and evaluation.

The usual way of looking at differentiation is to differentiate either by task or by outcome. Differentiation by task means that pupils are set a range of tasks so that all are working on a challenge appropriate to their ability. Differentiation by outcome involves setting the same task for all pupils but expecting different answers from pupils of different abilities.

It is worth looking at the kinds of tasks which teachers set. There are many ways of categorizing these. For the purposes of this chapter, that used by Simpson (1989) will be adapted to the PE context.

Practice tasks involve the repetitive application of a skill or procedure which the pupils have previously acquired or understood. There are many example of such tasks within PE as pupils attempt to refine previously learned skills. Children may practise rolling forwards in a gymnastics lesson. The least able will concentrate on rolling safely to a sitting position. The most able may practise rolling to finish in a straddle or a box splits position. In the games context, pupils may be practising throwing and catching. The difference between the task for least and most able or between the least and most physically mature may relate to the kind of ball being used with the least able using a large lightweight ball and the most able a cricket ball.

Incremental tasks involve introducing new work, developing previous work further or doing something with which the pupil has a problem. Pupils who have learned basic rolling actions in gymnastics could be introduced to different starts and finishes, either through examples given by the teacher or by being asked to invent their own. Pupils who have learned basic throwing in the games context could learn to differentiate between the types of throw used, for example, in netball or basketball, such as the chest pass, the overhead pass and so on. Again differentiation by task could involve giving pupils of different abilities or maturity levels balls of different sizes and weights.

Restructuring tasks are those where the pupil works with familiar materials but is required to discover, invent or construct a new way of looking at them. For example, pupils may have composed sequences in dance or gymnastics which follow a particular floor pattern, maybe a straight line. They might be asked to use the same actions to compose a sequence which followed a different floor pattern, maybe a circle or a 'Z' pattern. In games, pupils who have learned a number of basic skills using a netball could be asked to make up their own game using the same skills but with a court area and goal which were new to them. The size of court could be set by the teacher taking account of individual groups' abilities to cope with a large or small space. Scoring could also be differentiated by giving groups a large or small target at which to aim.

Enrichment tasks involve the use of familiar knowledge concepts or skills in unfamiliar contexts. Thus the pupil may have acquired the skills of rolling or balancing on the floor in gymnastics but is now asked to use the same skills on apparatus, for example, rolling along a padded plank, or balancing on a high table. In the games context, the pupils may have used throwing and catching skills in a game of netball but now be asked to use them in the context of a touch rugby game.

Revision involves the performance of skills or procedures which have been set aside for some time. Given the seasonal nature of many PE activities, there will be occasions each year when this kind of task is appropriate, for example, if fielding games are only played in the summer term.

The approach to differentiation chosen will depend in part on the teaching style chosen by the teacher. For example, pupils might be asked to show ways of taking their weight on their hands. For the more able child, this might involve a two-footed take-off from a straddle position, lifting into a handstand. Another child might kick up from a single take-off into a handstand. Yet another might use the wall for support in order to lift both feet off the floor for an instant. In the games context, the task might be to pass the ball to a partner. Some pupils might use a high double-handed throw as used in, for example, high-level netball, to pass the ball over a long distance. Others might use a two-handed underarm action over a short distance in a style which would answer the task, but would be less effective than the first example in outwitting opponents in the game situation. Whether pupils are set the same task and allowed to choose their response or whether the teacher makes the decision about who should be involved in which activity will depend upon the extent to which independence and decision making are priorities for the teacher involved.

It is important that the teacher is clear about the kind of differentiation being used and checks to see that the pupils interpret the tasks set in the way which was intended. For example, the teacher might set a task which was intended to have an enrichment or restructuring focus but which some pupils interpret as practice with the consequence that they restrict themselves to practising known skills rather than extending their range of movement by adding to them.

PROGRESSION

Because of the range of physical differences alluded to earlier, and because differentiated provision will often produce differentiated outcomes, progression will need to be considered in relation to the individual child rather than to the class as a whole. This will require effective assessment or recording of achievement. The statutory requirement to report to parents in relation to end of Key Stage statements (EKSS) will provide a brief comment on each individual's achievement in PE, but records of achievement are likely to be of much greater use to the teacher who needs to know how the child is progressing in more detail. Various strategies may be used including personal diaries and involving children in commenting on or recording aspects of each others' performance. A number of examples of good practice are to be found in the SEAC (1990) publication *Records of Achievement in Primary Schools*. The use of questions, class discussion and comment to help pupils to assess both their own work and that of their peers as part of either building personal profiles or keeping personal progress files was noted by HMI as an indicator of good primary practice (DES, 1991).

Progression can be defined in terms of: range of movement vocabulary; difficulty of movement vocabulary; or quality of movement achieved. Also important are the ability to plan, evaluate and work independently. Each is now considered in turn.

Range of movement vocabulary

Pupils should be expected to show an increased range of skills within the different activity areas. For example, in the games context, pupils would be expected to learn skills which can be deployed in an increasing variety of games contexts. Throwing and catching, for example, would progress from basic skills using a ball of the pupil's choice to achieving that skill using balls of a variety of shapes and sizes (rounders ball, tennis ball, rugby ball, netball, soccer ball and volleyball), and in a variety of games situations such as fielding in rounders or cricket-related games, passing in rugby, netball or basketball type games. In gymnastics, pupils could be expected to learn to perform an increasing number of variations of basic skills such as many different starts and finishes to a forward or backward roll, or a range of ways of coming down from taking the weight on the hands, or a widening range of balancing skills.

Difficulty of movement vocabulary

As well as an increasing range of movement, pupils should be challenged to learn skills of increasing difficulty. For example, pupils who can pass the ball effectively unchallenged, should progress to demonstrating the same skill with the pressure of opposition. Pupils who have learned a wide range of balancing skills should be encouraged to progress to achieving balances upon smaller points of support thus increasing the difficulty. This may be achieved through reducing the size of the supporting base on the floor, such as balancing on one shoulder rather than two, or by attempting the balance on apparatus which has a small supporting area such as a headstand on a bench or high plank rather than on the floor. Difficulty can also involve understanding and memory as in the learning and repeating of increasingly complex sequences in dance or gymnastics.

Quality of movement achieved

Pupils should be encouraged to continue to refine their performances. This aspect of progression is very clearly seen in gymnastics and dance where good style in performance should be developing by the end of Key Stage 2.

Ability to plan

PE for this age group offers many opportunities for planning, both alone and with others. A task involving games making could involve small group planning, not only challenging the pupil's ability to think through the planning process but also demanding the co-operative social skills needed for effective group working. Within the gymnastics or dance context, there is much scope for planning performance both solo and with others.

Ability to evaluate

While Key Stage 1 pupils are quite capable of making simple judgements about performance based on criteria given by the teacher, by the end of Key Stage 2, children have the potential to make quite sophisticated judgements provided that the opportunity to do so has been a regular feature of their PE programme.

Ability to work independently

If children are to become 'thinking' performers, they should be encouraged, from an early stage, to take responsibility for themselves where appropriate. The ability to work independently can manifest itself in many ways. Pupils at Key Stage 2 should be capable of practising for a sustained period without constant intervention by the teacher.

Progression through Key Stage 2 demands co-ordination within the school and leadership by the head or curriculum leader. It is also dependent upon the ability of the teacher to use a range of teaching styles and strategies.

PARTNERSHIP

The National Curriculum Physical Education Working Group supported the active involvement of various partners – such as parents, local authority organizations, Sports Council and local clubs – in order that pupils can realize their full potential in PE. They note, however, that the school is the main provider at Key Stages 1 and 2. Partnership at Key Stage 2 is therefore more likely to involve outside agencies visiting the school than vice versa.

There is plenty of precedent in other curriculum areas – parents coming into school to hear children read; parents or governors with particular skills being invited in. For example, a governor with many years' experience in the computer industry spent one day a week in a primary school working alongside the class teacher to enable all pupils to extend their information technology experience. Parents also act as classroom assistants. Local writers visit schools to run writing workshops for pupils.

Partnership in the context of Key Stage 2 PE can serve several purposes:

1   New activities can be introduced.
2   Access to the curriculum can be increased for some pupils.
3   Learning opportunities can be extended.
4   Teachers' subject knowledge can be improved.
5   New teaching approaches can be tried.
6   Extra curricular provision can be made or extended.

It should be stressed that any partnership-based activity should be related to and integrated with the aims and experiences described in the school's scheme of work. Although current National Curriculum Orders require the inclusion of all six activity areas at Key Stage 2, there remains considerable flexibility within this requirement. For example, schools can choose the games which they include. This opens up possibilities for parental involvement or for work with a youth development officer, thus widening pupils' experience of games in order to meet the Programme of Study element which states that pupils should,

> develop an understanding of and play games created by the teacher as well as small sided simplified versions of recognised games covering invasion, net/wall and striking/fielding games.

For this approach to partnership to be effective, the teacher should work with the partner rather than handing the class over. This could involve splitting the class so that, for example, half of the class work with a badminton development officer indoors while the other half work outside with the teacher on short tennis. Pupils are given a broader experience of racket games while also receiving more attention and feedback because of the reduced size of the teaching group. An alternative approach could be for a parent or a coach to introduce aspects of cricket to the whole class with the teacher playing a supporting role. This would be particularly appropriate if the teacher's own knowledge of cricket was limited. The same approach could be taken with hockey or rugby. It will be particularly effective if the result is to give pupils role models from both sexes, given that many Key Stage 2 classes will be taught in class groups by the class teacher.

Pupil experience of outdoor and adventurous activity can also be enhanced by a similar partnership approach. The precise activities to be included are not specified in the 1992 Order nor in the SCAA proposals. Some require additional adults for largely supervision purposes, for example, when undertaking problem-solving activities in order that a larger area can be used. Others require particular skills or qualifications if they are to be taught at all, for example most water-based activities such as canoeing or sailing.

Increased access to the curriculum will be particularly relevant for pupils with special education needs within the class. Where these pupils have a statement, appropriate support might be expected, but the reality is that this is not always the case as far as PE is concerned. A child with epilepsy may not be allowed to participate in swimming because of a concern for safety, but the presence of an adult whose specific brief is to act as 'minder' for that child may be all that is needed to make the curriculum accessible. Children with visual impairments can be excluded from PE lessons because of fears for the safety of other pupils as well as for concern for the disabled child. Again, the presence of a helper can make the curriculum accessible. Similar issues where children are in wheelchairs can be solved in the same way.

The extension of learning opportunities may be brought about by visits from outsiders who have particular knowledge. For example, dance animators may be invited either from professional dance companies, most of which have an education section, or from local providers with particular expertise.

The opportunity to work with an advisory teacher has offered many Key Stage 2 teachers a chance to improve their own knowledge with consequent benefits to pupil learning. Although many areas have cut the levels of advisory support available and now have to charge for services which were previously available as part of the local education authority service, opportunities do remain. Where this is so, the chance to work alongside an expert in one's own school environment and with one's own pupils offers an excellent route to more effective teaching and learning. Elsewhere, a variety of schemes have been initiated which aim to offer professional development, often accredited, for the Key Stage 2 teacher. An initial course held at the local teacher's centre or at a local university can introduce teachers to different approaches or to new content. This may be followed by individual project work which involves the design of a curriculum module by the teacher, with professional support. The teacher then teaches that module, again with access to advice and support and, following modifications where necessary, can offer it for others in the school to use.

It has sometimes been observed that, while Key Stage 2 teachers make considerable use of group work, individualized learning and a variety of other teaching approaches within their classroom-based work, they tend to resort to a much more didactic approach within PE. This is particularly true of areas where the activities involved are perceived to be high risk. Confidence in one's subject knowledge and the ability to teach it are needed if the teacher is to feel able to manage a class working in groups, all on different activities, some of which are felt to be potentially dangerous. The presence of a classroom assistant may help to allay anxieties about safety by providing a second pair of eyes to watch for any problems which might develop. An advisory teacher, coach or youth development officer may fulfil this role; they may also encourage the use of new teaching approaches through helping the teacher to improve his or her subject knowledge thereby extending confidence.

Extra curricular provision at Key Stage 2 is often uneven and frequently disadvantages girls. Although female teachers outnumber male teachers, they remain less likely to become involved in extra-curricular activity than their male counterparts. More schools offer soccer than netball for example.

SUMMARY

Successful PE provision at Key Stage 2 requires an understanding of a range of developmental factors of how they relate to the Key Stage 2 pupil and of their implications for good practice. If all pupils are to receive their PE entitlement, the curriculum needs to offer equality of opportunity through differentiated programmes which have a clear line of progression. This is a tall order for the non-specialist Key Stage 2 teacher and partnerships with outside agencies, sensitively handled, have considerable potential for enhancing the curriculum experience for this age group.

REFERENCES

Armstrong, N. and McManus, A. (1996) 'Growth, maturation and physical education', in Armstrong, N. (ed.), *New Directions in Physical Education: Change and Innovation*. London: Cassell, pp. 19–32.

DES (1990) *National Curriculum Physical Education Working Group Interim Report*. London: HMSO.

DES (1991) *Aspects of Primary Education: The Teaching and Learning of Physical Education*. London: HMSO.

DES (1992) *Physical Education in the National Curriculum*. London: HMSO.

Fox, K. (1992) 'Physical education and self-esteem', in Armstrong, N. (ed.), *New Directions in Physical Education*. Leeds: Human Kinetics, pp. 33–54.

SCAA (1994) *Physical Education in the National Curriculum: Draft Proposals*. London: School Curriculum and Assessment Authority.

SEAC (1990) *Records of Achievement in Primary Schools*. London: School Examinations and Assessment Council.

Simpson, M. (1989) *Differentiation in the Primary School, Investigations of Learning and Teaching*. Aberdeen: Northern College of Education.

Chapter 6

Physical Education at Key Stage 3

Brin Martin

INTRODUCTION

This chapter will not offer a commentary on the Orders for Physical Education (SCAA, 1994a); instead, it will hope to analyse the nature and purpose of the Key Stage 3 National Curriculum proposals and attempt to offer a rationale for the Key Stage, in a generic sense. These generic characteristics will then be related to the subject specific principles with regard to PE, and will suggest that the essence of the curriculum at Key Stage 3 is transitional, to inform choice and to enable independence on the part of the learner.

The chapter will widen to debate the key issues that support this view, based upon the statutory three-year span of the curriculum. It will focus on two central features: the delivery by the teacher; and how the learner can accommodate this independence.

THE NATURE OF THE CURRICULUM AT KEY STAGE 3

This section will focus on the curriculum in a generic sense, as it applies to all curriculum areas rather than from a subject-specific standpoint. The discussions elsewhere in this collection, dealing with physiological and psychological issues (Armstrong and McManus, 1996; Lee, 1996) will also shape the structure of this debate. It will, as always, be a compromise of expediency in relation to the values held to be important at any one time and the information gained through research to further thinking. To carry out this analysis, there will be an attempt to rationalize the curriculum at the points of transition to Key Stage 3, before coming to conclusions about the nature and purpose of the 11–14 curriculum. Lastly, it will raise issues that also impinge upon the context of curriculum design at this stage.

The process that underpinned the review of the National Curriculum was common to all subjects. It is not the place of this work to reiterate all of the arguments that led to the curriculum review, except where they are pertinent to the thinking behind this chapter. The fact that PE was treated in common with all other subjects is perhaps the most important issue. The review process itself was extremely focused and intense, and supported by strict guidance and ground rules. These two elements were the only agenda, overt or otherwise that shaped the new curriculum. Meetings came in a timetabled cycle, of subject advisory groups followed by Key Stage specific groups finally to co-ordination groups and so back to the start of the next cycle. Effectively, groups had to follow the principles set out in the final report of the Dearing review (SCAA, 1994a), to address specific points raised in the consultation documentation and, most importantly, indicate in their opinion what could be feasibly delivered in time allocations based around the notion of freeing up a certain percentage of the school week. This last fact has caused more discussion and argument and has been the cause of more misinterpretation than any other single issue. Far more important than time allocation is the use to which that time is put. There now follows an outline of the principles of each of the Key Stages as set out in the final report.

Key Stage 1 should lay the foundation for all future learning. (This does not negate the contribution made by pre-school education in its widest sense, particularly important in PE.) The curriculum should ensure that learners acquire the whole range of basic skills, and the knowledge and understanding that underpin such skills. This learning should take place in an environment that will promote positive attitudes towards learning. It is also centrally concerned with the development of the social skills that are essential in a shared community. These principles are founded in developmental theory, and stress the importance of the acquisition of the performance of basic skills, over and above the support, in a relative and appropriate way, by the process elements recognized by each subject.

These principles, it is suggested, are sensible and should not be a cause for debate. Essentially the curriculum focuses on the acquisition of a foundation of basic skills. This is the purpose of Key Stage 1: skill development, be it reading, number, social skills including reinforcing the work of the home, personal skills such as appropriate responses to situations, or even PE skills, such as finding space, catching or changing quickly. The function of teachers is to provide situations that will enable the learners best to acquire these competencies. Inherent in this belief is a recognition of a hierarchy of importance, genuinely held views that some skills are more important than others in the development of a foundation of skills from which to build.

At Key Stage 2, the situation is different in as much that it is prudent to carry out planning in two specific transitional phases that reflect the developmental ages of the learners at the appropriate times. The purpose of the early phase would be to consolidate and develop the basic skills established in the previous Key Stage, and to increase the range of applications to which these skills can apply. In the second phase, concentration should be on developing higher-order skills, alongside subject specific knowledge. Planning should take account of this progression in the balance of skills knowledge and understanding across the Key Stage.

Therefore the purpose of the Key Stage 2 curriculum is twofold: initially to consolidate and develop the foundation skills established in Key Stage 1, and to extend and apply these skills to an increasing range of specific situations. Essentially, it is concerned with consolidation. The function of teaching therefore is to construct situations that will allow this consolidation and development to take place. The debate concerning overcrowding that prompted the curriculum review was most prominent at this Key Stage. The hope is that the proposals go some way to alleviate the problem, even accepting that the number of activity-specific Programmes of Study have not reduced in number, only in content. However, if the purpose of the Key Stage is to extend further the skills and to apply them to a specific context, how can this be achieved through a teaching force that consists mainly of non-specialists, with the possible exception of middle-school staff? I am confident that primary colleagues are more than able to take and apply the work started in the previous Key Stage, and that their particular expertise in teaching children, combined with their exhausting ability to update their specialist knowledge will ensure that the task of consolidation and application of skills, knowledge and understanding, in their broadest sense, is well managed.

The Key Stage 4 curriculum is based upon the particular interests, talents and aspirations of the learner. The opportunities at this Key Stage should reflect such diversity. The principles of the curriculum should be to provide an education that is appropriate, challenging and meets the needs of the individual. It should build upon the breadth and balance that have been established, and provide a range of learning options to encompass all these diverse needs, and equip the learner with the capacity to respond and even anticipate changing situations.

The purpose of Key Stage 4 is to provide choice to encompass the needs of all learners. The function of teaching is to facilitate meeting these needs. This is a tall order and one that will require flexibility of interpretation and delivery.

Underlying all of this debate has been, for want of a better phrase, the 'back to basics' movement from the sports lobby. Although the high profile contributions made in this respect should have no direct influence on the curriculum, they nonetheless still need to be addressed. Sport is, always has been and always will be a significant part of PE.

So to Key Stage 3. The guidelines that shaped the slimming down process state (SCAA, 1994b, p. 17):

> In this key stage pupils should be *provided with* [my emphasis] opportunities to acquire, develop and apply a range of more advanced knowledge, understanding and skills. . . . breadth, depth, access and entitlement are particularly important . . . to ensure that pupils are given a sound basis from which to take advantage of choices at Key Stage 4. . . . Pupils should know enough about the nature of subjects to allow their decisions about future study to be informed ones . . . Pupils in this key stage are becoming more independent and clearer about their own interests.

The challenge at this Key Stage is to enable balance between the need for flexibility and continued achievement in all areas.

The purpose of the Key Stage is therefore less than clear, and the function of teaching also not as well-defined as in transitional phases. It is difficult to identify clearly specific characteristics of the Key Stage that indicate a unique contribution that it can make to compulsory education, such as is the case at Key Stage 1 with the promotion of foundation skills. There is no realistic function defined. The essential characteristic of Key Stage 3, in a generic sense, is that there are no essential characteristics! As such there does evolve a specific, discernible and achievable function of the Key Stage. Furthermore, this function makes a significant, perhaps after Key Stage 1 the most significant, contribution to the career of the learner. Key Stage 3 is there to bridge the gap between consolidation and extension at Key Stage 2 and choice at Key Stage 4.

However it is achieved, the purpose of Key Stage 3 is to serve this transitional phase. The function of teaching is to ease this transition from two distinct styles of curricula. These characteristics are by no means of a lesser order than other phases due to their lack of intrinsic definition. Indeed, the task of the Key Stage 3 curriculum is overtly harder as a consequence of being answerable to two other Key Stages, rather than having a concrete outcome driven by its own characteristics. In addition, the outcomes are also subject to greater external pressures than other Key Stages, perhaps more significant in our subject than others. With regard to the specific nature of the learner, the direction taken by the Key Stage can be the single most significant factor in either promoting or ending their physical career. Too many times, we have seen an inappropriately delivered programme, either due to inadequacy of curriculum, philosophy or style, conflict with the needs of the learner. This disenchantment is compounded by social factors that did not exist a generation ago, such as the inability to allow children to play in the park unattended. In addition, pressures upon teaching exist more so now than at any other period in recent times. The interpretation of internal bandwagon or critical influence is at the discretion of the department, but influences such as the sport, health or academic lobby take up the developmental time and energy of staff, even if they are eventually dismissed. Clarity of thought and direction have been confused by pressures of accountability, where focus has shifted from what the teacher does to the outcomes of the child. In the next section, this view will be developed as it directly applies to PE, and identifies the influences that will have a salient impact on the success or failure of the Key Stage 3 curriculum.

KEY STAGE 3 PHYSICAL EDUCATION

Accepting then for the time being that the purpose of Key Stage 3 is to ease transition from consolidation and development to choice; and bearing in mind the ground rules of reduction, this chapter will now consider the proposals for PE.

The stated need for all subject areas to allow flexibility, yet still enabling study in depth of one aspect has been encompassed by the curricular arrangement that allows a core and extension in all Programmes of Study except games. This situation is a compromise that has both advantages and disadvantages but, I would suggest, will allow the purpose of the Key Stage to be achieved. If in order to reduce content you do not want to either devalue the integrity of the activity, or risk providing content that would not stretch the most able, effectively a possible solution would be to offer some form of modular curriculum.

The structure of the proposals allows choice on the part of the teacher. By having the option to introduce, at core level, an activity will in fact offer access to areas otherwise denied under the original structure. For example, teachers with commitment to, but little confidence in, activities such as dance or outdoor and adventurous activities no longer essentially have to choose between the two, as the core level could well be within their competencies, whereas the full Programme of Study would not. This choice also allows for depth of study in at least two activities, while retaining the flexibility required in order to prepare learners with the experience to make rational and informed choices. It should also be remembered that the proposals do not necessarily form the complete curriculum for PE. Depending on curriculum organization and deployment of resources, it may be possible to have non-National Curriculum units of work of varying length that serve purposes other than fulfilling the statutory requirements. Again time is not the issue, it is the use to which that time is put.

The proposals reflect a balance therefore between depth and breadth of study. However significantly the commitment to games, gymnastics and dance made in earlier Key Stages is maintained, while still developing the contribution of the other three Programmes of Study, including the introduction of swimming as a discrete area in its own right for the first time at this Key Stage. This move, although only affecting a minority of curricula, should be commended as going a long way to achieving the global aims of PE.

The task to implement a purposeful and relevant curriculum that achieves the aims of the Key Stage will require thought on the part of departments in interpreting and implementing a curriculum that is first and foremost relevant to the needs of their learners, and secondly within their capacity to deliver. The time required to deliver particular Programmes of Study will be an issue. It was not the intention to require that the same time is needed to deliver either full Programmes of Study or core and extension units across different areas of activity. Creative timetabling will allow flexibility in this area, either to create time for study in greater detail, or to allow pursuit of other aims still within the medium of the activity. What it should do is move departments away from the 'pick and mix' curriculum that allows little depth of study, while still not allowing sufficient time to inform choice of future learning. Balance should also require the curriculum to offer sufficient time to games teaching that recognizes its importance, but not at the cost of other Programmes of Study.

It should also be remembered that, in most cases, it will be the teachers who decide the curriculum. It is essential therefore that liaison is established and functional, so that the design of the curriculum reflects and builds upon the best of what has gone before, yet still attempts to interpret the purposes of the Key Stage. Departments will need to audit their provision carefully, and to monitor the outcomes in a far more systematic and searching way to ensure that they truly are meeting the actual needs of the learners rather than meeting their perceived needs. The issue of continuity from Key Stages 3 to 4 should be of no greater concern than the diversity of strengths that comes from a number of individual feeder schools. The curriculum requirements may indeed facilitate discussion and action towards a shared curriculum for these schools, through negotiation and understanding rather than expectations. Progression at this Key Stage should, in reality, be less of a problem within Programmes of Study than at other Key Stages. The unitary structure of the Programmes of Study should be regarded as providing a framework on which to build schemes of work rather than being a total entitlement, and individual preferences with regard to the order of material will be catered for through this mechanism. Progression within the strands of the attainment will require greater tracking across Programmes of Study due to the increasing equity between the planning and evaluating and the performance of activities. The establishment of intended learning outcomes, derived from the end of Key Stage statements (EKSS) will facilitate this tracking exercise.

The task of meeting the purpose of the Key Stage should offer challenge and reward in inventive and characteristic curriculum design opportunities. Challenging in as much as departments will need to reconsider practice in light of the new requirements, and to arrive at a compromise between idealism and reality. The reward will come from satisfaction in the outcomes of a curriculum that will meet the needs of learners and prepare them to rise to opportunities offered at Key Stage 4. The purpose of PE at this Key Stage as opposed to the whole Key Stage 3 curriculum should be first to inform this choice and second to provide learners with the skills necessary to take full advantage of choice, and the responsibility that such independence entails.

This task is the function of teaching at Key Stage 3 in PE. Teachers must provide sufficient skills, knowledge and understanding in appropriate activities that will allow decisions to be made on the part of the learner. The central role of the teacher therefore is to balance between being a provider and an enabler, offering strategies towards independence. This will require the teacher to employ suitable methods to allow the learner to respond initially to this offer. Both the offer and the response are still, at this Key Stage, the task of teaching. In the next section, I will look at how the ownership of this offer should pass to the learner.

INDEPENDENCE AND RESPONSIBILITY

It is apparent that independence and responsibility are not the same thing; the teacher can delegate responsibility to the learner for a greater or lesser part of the learning process, but this in itself does not indicate independence from the teacher. The teacher should be seen as a provider, a facilitator to kickstart learning, to let things happen, which in itself offers a pseudo-independence to the learner. The teacher is still dictating the majority of the elements of the learning process and, on the surface, would appear to be offering little overt responsibility or independence, although doing exactly that. However, significantly even from the outset, the teacher can only indicate, offer to the learner a particular commodity, be it a process, product or other 'offerables'. The teacher then becomes powerless in the learning process until this offer is taken up, and the learner accepts the offer. Even this acceptance does not infer a step towards learning; the offer could be accepted but its intent misunderstood; it could be accepted but its relevance not recognized; or indeed it could be merely accepted under duress. It is the learner that is empowered to change practice, and as such the movement towards improvement is out of the teacher's control at a very early stage. For the learner first to accept and second to act upon or utilize the offer, it must be sincerely given by the teacher, be perceived as such by the learner, and also be honestly received by the learner. Once these preconditions have been met then a true partnership has been established and the potential exists for learning to commence, eventually evolving to allow the learners to lead themselves towards a change in behaviour and hence learning.

The phrase 'pseudo-independence' mentioned earlier refers to the first tentative steps towards a learning partnership, as initially at least the teacher initiates the decisions pertinent to the learning process. This reiterates and reinforces the power differential that does exist between provider and acceptor. However, if and when a learning partnership can be forged, this differential holds far less significance for the learner. The true success of the development of an independent learner must surely be if the learner is able to pursue their learning career once the teacher has been removed from the interaction, or on leaving school.

The task of teaching, therefore, at Key Stage 3 is to both enable independence and inform choice. This is entirely dependent initially upon the teacher to start the process, and will require a deal of thought concerning the use of appropriate and varied teaching strategies. True independence is a commodity that has to be learned, and one that implies a number of abilities on the part of the learner. As mentioned, independence implies the acceptance of and action upon given responsibility; it implies the ability to make reasoned and informed choice based upon needs rather than external pressure. However, significantly it also requires the development of a battery of skills in the ability to learn, described elsewhere as learning competencies. These will include aspects of questioning and evaluation and the ability to make judgements based upon the results of this enquiry, not with regard to aspects of PE but concerning generic learning abilities. It requires the ability to solve problems and to take learning from one context and to be able to transfer any new or amended constructs into different situations. More systematically, it requires of the learners, efficiency in organizational and personal administration, being able to select appropriate responses to differing situations, to take the initiative and to have a clear understanding of their role as individuals in the learning task. These skills will enable, complement and, to a great extent, overlap our own subject requirements to plan and evaluate aspects of performance, although actually delivering the goods should not be underestimated. Finally, and in a sense much harder to pursue or enforce, is the development of a positive attitude towards learning. To develop independence, the learners must develop a positive attitude and desire towards their own learning, and the subsequent motivation to continue learning once the direct extrinsic influence is either played down or removed entirely. This requires commitment to the learning process.

TEACHING STRATEGIES

The above agenda is a tall order for the teacher to accomplish, especially when the different learning rates of children are taken into account. Teaching children independence cannot be achieved through the use of a narrow conception of teaching methodology. Traditional command and didactic teaching strategies play a very important role in teaching certain aspects of PE at any age, including Key Stage 3. However, it is important to select the appropriate style for a specific purpose, and the movement towards independence will require suitable methods to be successful, fitness for purpose. Furthermore, what is appropriate in one year group is not necessarily the most fitting in another. Movement and flexibility will be required throughout the Key Stage to accommodate different stages of independence and different learning foci at a particular phase. For instance, in the early years of the Key Stage, teaching may wish to centre on the development of learning competence, while towards the transition to Key Stage 4 attention may shift to enabling informed choice.

What is required is a coherent and planned overall strategy in the direction of teaching towards independence. As with any strategy, this will include a combination of tactics, or styles of teaching, pertinent at a particular time for a particular purpose, but still maintaining the overall shape of the strategy. In planning for this movement, schemes and units of works should include sections on the required learning outcomes desired, and suggestions on the most appropriate teaching methodology that could be employed. It should be remembered that as long as the desired outcome is achieved, the particular style used to achieve that outcome is to some extent secondary. The focus is on the learner rather than the teacher. However, it is obvious that the impact of the teaching will be far more successful when planned and purposeful techniques and interventions contribute in a significant way towards the achievement of the intended learning objective. Learning can develop despite teaching, but independence cannot. Planning will therefore encompass more than one agenda, and should include progressions towards all desired learning outcomes. A unit of work on basketball in Year 8 for example may well include objectives indicating stages in the development of performance, but may well also refer to process elements such as planning or evaluating strands; areas that focus more on the learning competencies, such as the ability to react to changing or unfamiliar situations; or that allow shift in responsibility and decision making towards the individual.

Most secondary specialists will be familiar with the Mosston and Ashworth (1986) spectrum of teaching styles, a continuum of styles indicating differing degrees of responsibility and decision required on the part of the learner, and it is not the place of this chapter to elaborate on the particular merits of the various styles within the spectrum. What is required is a coherent overall strategy that at various stages employs a range of styles from this spectrum towards a particular end. Teachers should not slavishly adhere to the letter of the characteristics of particular styles; rather, they should follow the principles that underpin a particular methodology. Indeed, in reality, teachers will adapt or consolidate similar styles in a more general way. For instance, most teachers already employ a combination of the command and practice styles when performance elements are to be stressed with a unit of work. The point is that when working towards independence, and the elements inherent in such a policy, other styles may well be more appropriate. For example, if the learning objective focuses upon the learners' ability to evaluate, then some form of reciprocal or self-check technique could be used. The decision to select a particular style should be based upon the needs of the learner rather than the dominant or favoured style of the teacher. Whatever style is considered to be the most appropriate at a particular time, it should be pursued with integrity and honesty on the part of the teacher. Furthermore, the teachers should accept the results of their actions, and honour the outcomes from the learners. Only when teaching for independence is delivered with intent and wholeheartedness on the part of the teacher can it fulfil its contribution towards the principles of the Key Stage.

SUMMARY

In conclusion, I have attempted to draw out the characteristics of the Key Stage in a generic sense, and then developed how these principles were translated through the PE orders. It evolved that the essential characteristics of Key Stage 3 are that there were none, exemplified by the transitional nature of the Key Stage. This has been accommodated through a flexible interpretation of depth and balance. This will prove challenging for teachers in attempting to develop the outcomes desired from the learner to cope with this transition. These skills in particular are: to inform choice, which is a matter of skilful and appropriate curriculum design; and to encourage independence, through the honest and wholehearted use of a suitable and coherent strategy with regard to methodology.

The task of teaching at this Key Stage is therefore inherently more difficult than at the Key Stages, where the purpose is to teach and to enable respectively. Key Stage 3 is between these two camps, which is the reason why it should prove to be both challenging yet rewarding for the teacher, and purposeful and inspirational for the learner.

REFERENCES

Armstrong, N. and McManus, A. (1996) 'Growth, maturation and physical education', in Armstrong, N. (ed.), *New Directions in Physical Education: Change and Innovation*. London: Cassell, pp. 19–32.

Lee, M. (1996) 'Psycho-social development from 5–16 years', in Armstrong, N. (ed.), *New Directions in Physical Education: Change and Innovation*. London: Cassell, pp. 33–47.

Mosston, M. and Ashworth, S. (1986) *Teaching Physical Education*. London: Merrill.

SCAA (1994a) *Physical Education in the National Curriculum Draft Proposals*. London: School Curriculum and Assessment Authority.

SCAA (1994b) *Review Handbook for Subject and Key Stage Advisory Groups*. London: School Curriculum and Assessment Authority.

Chapter 7

Physical Education at Key Stage 4

Joy McConachie-Smith

INTRODUCTION

Key Stage 4 is becoming the most significant segment of the whole school curriculum. Post-14 education has assumed a significant role in helping the government to meet its national education and training targets. There are a number of policy issues which have influenced the 14–16 debate (Baker, 1994). The centre of the debate is the academic/vocational divide or alternatively the potential balance between them in the education of this age group in particular. The development of competence-based vocational initiatives has been remarkable in the drive to prepare young people for the world of work. This is challenged by Drucker (1993, p. 34) where he makes reference to 'the knowledge revolution' which is based on the premise that 'the basic economic resource already is and will in future be knowledge'.

The only realistic solution would appear to lie in an integrated academic/ vocational modular system which is available to, and from which, all 14- to 16 year-olds can make personal election within the limits of the resource of the school. This would guarantee that an appropriate balance of skills, knowledge and understanding could be achieved. This flexibility will mean quite a radical shift of thinking away from what has traditionally been the delivery of a controlled and planned common curriculum.

Now, 14-year-olds may select, alongside the statutory National Curriculum for Key Stage 4, to follow courses from General Certificate of Secondary Education (GCSE), National Vocational Qualifications (NVQs), General National Vocational Qualification (GNVQs) and specifically in relation to PE, the Certificate of Further Studies – Sports Studies and Central Council for Physical Recreation (CCPR) Sport Leader Award. Also available are schemes that developed in the first instance as local initiatives designed to meet local needs. One of these is the ASAD Youth Award Scheme which is now integrating with the NCVQ Core Skills national pilot scheme.

It is not the intention that, within this chapter, provision will be made to discuss the complex details of all these syllabi. This knowledge, or its ready availability, is assumed. The chapter will instead focus on the context within which critical decisions about Key Stage 4 will be made, and will attempt to provide a framework for approaching the design and implementation of a coherent educational experience from such a range of different courses.

It is at this somewhat earlier and critical point in planning for the curriculum – for 14-year-olds rather than 16-year-olds – that the dichotomy between academic tradition and vocational innovation is now going to become a real issue and must be addressed. Dearing's (SCAA, 1994) revision to the National Curriculum has strengthened 14–19 as a complete segment of education thus reducing the separation of Key Stage 4 from the 16–19 segment that we have known so far.

GNVQs are now well established and pilot proposals for 1995 to bring Foundation and Intermediate GNVQs forward as Part 1 into the 14–16 age group will present some interesting and unavoidable challenges to both pupils and teachers; challenges, which, if met well, could alter significantly the course of education for 14–(16)–19 year olds. I will argue later in the chapter that this could have very special implications for PE.

Innovations within the 14–19 segment of the curriculum would appear initially to be considerable, but it is important to note that for Richard Pring (1994) current innovations do not necessarily mean change. He argues that (Pring, 1994, p. 34):

> nothing of significance is happening – that an opportunity is being lost for transforming the impoverished and limiting traditions that we have inherited, into something worthwhile for everyone . . . amidst all the changes, the curriculum and the education system remain much the same.

There is no doubt that it is still in the hands of both teachers and pupils together to influence the quality of any changes, even where external pressure seems at its greatest, and to ensure that those proposals for change that are of potential value to young people result in real innovation. It is critically important that some change in traditional thinking among curriculum planners is taking place which is coupled with a will to action which will affect daily practice. Otherwise, these new developments in both vocational and academic education will simply become absorbed into the status quo. This will indeed be a lost opportunity for PE which, as a subject, has long argued for a better balance between the academic and vocational and between the practical and theoretical in the substance of its courses.

The structure of this chapter will be in two sections: the first will address the major issues facing curriculum planners of the 14–19 segment; and the second will consider the implications of these issues for Key Stage 4 in PE in particular and will propose some possibilities of addressing them in more specific ways.

MAJOR ISSUES FOR THOSE PLANNING THE 14–16 CURRICULUM

The issues that follow will be raised initially as general issues in relation to the total school and are not directed at this point specifically to PE. It is hoped that the reader will make the relevant extrapolations as the section progresses in anticipation of fuller, more specifically targeted, discussion later in the chapter. It is important to consider Key Stage 4 and, in particular, PE in Key Stage 4 in the context both of a vertical and a horizontal school curriculum – otherwise the potential for development and extension will be reduced substantially.

14–19: Where is Key Stage 4?

Key Stage 4 is still clearly in evidence within the revised proposals for the National Curriculum and is due to be implemented in August 1996. For PE, these proposals set a particular challenge and have provoked some strong responses from the profession, especially in relation to the prescription for team games for all. This specific issue will be considered in more depth at a later stage in the chapter in relation to learners and learning. What is at issue at this point is the potential for loss of identity of Key Stage 4 as a whole, as it slips into an extended 14–19 concept. This may not be a bad thing, especially for PE, but the implications need to be considered very carefully. Other issues as they emerge will inform this specific discussion, but it is clear that decisions made about Key Stage 4 cannot be isolated from what has gone before nor from what will follow.

Integration within the curriculum

This is a topic which merits a chapter in its own right but which is explored here to a limited extent within the context of a focus on Key Stage 4. Integration is a complex but very significant concept within the system as it is now developing. There is a grave danger, both of our losing sight of the individual learner in the plethora of modes and pathways that will be on offer, and also of the educational experience for any one pupil being unconnected and meaningless. There is a will, however, to address this issue and the proposed new General Diploma combining GCSE core and vocational equivalent is an example of this, although according to Baker (1994, p. 27):

> The General Diploma, proposed in the government's joint education/employment *Competitiveness* White Paper, for students with five or more A–C GCSEs or their vocational equivalents, is only concerned with the retrospective recognition of equivalence, not the ongoing integration of all forms of learning.

With the impressive development of vocational education in recent years in terms of both speed of implementation and also of numbers of students taking part (70,000), there is a real challenge for those who would wish to see the educational experience being offered to young people as logical and meaningful in terms of a relevant education. There are some major obstacles to integration created by the separation in GNVQs of skills from knowledge.

Immediately follows the next question What is a relevant education? What is relevant PE and what is its relationship to the whole?

The implications of integration will be considered within each of the following:

- liberal/vocational divide between courses;
- horizontal integration across the curriculum;
- vertical progression over time; and
- coherent educational experience for the individual.

Liberal/vocational education

The traditions of liberal education are being severely challenged in the light of the perceived need to equip the next generation to cope with a world that, in Pring's (1994) terms, is often humdrum and hostile. Education is now facing the challenge of relevance to young peoples' needs that revolve round such things as finding a job, developing skills and competences, practical utility, personal development and personal effectiveness. To acquire in-depth knowledge, for its own sake, is still a desirable and laudable aim but if that is all that is on offer to the 14-year-old then the relevance of intellectualism to pupils' own lifestyle must be proven and rendered acceptable to them. Such an academic model should be available to those who wish it, but there is no doubt that the current climate for all young people making their way in the world points very clearly to a strong vocational element within their chosen courses.

In most schools, there is still a clear distinction between the two forms of education and as Pring (1994, p. 35) observes:

> There are, then, different languages about education – the language of intellectual excellence for some and the language of vocational competence for the others.

This split is reinforced according to Pring, by divided modes of assessment and a divided population. Despite all attempts to change traditional attitudes, the products of vocational education are still considered to be inferior to the real achievement of a liberal education. The climate for a radical change in this has never been better since the possibility of a good vocational education is now within the grasp of all. From the point of view of current learners, it would seem that, far from being inferior, the courses within the new GNVQ provision are being voted by the pupils as superior: in the degree of independence allowed; in the collaborative relationship with teachers; in the breadth and scope of courses; and in experience of the outside world that is being made available, within courses.

Other, more traditional, established courses, could do worse than consider carefully the model adopted by GNVQ courses, especially in the teaching and learning modes employed.

Integration between the academic and the vocational will need to be addressed at the level of central planning so that each pupil can select modules that will provide the balance that is felt to be appropriate for them. It is indicative of the piecemeal approach to central planning for the curriculum, that such diverging approaches have developed within that which should be an integrated whole for each individual. How much this can be offset by careful planning within each school or even subject area as opposed to a national initiative, is yet to be shown but it would seem that PE, because of the way it has developed and because of the intrinsic nature of the subject being about competence in and knowledge about physical activity, is well placed to present a model of integration of liberal and vocational courses that is viable both to PE itself and, possibly, also to some other subjects.

Horizontal integration across the curriculum

Oates (1994) has an optimistic view of the potential for a more integrated system. He is confident that there is strong public and government desire for this, it being the intention behind the introduction of GNVQs. While it is possible to construct integrated programmes within each school he considers this 'inadequate and limited as a response to the issues' of integration which should be a national priority. He cites the definite moves towards the provision of modular courses as positive, in making it possible for articulation within and between GNVQs and NVQs. With similar articulation between Key Stage 4 and GCSEs, this should lead to a fully integrated system where an individual pupil should be in a position to design an individual and more personal curriculum with the appropriate mix of vocational and academic courses.

What is urgently needed to effect this, and what is not available at present, is that all modules and modular courses need to be stated in the same way. Assessment procedures and structures dovetailing, and teaching and learning approaches coming closer in mode, would avoid the situation where pupils cannot move easily from one system to the other without becoming completely confused by the divergence and sometimes competing nature of demands.

A critical factor in the concept of integration of liberal and vocational education is to establish parity of esteem for both aspects of education. There seem to be few problems in this for the pupils themselves and we should look to them for a lead. 'British' attitudes to this are hard to move and the strong belief that the best education is that of the liberal/academic may be too well established, within an Oxbridge tradition, to effect a change of attitude in the schools. There is a growing conflict between a rising and recognized need for a focus on vocational education and the now established production of league tables. Perhaps it is here more than anywhere else that PE can look back on years of similar experience and feel that the world is coming to join in our battles for recognition. We have much to offer to our pupils by engaging in the debate about appropriate and relevant education systems at this critical stage in young peoples' careers.

Vertical progression over time

Most references, specifically to Key Stage 4, are normally in relation to National Curriculum Orders. This area has been the sole responsibility of the Schools Curriculum and Assessment Authority (SCAA) and only after age 16 does this responsibility for the curriculum widen to other accreditation bodies responsible for the specific aspects of the vocational curriculum.

With the proposals to introduce GNVQs and NVQs to pupils at 14 this unitary control is no longer and, where integration is feasible, potentially there is now a shared responsibility. The concept of a logical single progressive system from Key Stage 1 through to Key Stage 4 is no longer viable.

Each of these accreditation groups, now involved in Key Stage 4, has a different set of regulations to which they work and this will cause significant problems for pupils in Key Stage 4 who wish to combine some academic with some vocational courses – a very attractive option which should now be open to them but which could prove to be difficult to implement.

Oates (1994) notes that, in each of the vocational courses, an increasing amount of detail is being planned within the content. This seems to be in direct conflict to what is happening within the National Curriculum – in PE at least, where the curriculum content is being slimmed down with each revision. Oates is of the opinion that this increase in vocational detail does not mean automatically more content but more likely greater depth within the same framework.

The changing nature in terms of shift to vocational emphasis, of what is being made available at 14, makes it necessary, therefore, to reconsider the implications of what has been achieved in Key Stages 1–3 and what vertical progression might look like. For example – can vocational competences be seen to have any roots within the end of Key Stage statements (EKSS) of Key Stage 3 or even Key Stages 1 and 2? Should these competences be traced back to ensure that early educational experience is the beginning of a logical progression of learning including specific skills and competences. One of the possible losses in Dearing's streamlined version of the National Curriculum in Physical Education (NCPE) is that of the carefully detailed progression in content from Key Stages 1 to 4 which was much in evidence in earlier versions of the curriculum.

To rethink the nature of progression in relation to competence rather than content would seem to be a viable proposal, at least in relation to the core skills of G/NVQs which are: application of number; communication; information technology; personal skills and problem solving. Much of this is already implicit in the PE curriculum and so it should be possible to make it more explicit and systematic as we move towards greater integration.

The development of credit recognition and transfer is yet another aspect that has relevance for the nature of progression, certainly within the 14–19 segment. This is an area fraught with complications and will require careful central planning if the system is going to work smoothly.

Moderation and standardization within the criteria of transfer will be critical if this is to function at national level, which is its main justification. There are financial implications which need not concern us in this chapter. Where integration has been achieved within a school or even a subject area then credit transfer should be a real option where pupils can count some vocational units towards an academic qualification and vice versa. This will allow for true flexibility and for courses to become fully relevant to individuals. This is intrinsic to both horizontal and vertical integration.

Coherent educational experience for the individual

Coherence as a concept features regularly in documentation on the curriculum. The 'broad, balanced differentiated and coherent curriculum' has become almost a household phrase but, as Ruddock *et al.* (1994) point out, the concept of coherence has gradually become less prominent in implementation.

Ruddock suggests that 'its virtue is assumed rather than justified and definitions are vague' and she goes on to say (Ruddock *et al.*, 1994, p. 197):

> there is an easy slippage between 'coherence' and 'commonality'; a more predictable slippage between 'coherence' and 'consistency'; and an easy association of 'coherence' and 'tidiness'.

All these are references to coherence that stem from managerial concerns and are related to control and organization. As such, they reinforce a set of values rooted in having a curriculum which is focused on centralized and stable structures.

Ruddock contrasts this with the concept of coherence being about individual meanings rather than common structures and specifically about meanings for the learner being about 'connectedness'. It is this approach to coherence that is important within PE such that the pupils can see some overall meaning in the courses that they select and have some confidence in the relevance of these courses for the future. This raises an issue which is becoming more and more critical within PE – that of recognizing the ever-increasing range of possibilities within the subject and making deliberate attempts to prepare pupils for sensible selection in a systematic way such that they may pursue meaningful courses towards planned employment.

Ruddock *et al.* (1994, p. 198) conclude that the climate of current educational organization is not one in which:

> we can expect coherence to flourish and it is not surprising . . . that the word has been moved out of the spotlight on national policy documents.

We cannot afford to ignore coherence in terms of connectedness within an individual course structure if we are going to offer a meaningful experience to young people from within the fragmented and wide-ranging opportunities now available.

Summary

Issues that are of significance to the curriculum at Key Stage 4 relate to the fact that the opportunities for 14- to 16-year-olds have expanded. The challenge of confirming both vocational and academic courses as having equal status must be addressed. Planning the curriculum in respect of both offering and meeting realistic pupil choice will mean that the process of integrating all available elements must become increasingly sophisticated so that coherence of experience is related to learning as far as possible.

PHYSICAL EDUCATION IN KEY STAGE 4 – THE ISSUES CONSIDERED

This section of the chapter recognizes the critical significance of the issues discussed in the first section and will now attempt to absorb them and allow them to illuminate possible answers to some key questions about what we can and should be offering to 14-year-olds within PE. The approach taken will, as far as possible, focus on the learner rather than on the curriculum, as the curriculum should be there to provide for the learner's needs and should be planned accordingly.

The section will be structured as follows:

- the nature of Key Stage 4 and the learner;
- the balance of theory, and practice, and progression within academic courses;
- integration of academic and vocational courses; and
- recommendations for teachers and lecturers as curriculum planners.

The nature of Key Stage 4 and the learner

The intended learning outcomes for Key Stage 4 relate to the final stages of a statutory framework for a learning process which is considered academic in mode. Each pupil, as a result of the experience gained throughout the previous three stages of the NCPE, is expected to be ready to develop further throughout this stage in three ways and to achieve the following outcomes:

1 to master two activities in terms of both performance and understanding;
2 to be able to contribute to the setting up and organizing of activities for others by adopting different roles; and
3 to acquire and articulate attitudes to activity, both in relation to self and others that can be monitored in their implementation.

The recent changes resulting in the new streamlined curriculum of 1995 give some cause for concern in that these outcomes now may be difficult to meet.

By this stage in the education process, and especially after successful Key Stages 1–3, each individual should be aware of personal preferences and styles in relation to learning and participation, particularly in a practical mode.

It is by Key Stage 4 that the individual pupil is ready to appreciate the deeper meanings and successes of taking part seriously in activity; and this will only be truly experienced where each individual can become engaged in activities the demands of which can be well matched by the individual's expertise. Freedom to choose against this knowledge is therefore of critical importance. The fact that the curriculum as proposed has restricted this choice is regrettable and will have serious implications for some pupils being able to achieve the learning outcomes referred to above.

There are a number of criteria that are used to distinguish the ways in which different learners become successfully engaged in the process of learning about a physical activity. They are not all relevant to this issue but two of them have a significant contribution to make to an understanding of why the curriculum as proposed at Key Stage 4 will exclude some pupils. These are:

1 some pupils learn better in an individual setting and would naturally select activities that are dependent on individual participation; and
2 some pupils do not succeed in a competitive context and only fully achieve in activities where success is measured in other ways.

Full commitment to an active lifestyle and the holding of positive attitudes can only follow from real success within a comfort zone of performance and participation. Within the revised National Curriculum at Key Stage 4, some pupils will inevitably be functioning outside their comfort zone. The high levels of performance and under-standing expected at Key Stage 4 must be built on a good foundation in the previous stages. Learning in a physical mode is not achieved in a short time-scale. Exposure to the experience must be given through repetitive and regular periods over time. With the possible reduction to half units in Key Stage 3, this will be difficult to achieve. Pupils will need to be carefully guided in their choices to avoid unnecessary fragmentation.

Balance of theory and practice, and progression within academic courses

In relation to academic courses, it is important to consider the total 14–19 concept of the curriculum and to see Key Stage 4 as nested in this larger framework. Concern has been expressed already on a number of occasions about whether we have the balance of theory and practice correct across all the courses, both academic – leading to examinations – and vocational, that are offered now under the umbrella of PE. There is growing concern that vocational competences are incomplete in their value to the individual without some measure of knowledge and understanding. It is time that once again we made some very clear statements about the integrity of the subject being rooted in practical experience underpinned by relevant knowledge and understanding; and that we review the courses that are on offer to establish once and for all that we have come of age sufficiently to present viable and reliable courses and examinations that reflect this balance and meet both academic and vocational criteria. The changes that are proposed for GCSE courses confirm the study of physical activities as the central core of the syllabus in the way in which both coursework (60–70 per cent) and terminal examinations (30–40 per cent) are structured. The result is a much closer relationship of theory to practical participation. In terms of the practical/theory balance across the total examination spectrum, however, the current position in relation to the pupils' experience within the examination structure is neither consistent nor clearly progressive. It is obvious that different rationales on the balance of theory and practical are applied to the form of examination at each tier of the structure as it stands at present (Figure 7.1).

The progression of knowledge and understanding, however, as manifest in the three tiers of examinations could be identified as:

● general principles and practical application;
● knowledge of framework(s) and theories;
● critical evaluation and comparison of theories; and
● interrelation of theories and formulation of principles of differentiated application.

If this progression were applied to each stage of the examination process, it would go a long way to clarify the rationale for the way in which each academic course and its examination programme was structured; and it would offer a logical coherence both to the experience of the pupil/student and also to the teacher in school and the further or higher education lecturer in planning a continuous curriculum.

To preserve the integrity of the subject and thus strengthen both vertical and horizontal coherence, we need to apply less of the traditional academic, discipline-based model and move nearer to the arts model of study in selecting the theory–practice focus and balance. It is time to challenge strongly the prevalent school of thought that believes that practical competence in physical activities should not be included in assessment at 'A' level. In drawing parallels with art and music, would we expect ability and competence to be excluded similarly from their examinations? The argument that abilities that are influenced by inherited potential should be excluded from assessment because of unfair disadvantage is hard to sustain when no adjustments are applied for innate intelligence in other examinations.

There seems little logic in omitting such a critical area/mode of study and its

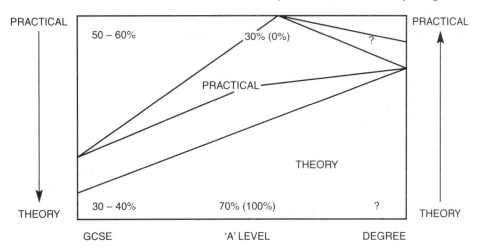

Figure 7.1 *Balance of theory and practical as applied to current examination structure.*

assessment at one level of the process ('A' level) when it returns at the next (degree study).

A greater emphasis on the practical mode as the core of in-depth study of our subject will necessitate the revisiting of assessment modes and their application. It has been shown that the most effective way to change the curriculum is to approach it first through assessment. It may be appropriate then to ask the question: How would we wish to describe the successful student(s) of PE at each stage in the learning process? The answer to this should show clearly the logical progressive development of the subject as a coherent area of academic study with a practical core while at the same time giving scope to describe the competences that should underpin the preparedness for vocational practice that will be the appropriate application of this academic knowledge.

Integration of academic and vocational modules – a working model

The following is proposed as a model for curriculum planners in PE at Key Stage 4. It is based on the assumption that there are different 'kinds' of modules that can be integrated into coherent courses which are relevant to different needs. At this point in time, the model may be too ambitious for implementation in schools but it raises questions of principle that could inform decision for a less coherent and ambitious process in this interim stage.

The different kinds of modules can be grouped under those that come from academic courses – i.e. Key Stage 4 National Curriculum and GCSE – and those that derive from vocational courses – i.e. GNVQ (Health and Health Care, Performing Arts, and Leisure and Tourism) and NVQ (Sport and Recreation). Together these can make available a very broad selection of modules that relate to theory, practice, personal competence and/or professional competence (Figure 7.2).

Those pupils who intend to pursue tertiary education and a career in an area related to PE, sport or leisure will seek advice as to the best pathways to follow from an

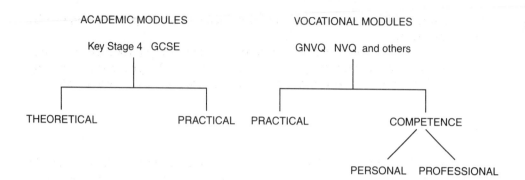

Figure 7.2   *Academic and vocational modules.*

Selections for course design might be as follows:

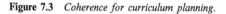

ROUTE	KEY STAGE 4	GCSE	GNVQ	NVQ
ROUTE A – towards sports science	2 games	sports studies	health and health care	sport/ rec.
ROUTE B – towards exercise science	2 games or 1 game + athletics/gym	sports studies	health and health care	sport/ rec.
ROUTE C – towards leisure	1 game + 1 other sport or dance	sports studies or dance physical educ.	leisure and tourism or performing arts	sport/ rec.
ROUTE D – towards physical education	1 game + 1 other sport	physical educ. dance	healthcare performing arts leisure and tour	sport/ rec.

Figure 7.3   *Coherence for curriculum planning.*

earlier point at the beginning of Key Stage 4. As professionals we must be ready to advise them. The challenge of the academic/vocational divide now features in further and higher education as much as it does in school curricula, and so decisions made at this stage will influence later experience.

Figure 7.3 gives a guide to the coherence of curriculum planning that is possible, from Key Stage 4 right through to degree study, indicating how important it could be for the appropriate decisions to be made at the correct time.

Recommendations for teachers and lecturers as curriculum planners in PE

1   Consider the total experience for pupils as beginning at 14 and moving through to either employment or a university course.
2   Be prepared to be innovative in the opportunities that are available within the curriculum for pupils from 14 onwards.
3   Be prepared to create bridges between academic and vocational courses.

4 Have a rationale for the coherence or connectedness of the pathways chosen by individual pupils.
5 Be ready to give counselling advice as to options and the implications of choices.
6 Be ready to rethink the whole approach to the educational experience that is being prepared for pupils and to relinquish the 'sacred cows' if that is appropriate.

CONCLUSION

The time is right to reconsider the future of PE in the secondary school. This will involve a strengthening of the commitment to the integrity of the subject being its practical core expanded as performing, planning and evaluating. We, as curriculum planners, need to take note of the attitudes of pupils to our subject and to respond to the fact that the number taking the formal academic examinations is increasing almost one hundred fold each year. Not only that but numbers applying for courses that relate to a career in the areas of PE, sport and dance are in a ratio of approximately 20:1 to those who are successful in securing a place on a university course. With declared interest of this magnitude, we must ensure that the best is offered and that the commitment is matched by the quality of provision in all courses. But, more importantly, we must raise the profile of our subject as one arising from successful and satisfying participation for all, in that each individual's needs can be met from the range and diversity of what is available.

REFERENCES

Baker, K. (1994) 'Open to debate; the NUT and 14–19 issues', *Education Review*, **8**, 27–31.
Drucker, P. (1993) 'Post-capitalist society', in Report of the Paul Hamlyn Foundation National Commission in Education, *Learning to Succeed*. London: Heineman, p. 34.
Oates, T. (1994) A converging system? Explaining differences in the academic and vocational tracks in England and Wales. Paper presented to the *3rd International Interdisciplinary Conference of the International Research Network for Training and Development*.
Pring, R. (1994) 'Innovation Without Change', *Education Review*, **8**, 34–9.
Ruddock, J., Harris, S. and Wallace, G. (1994) 'Coherence and students' experience of learning in the secondary school', *Cambridge Journal of Education*, **24**, 197–213.
SCAA (1994) *Physical Education in the National Curriculum. Draft Proposals*. London: Schools Curriculum and Assessment Authority.

Chapter 8

Physical Activity Promotion and the Active School

Kenneth Fox

INTRODUCTION

Throughout its history, PE has struggled for a justification for its existence. The development of sport and motor skills has always been a central feature but a focus on health has also seen its moments. It was not many decades ago, for example, that we might have seen regimented calisthenics in the playground not dissimilar to the exercise breaks of the current Japanese corporate sector, all in the name of fitness, good posture and self-discipline. In the past ten to fifteen years, there have been renewed attempts to provide a health rationale for the PE curriculum. However, it has become apparent that this recent re-emergence has taken on a distinctly different flavour. For the first time, we have begun to hear the language of the psychologist, sociologist and health economist enter discussions. Terms – such as attitudes, beliefs, expertise, lifestyles, lifetime fitness, life quality and cost effectiveness – have crept into the rhetoric with increasing regularity. To promote volitional change, the target for the curriculum has strategically shifted to include the youngster's mind as well as the youngster's body and its capabilities. Given similar health-promoting initiatives at the national level, this recent shift in PE has the potential to become firmly embedded in broader-based public health strategies.

The purposes of this chapter are threefold. The first part provides a contextual analysis of the recent emergence of interest in fitness, exercise and health. The second part, in the light of this analysis, is a presentation of developments in rationale underpinning recent public health initiatives concerning physical activity promotion for public health. The last part of the chapter applies this information to physical activity promotion policy for schools so that they might be seen as effective vehicles for change.

THE DEVELOPMENT OF EXERCISE AND FITNESS PROMOTION IN THE 1980s

The health-related exercise movement that became increasingly identifiable in schools from the late 1970s did not take place in a socio-political vacuum. It was accompanied by a rapid expansion of the exercise sciences that were beginning to establish stronger and stronger links between inactivity and ill-health. At the same time, a social change was taking place, catalysed by the media and advertising, towards the acceptability of exercise and fitness as a socially desirable trait. Fitness was becoming fashionable. As we stand in the mid-1990s, we are faced with a melting pot of educational, scientific, medical and media visions of exercise that is sometimes difficult to interpret. The reasoning and assumptions behind these different forces require some historical analysis as they have important implications for future physical activity promotion policy, particularly when considered from a public health perspective.

THE GROWTH OF EXERCISE AND FITNESS IN SCHOOLS

The current health-related developments in school PE closely followed the application of epidemiological and medical sciences to exercise. This fusion elaborated the links between lack of exercise and fitness, and serious disease, disorders and mortality. Coronary heart disease captured the bulk of attention as it had become the leading dealer of premature death in the developed world. This provided valuable ammunition for the proponents of the 'health-related fitness curriculum' as it became known in the early 1980s. At last, a strong medical and scientific prop was available to support the argument for PE as a core item on the school agenda. This new-found strength was welcomed by many teachers, and pockets of change in schools became more numerous as the decade advanced. Successions of articles appeared in the professional journals espousing the hows and whys of health-related fitness, and the trails of increasingly weary in-service preachers delivering the new gospel of lifetime fitness could be traced throughout the country. In the late 1980s, it was beginning to be more widely realized that, in children, physical fitness had a strong genetic element, and that the process of exercise was far more important in the determination of current and future health. 'Health-related exercise' became the favoured terminology and the issue became behaviour change. In the early 1990s, the National Curriculum panel examined the role of health in the PE curriculum and sealed its fate as an all-pervasive element (National Curriculum Council, 1992). It would permeate all Programmes of Study and would receive explicit reference in Attainment Targets (ATs) and end of Key Stage statements (EKSS). Since that time, health-related exercises, in varying degrees of depth and complexity, seem to have found their way into almost all school PE curricula, and health-related exercise teaching continues to be in high demand as in-service work (Harris, 1994). In summary, in PE, there has been a gradual shift in emphasis from fitness to exercise as a lifestyle behaviour.

THE GROWTH OF FITNESS AND EXERCISE IN THE MEDIA

In the media market-place, fitness has also experienced a boom era. The general public have been steadily fed a new package of personal values. By the early 1980s, healthism and consumerism were beginning to fill the void left by the hippie culture of the 1960s. Joggers were no longer seen as freakish and the image of the fit, clean-cut, athletic and muscular male, had replaced long hair and flower power. Women found their own way of expressing this metamorphosis. Pop-mobility emerged and was soon to graduate to aerobic dance and step aerobics, as lycra and leotards took over from gym slips and knickers. In a relatively short period of time, it once again became respectable to be seen to be looking after one's body, and sweat and strain had become an essential part of the health formula. The advertising industry promoted the latest symbols of social status, and it was clear that exercise and fitness had become a marketable commodity as it outgrew its old-fashioned image and became a key to attractiveness and sexuality. Fitness became as important an acquisition for the professional classes as the BMW or mobile phone, and the new language it brought offered the same impressive social currency as the world of information technology or gourmet cooking. It is a matter for debate how much this growth has been truly allied to the public's concern for their health, but to exercise and eat sensibly certainly became well-espoused messages by the end of the decade.

On the surface, the high degree of public exposure that the media has offered the fitness movement looks good. However, when examined more closely, it poses two serious problems that in the long-term may work against public health. First, fashion accessories have a limited lifespan and fitness is in danger of becoming as outdated as the typewriter. From a public health perspective, this is nonsensical. Second, when a behaviour becomes a measure of social achievement, a system of indicators soon develops in order to allow people to both rate and display their performance. Slimness, muscularity, strength and 10K times all begin to take on a social salience as measures of competence and success. Some individuals score well, but implicitly, others become labelled as incompetent. The competent increase their commitment and the social system works to exclude and ostracize the incompetent. This is a powerful phenomenon and helps explain why the bulk of the population, including many youngsters, shy away from sport, sports centres, health clubs and other formal fitness and exercise settings. For them, the simplest solution is to avoid exposure and threat of failure by staying clear and spending time with other more rewarding pursuits. In essence, a fitness movement that has its foundation in status and social achievement, by its very nature will ultimately deny opportunity to those who need exercise and fitness most. The inevitable consequence is that the fitness rich will grow richer while the fitness poor grow poorer. In summary, the media clearly have a powerful influence over the public's view of fitness and exercise. Left to its own devices, however, it is likely that the images portrayed exclude those in most need, and therefore contravene good health promotion policy.

THE EXPANSION OF EXERCISE SCIENCE

The development of exercise science has been heavily dominated by the disease orientation of the medical profession. In search of credibility, exercise scientists have been desperate to establish the links between lack of exercise and disease and early death. This has been successful and the acceptance of sedentary living as the fourth primary coronary risk factor in recent years by the American and the British medical fraternities provides testimony to their efforts and to the importance of exercise. On the other hand, this drive has also restricted vision and constrained progress. Optimizing cardiovascular fitness became the key issue by the mid-1980s, and this was often at the expense of other important benefits of exercise. For example, there is a growing literature on the impact of physical activity on psychological well-being that has been virtually ignored by the medical profession (Seraganian, 1993). Yet, ironically, mental ill-health, depression and anxiety are as widespread as coronary heart disease, and also incur substantial costs both financially and in terms of human suffering.

Furthermore, it is ironic that the emergence of the exercise sciences within the medical model not only provided a strong rationale for the health-related fitness movement in schools, but also fuelled the media-generated fitness fashion. It provided the commercial market place with the luxury of scientific, medical and technical credibility. The catechism of the American College of Sports Medicine was soon learned by the fitness and aerobics workforce. Three or four times per week with heart rate between 60 and 80 per cent of maximum for at least twenty minutes become the magical pill of exercise prescription. Thousands of carotid pulses were located on thousands of sweaty bodies as we learned to count heart rates. The skinfold caliper was soon to become the most potent weapon of the fitness professional. Narcissism was satiated as people could not resist the temptation of confirming how lean and fit they were through the numerous fitness testing services that sprung up. In the meantime, the overweight and unhealthy learned to stay well clear.

For a while, the health-related fitness movement was the exclusive domain of the exercise physiologist, as the demand increased for more knowledge of exercise training effects and better testing techniques. However, in the late 1980s, with a gradual change in orientation towards exercise and fitness, a new breed of exercise scientist was emerging. The exercise psychologist was more concerned with facilitating behaviours rather than the measurement of fitness. Links were forged with health psychology (Biddle and Fox, 1989) and health promotion which had been researching other health behaviours such as smoking and eating disorders for some time. There was also an increased interest in the mental benefits of exercise. This development is representative of the gradual move from the product orientation of fitness towards the process of exercise that was taking place throughout the educational and scientific community in the late 1980s.

IMPLICATIONS FOR PHYSICAL ACTIVITY PROMOTION POLICY

The interrelated developments of exercise and fitness in the exercise sciences, education and the media have resulted in a confusion of sometimes conflicting messages which today can confound those entering the physical activity promotion debate. The philosophy of most physical educators, which is to help all to enjoy physical activity, regardless of shape, size or current fitness level, contrasts sharply with the exclusivity of the glamour and high-performance image of fitness portrayed by the media. Similarly, the emphasis on lifetime behaviour change stands in opposition to the all-powerful sales and magic pill approach of the commercial world to fitness and weight loss. The disease and illness orientation of the medical tradition dominates over a more holistic and positive health promotion approach to the improvement of well-being and quality of life. The over-emphasis throughout on cardiovascular fitness has been at the expense of exercise for weight control, mental health, lower back health and skeletal integrity. It has also focused attention on high-intensity exercise at the expense of the type of activity the general public are more likely to take on board. Given these conflicting visions and the differing degrees to which we have been exposed to them, it is not surprising that educators, medics and research scientists vary in their views on the critical exercise and health issues. It is equally unsurprising that the general public are in worse disarray. However, unless understood from a historical perspective, the multiple reality of exercise and fitness will be missed and physical activity promotion strategies will be less effective or will fail in public health promotion. Fortunately, in the last two or three years, there have been substantial developments at the national level in public health policy which have taken on board some of these paradoxical but crucial promotional issues.

RECENT NATIONAL DEVELOPMENTS IN PHYSICAL ACTIVITY PROMOTION

After considerable delay, physical activity has at last been taken on board by the health policy-making machinery in Britain. In the past two or three years, important steps forward have been taken. The Allied Dunbar National Fitness Survey was commissioned by the Health Education Authority and Sports Council (Activity and Health Research, 1992). This helped to establish just how little physical activity was being undertaken by people of different ages, with the middle age to older sector proving least active. The government's 'Health of the Nation' strategy was launched and a Physical Activity Task Force selected that is currently in session. The objective of this group is to set physical activity promotion policy and strategy until the turn of the century. Furthermore, an expert symposium has been called by the government to produce strategies to reduce the rapidly increasing incidence of overweight and obesity. Great significance is being attached to the role of physical activity in the solution to this problem. The Health Education Authority (1994), with the help of experts from all over the world, have taken all the evidence and are busy establishing a truly health-related rationale for physical activity to guide promotional strategies. It is pleasing that several physical educators have contributed to these lengthy discussions. It seems that although the interest of national policy-makers is long overdue, at least the physical activity philosophy, assumptions and messages seem sound. Several fundamental statements pervade discussion and it is likely that these will form the basis of future national initiatives for physical activity promotion. Paraphrased, these are as follows:

1 Physical activity is for all, but the focus should be on attracting the lesser active sector of society as they stand to gain most in terms of health.
2 There should be a shift in focus from higher to moderate and lower levels of physical activity. These levels have important benefits for health and they are more accessible to a larger sector of the population.
3 There should be a shift towards activities that can be accomplished by small changes in lifestyle, such as walking more often during the day. It is likely that guidelines will include encouraging people to exercise the equivalent of thirty minutes walking each day.

4   Steps should be taken to modify the environment and transport system to make
    physical activity more appealing and accessible.

These statements clearly represent a concerted move away from the dominance of
the American College of Sports Medicine exercise prescription approach that has been
deeply embedded in the system. Discrete bouts of moderate- to high-intensity exercise
such as aerobic dance or jogging that have been the hallmark of the exercise industry
to date are replaced by a re-orientation based on lifestyle activity, and activity as
leisure and transport. That is not to say that the small percentage of the population
involved in higher-intensity exercise should cut down. It is a sensible attempt to market
activity at a more acceptable level to the general public. It is also based on the
realization that lower-intensity activity has many important health benefits, such as
obesity prevention, improved skeletal health and mobility, and mental well-being.

Exercise demand has typically been absorbed by leisure centres and commercially
run health clubs. Several institutions are now seen as potential contributors to a
broader front of physical activity promotion. These include primary health care, the
media (with updated messages), community and leisure services, and corporations. In
addition, the policy of several of the government departments have been implicated
including those concerned with traffic, transport and environment, culture and heritage
(sport) and, of course, health and education.

Already, some sectors are undergoing change. For example, over two hundred
physical activity promotion schemes in the primary health care setting have been
identified (Biddle *et al.*, 1994). On the other hand, the larger British corporations have
been slow to mirror the rapid growth in the corporate sector in the US. Certainly, the
education system and schools in particular are seen as a critical component in the
jigsaw puzzle, although it has not been clearly stated in what ways they might
contribute. It is well recognized, however, that schools provide one of the few
opportunities to address the full range of individuals in a population, and a last chance
to access, at no extra cost, a captive audience. It is also appreciated that today's
youngsters become the next generation of adults and that any positive impact has the
added potential of having a lifetime, as well as an immediate, effect.

PHYSICAL ACTIVITY IN CHILDHOOD AND ADOLESCENCE

Although the potential for schools to have a long-term effect on public health through
the education of a future generation of more healthy adults, it is appropriate to
provide a brief update on the evidence for physical activity promotion for the current
health of youngsters. Research continues to identify stronger links between adult
activity, absence of ill-health and presence of mental well-being. The health/physical
activity relationship with children and adolescents is not so well-established. The
epidemiological approach which relies on disease and death rates is not applicable in
youngsters as fortunately not enough of them comply with the demands of the end
point! We are left to examine the results of exercise training and physical activity
programmes on risk factors rather than incidence of ill-health. The purpose of the
recent International Consensus Conference on Physical Activity Guidelines for
Adolescents held in San Diego was to gather the available research data on this topic.

Several reviews were commissioned that have since been published in an edition of *Pediatric Exercise Science* (Sallis and Patrick, 1994). The conclusions from these reviews were somewhat weak, primarily because of the limited amount of well-conducted research that is reported, but also because of the added difficulties of measurement in maturing youngsters, and the likelihood that unhealthy habits have had insufficient time to take their toll. However, the final comments of the consensus panel (Sallis and Patrick, 1994, p. 311) were optimistic:

> Despite the limitations of the current database, there is substantial evidence that regular physical activity produces multiple beneficial physiological and psychological outcomes during adolescence. The strength and consistency of these findings lead to recommendations for all adolescents to be physically active on a regular basis.

CATEGORIES OF PHYSICAL ACTIVITY

There appears, therefore, to be some immediate support to establish physical activity promotion strategies for adolescents. Unfortunately, the same consistency of information is not available for younger children. However, there is no reason to suspect that the same principles do not apply, although the implications for educational policy may be quite different. The consensus panel recommended that two elements of physical activity should be developed. These are that all adolescents should (Sallis and Patrick, 1994, pp. 307–8):

1 be physically active daily, or nearly every day, as part of play, games, sports, work, transportation, recreation, physical education or planned exercise, in the context of family, school and community activities;
2 engage in three or more sessions per week of activities that last twenty minutes or more at a time and that require moderate to vigorous levels of exertion.

These categories fall in line with the trends in recommendations for adults described earlier, and are primarily distinguished by level of exercise intensity. They are derived because each has the potential to satisfy specific physiological and psychological needs.

Activity for the body

This refers to locomotion involving carrying the weight of the body over distance. This is required to prevent overweight and obesity, and to ensure the development of a strong bone structure. Total daily activity of this type may also have a cumulative effect on aerobic fitness. Currently, there is an overweight and obesity boom in British adults, and the limited evidence available points towards this trend being mirrored in children. Although conclusive data are not available, there is a strong likelihood that social change is being accompanied by a gradual lowering of physical activity and daily caloric expenditure. The reductions in energy expenditure caused by an increasing dependence on labour-saving devices and motorized transport has not only affected adults. For example, Hillman (1993) has reported comparisons between surveys in 1971 and 1990. Over that period, there was an increase of almost four times in the percentage of children taken to school by car. In the same period, adults became increasingly wary of allowing their children to cross or cycle on roads, go to leisure events, walk home from school or catch the bus alone. A fear of heavier traffic and the more frequent reporting in the media of incidents involving child molestation seem to have been responsible. Girls are allowed considerably less activity independence than boys. The end result is that some children rarely transport their bodies under their own steam for significant distances, and time and licence allowed them for active outdoor play has reduced. There are other cultural changes at work also. The tremendous rise in computer-based leisure for children may be having a serious effect on the time spent active in leisure, although this has yet to be fully established. There is likely to be considerable variability among individual children and the social context in which they are placed. Absence of suitable play areas in a busy inner-city development may restrict play whereas the suburban youngster living in a cul-de-sac where bike-riding is safe and which is within walking distance of school is likely to fare much better. This variance is also reflected in differences between the cultures. In The Netherlands, for example, over 60 per cent of journeys made by children are by bicycle, and this compares to 13 per cent of boys and 4 per cent of girls in Britain, even though 90 per cent own a bicycle (Rosenbaum, 1993).

At present, the evidence to support the decline in physical activity involving locomotion of the body remains somewhat circumstantial. However, given the social and environmental trends towards increased motorization and technology, convenience living and sedentary leisure pursuits, certainly there is cause for serious concern for the present and future.

Activity for the heart

The second recommended category of activity involves a level of intensity that will optimally stress the cardiovascular system and help youngsters to develop fitter hearts, muscles and oxygen delivery systems. In addition, there may be an accompanying improvement in blood lipids and reduction in blood pressure that could have an important positive effect on subsequent coronary risk. Considerable research has been published on the incidence of this type of activity as it can be more accurately measured through 24-hour heart rate monitoring. Research with adolescents (Armstrong *et al.*, 1990; Riddoch *et al.*, 1991) and primary school children (Armstrong and Bray, 1991; Sleap and Warburton, 1992) have produced consistent results. British children rarely engage in amounts of sustained activity of sufficient intensity to optimize their aerobic fitness. In one study, over a third of boys and half of the girls did not experience a sustained ten-minute period of moderate intensity physical activity. This may have important consequences for future health, particularly for girls.

It is not clear what percentage of children have traditionally been involved in prolonged activity that requires an intensity elicited by, at minimum, brisk walking. It is unlikely that youngsters raise their heart rate to these levels walking to school unless they have to hurry or walk uphill, as typically they stroll and chat. It could be achieved by bike-riding. For the majority, though, it probably requires formal and purposeful bouts of exercise such as those involved in relatively vigorous sports, or aerobics sessions, distance running or similar. Given the reported decline in extra-curricular school sport over the past decade, and the reduced PE curriculum time in

Britain when compared to almost all other European countries, there seems to be a serious threat to this type of health-enhancing activity. The implications for younger children are not clear, as they are less likely to exhibit patterns of activity that produce a steady-state level of elevated heart rate. An unresolved question is the extent to which the short bursts of activity, more typical of the kiss-and-chase activities of the primary playground contribute to young children's aerobic fitness and health.

Activity for the mind

There has been much less attention paid to the psychological health consequences of physical activity for adults as well as children. This has probably been a result of the traditional focus of the medical profession on disease rather than well-being. Several reviews now indicate that exercise can elevate mood, reduce anxiety and depression and produce improvements in self-perceptions and self-esteem with adults. Several of these effects are also identifiable with adolescents (Calfas and Taylor, 1994) although fewer studies have been conducted. An exception is the work on the self-esteem of children showing an overall improvement with exercise, particularly when fitness rather than motor skill programmes are used (Gruber, 1986). However, as with adults, the link between physical activity and psychological well-being is likely to be complex. 'Horses for courses' seems to be the rule of the day. Some youngsters will gain a great sense of thrill and achievement from high-intensity competitive sports, which for others would be anxiety-provoking. For some, a brisk walk and a chat at lunch time or a swim may provide exactly the diversion and relaxation needed, but for others it may be perceived as tedious. The point here is that physical activities have the potential to impact on a youngster's mental state in different ways. We have a long way to go before we are sufficiently knowledgeable to engineer the activity experience so that it maximizes well-being for all.

Activity for life

Clearly, concern for the immediate levels of physical activity, fitness and health of our youngsters is important and the evidence seems to be gathering to support this, at least with adolescents. Of particular significance to the educational setting, however, are longer-term objectives. The way exercise is presented to youngsters may carry important implications for future activity patterns and consequently their health and well-being as adults. In the captive environment of compulsory PE, it is possible to raise the level of children's physical activity as well as their fitness levels simply by working them hard at every opportunity. However, it is clear that our youthful exuberances cannot physiologically store up fitness and health for later in life. Maintenance of benefits relies on continued participation and therefore the PE experience has to be designed to make a positive impact on children's choices.

The extent to which physical activity as a youngster carries over to adulthood has not been answered adequately. At best, the limited research evidence is weak (Powell and Dysinger, 1987). There is support for the tracking of sport involvement into adulthood (Activity and Health Research, 1992; Kuh and Cooper, 1992) and this is not surprising given the links between perceived sports competence and participation. By the time adolescence is reached, those who are good at sport are selected into sports teams, and are also likely to remain involved into adulthood. However, this is not the majority of youngsters and the statistics on the tracking of physical activity levels in general, or health-related exercise into adulthood are not available.

In summary, the data on adults and children clearly point towards different activities and different activity levels being important for an individual's health for different reasons. However, the strength of relationships suggests that we should be encouraging youngsters to move more, more often, for the sake of maintaining good functioning of the body. Some of the movement should involve exercise at a sufficiently high intensity to stress the cardiovascular system adequately. At the same time, activities should be presented that can have psychological benefits and carry over into adulthood behaviour patterns.

DEVELOPING AN ACTIVE SCHOOL POLICY

Although current Health of the Nation strategies do not have a direct remit for children, the education system is recognized as an important agency in physical activity promotion and the prevention of obesity. It is seen as an appropriate inter-vention point because it (a) directly addresses children's physical activity levels, and (b) can raise awareness, set expectations, develop expertise, confidence and attitudes that might produce a more active and healthier future adult generation. Furthermore, as with any institution, it also has potential to impact on those who serve in it, in this case, teachers, governors and parents.

Recent research (Edmunds *et al.*, in review) has shown that schools can vary considerably in the amount and quality of physical activity opportunities that they offer to children. This is partly due to the policies they operate and the patterns of the school day, but also their location and surrounding environment. To maximize the number and quality of these opportunities, the concept of the active school is suggested. The active school will be aware of the importance of physical activity promotion and will be constantly working towards devising and operating policy that will increase the physical activity levels of children and staff in a way that is likely to have a positive and sustained impact on habits. There is no single formula for the operation of the successful active school. However, some general but critical suggestions are presented here as a starting point.

Policy-making machinery

Schools have many pressing priorities and have limited time and resources. Realistically, in order to compete, the successful active school is likely to have set up a formal vehicle for developing and implementing change. This may be initiated by a single-handed activity promotion champion who, for example might be an enthusiastic head of PE. However, because of the range of areas of the school that are implicated, it is likely that a physical activity task force is required, involving a range of staff and parents, to develop a business plan for activity promotion. The remit of such a group might be, for example, to keep the school informed of the national physical activity promotion picture, to evaluate existing activity levels among children and staff, as well as to identify targets of change, set achievable short- and long-terms goals and establish a means of assessing success rates. Other challenges might be to establish the need for resources, and a means of acquiring them, or to find innovative ways of creating an active school culture. It might also operate as part of a broader healthy school policy which takes on board issues such as safety, healthy eating, sexuality and smoking in school life and beyond. It could also serve to forge healthy alliances with other agencies such as the local community, leisure services and sports clubs, and to develop strategies for influencing local transport and environmental policy. The scope of such a task force is vast and is only limited by the time, energy, expertise and imagination of its contributors.

Developing physical activity profiles

The active school will not only use the terms 'health-related fitness' and 'exercise', it will use the all-encompassing phrase of 'health-related physical activity' in order to direct attention to the full range of physical activities that are important. Our recent research (Edmunds *et al.*, in review) has indicated that children are remarkably consistent in their activity habits during the school week when their time is relatively structured. There are five key elements that are useful in producing a youngster's weekly physical activity profile:

1   active transport to and from school;
2   informal active play that takes place at break and lunchtime, and after school until the evening meal (but extended into the evenings during summer months);
3   formal activity such as sport, training and practice that takes place at school or in clubs;
4   PE lessons; and
5   time spent watching TV and playing computer games.

Weekends are more variable and, of course, generally influenced by the family situation rather than school. Table 8.1 shows an example of a youngster's activity profile. The active school will consider each of these elements when creating policy for increased activity.

Activity as transport

A neglected area of physical activity has been the journey to and from school. This is because of the narrow focus in the past on cardiovascular exercise and fitness. The recent decline in walking and cycling to school may to some extent be reversible. There are several ways of addressing this important issue, some being easier than others. For instance, to increase the number of youngsters cycling to school, secure storage facilities for cycles and safe cycling awards could be offered. Schools might develop pressure groups for lobbying local authorities for cycling routes and traffic calming schemes. Children might be offered incentive schemes to walk to school in the safety of

Table 8.1 *William's daily physical activity profile: Tuesdays*

Category	Time	Example
Work	Before school	Paper round
Transport	Before and after school	Walk to and from school
Informal play	Break	Playground soccer
	Lunch	–
	After school to evening meal	Play out
Formal play	Lunch	Soccer team practice
	After school	–
	Evening	Karate club
TV/computer	Evening	1 hr TV 5–6 p.m.

groups, as often many come from the same close neighbourhood. Perhaps a percentage of the cost on bus fares saved might be retained by each student. For primary age children, perhaps schemes could be devised to encourage parents to walk their children to school more often. Certainly, children currently do not see the importance of this form of activity and it could form the basis of a project, lesson or discussion within curriculum time.

Activity as informal play

Given the choice, the majority of young children are active during break and lunch. Primary school children are involved in spontaneous activity as well as traditional playground games. Girls continue these games until about the age of 12 and then tend to spend their time in inactive social groups. Boys develop pick-up games of soccer and cricket with many continuing to play throughout their mid-teens. These activities are important and should be formally encouraged through school policy. However, as a matter of convenience, quite often schools work against playground activity. Often, all that is required is suitably marked out all-weather areas and a modest supply of equipment. Primary schools should consider adopting some of the active playground schemes that are currently being developed. Furthermore, attention could be paid to those children who prefer to be inactive at these times as they may represent a high-risk group.

Activity as formal play

Involvement in formalized sport and active leisure seem to carry over to adulthood. It is therefore critical that as high a percentage of children as possible leave school with a reasonable level of skill and enthusiasm in some type of formal activity. The decline of the school fixture programmes that took place in the 1980s could be seen as a blessing in this respect. Instead of the expense of transporting a small minority of students to distant corners of the county, a lunchtime and after-school activity programme could be developed that appeals to the full spectrum of youngsters' interests. Apart from the usual sports activities, some schools already offer lunchtime aerobics, swimming for fitness or aquaerobics, and outdoor pursuits clubs. This is no more labour intensive than running several age group school teams and, if competition is seen to be appealing and healthy for youngsters, then lunchtime or after-school tournaments and leagues in a range of sports would involve much greater numbers of students.

The school is not wholly responsible; as many children will take part in swimming, gymnastics, dance and other sport activities, as well as organizations such as cubs and brownies, generally on weekday evenings. Increasingly also, youngsters play sport through the club system on weekends and older adolescents are beginning to enrol in formal exercise classes and take membership at fitness clubs. An important role for schools is to make links and alliances with these alternative agencies. This is particularly important where youngsters are bridging the gap between school and community, which is a critical time for drop-out.

Activity through the curriculum

Much has been written about the role of the PE programme in promoting physical activity in children. National Curriculum policy now encourages schools to incorporate health-related aspects and this appears to be working. There is a political misconception that PE is totally responsible for the provision of children's physical activity. This is naïve given that two hours of PE per week throughout the school year represents only 1 per cent of the youngster's waking hours! Clearly, this precious amount of time exposed to experts should be used very wisely. It should be dedicated to learning the critical elements of skill, knowledge and understanding that are required to ensure 'physical education' in the truest sense, and not used as an excuse for recreation or even increasing children's fitness. This is explained in greater detail below, but the active school will ensure that PE receives adequate amounts of time on the school timetable.

Reducing inactive leisure

As far as active lifestyles are concerned, the amount of time spent watching TV and playing with computers is not necessarily detrimental, unless it diverts children away from active play and leisure pursuits. It is difficult for the school to have any direct influence on this time and clearly some children are more susceptible than others. However, the success of the school's formal and informal programmes should have a positive impact on children's decisions. Furthermore, the school could develop a policy of working with families to help them to deal with children who have inactivity problems around the home.

Encouraging lifetime physical activity

The active school will not be content with simply finding ways of increasing current levels of activity in students. The long-term product of empowered individuals who maintain active and healthy lifestyles will underpin all the activity promotion policy described so far. The empowered school leavers will have several attributes: they will be activity experts, and activity advocates.

The activity expert

Each student will be fully physically educated. This means that they will be knowledge-able, independent, skilled and expert in the area of exercise, fitness and health. Furthermore, they will understand key social and environmental factors that constrain healthy lifestyles, and be aware of the machinery that prevents and allows change. For example, they will be able to address issues such as body image problems, decisions about traffic, and the role of community in the local change process.

The activity advocate

Knowledge and expertise will not ensure but will enhance the chances of continued participation. Just as important is that each school leaver will leave education with a favourable attitude to at least some forms of sport, exercise or other physical leisure pursuit. This issue is well-recognized and a great deal has now been written about the social psychology of exercise and sport participation. This has been applied to the behavioural choices and decisions of children and adolescents with regard to long-term effects (Fox, 1991; 1994; Fox and Biddle, 1988). In summary, whenever exercise and physical activity experiences are designed for youngsters, their impact for the future always need to be carefully considered. The way the experience is processed in the form of beliefs, attitudes, self-perceptions and confidence are likely to be critical to future involvement. Children who learn that the benefits of taking part outweigh the costs, in whatever form that may take, are more likely to make the decision to be active when they are free to choose. Schools need to find ways of offering physical activity opportunities that children find fulfilling. This will involve offering a broader range of activities that are presented at different levels of competitiveness.

Creating a physical activity culture

The main factor that distinguishes the active school is that it has created a physical activity culture. This does not happen overnight; it requires a change in opinions, priorities and practices of a critical mass within the school. It may also mean overpowering an existing physical activity culture. For example, the school that has seen its prestige and ethos emanating from its competitive sports record provides a particular challenge. However, there are two policy issues that appear to be critical: generating enthusiasm across the board and public relations.

Generating enthusiasm across the board

Most successful corporate fitness programmes have their roots in an executive board who are personally committed to fitness. One way of convincing staff is to make exercise and fitness personally relevant to them. An exercise and fitness counselling service could be operated to help staff to increase their own activity and fitness, and to reduce their stress. Exercise sessions could be set up specifically for staff, governors and interested parents. Some schools have used this system very successfully. Even if it does not convince individual staff members to be more active, they may become sympathetic to the initiative and this will help to grease the wheels of progress. Furthermore, when pupils see that staff advocate physical activity policies, they are more likely to appreciate their importance. The concept of a crowd forming a crowd becomes highly applicable.

Public relations

The success of an overweight child becoming slim is not going to attract the same attention as the first XV winning the county championship. This is where the imagination, ingenuity and business sense of the physical activity task force is required. Fitness, exercise and health do still attract interest and the media can be used to advantage. Schools have used strategies such as open days, local sports personalities openly advocating the importance of exercise for health as well as sport, activity newsletters, and regular releases for the local press to establish physical activity policies with parents and the local community. All these factors can help develop a new active identity for the school.

SUMMARY

This chapter has attempted to describe the nature of the emergence of the latest wave of interest in personal fitness and health. The assumptions underpinning the development of health-related concepts in school PE have been different to the glamourized images of fitness and exercise extremes depicted by the media. These images have had a powerful impact on public perception of the meaning and importance of fitness, creating a perceptual barrier of inaccessibility to the majority. At the same time, educational attempts to develop fitness and exercise have been heavily biased by the concern of exercise scientists and the medical world for coronary heart disease and cardiovascular fitness.

Recent developments in public health policy at the national level have at last taken physical activity promotion on board. The messages are clear and the focus of attention is on helping the least active become more active. There is a move towards an emphasis on physical activity becoming more entrenched in lifestyles, as opposed to being restricted to discrete incidences in health clubs or leisure centres. The contribution of physical activity for mental well-being is slowly being recognized.

The concept of the active school has been presented in the light of these discussions. A basic framework of suggestions has been offered to demonstrate how schools might adopt a more extensive physical activity promotion policy. If schools were able to adopt such policies, the case for their inclusion as a critical element of the national drive towards increased physical activity for public health will be greatly strengthened.

REFERENCES

Activity and Health Research (1992) *Allied Dunbar National Fitness Survey*. London: Sports Council and Health Education Authority.

Armstrong, N. and Bray, S. (1991) 'Physical activity patterns defined by heart rate monitoring', *Archives of Disease in Childhood*, **66**, 245–7.

Armstrong, N., Balding, J., Gentle, P. and Kirby, B. (1990) 'Patterns of physical activity among 11 to 16 year old British children', *British Medical Journal*, **301**, 203–5.

Biddle, S.J.H. and Fox, K.R. (1989) 'Exercise and health psychology: Emerging relationships', *British Journal of Medical Psychology*, **62**, 205–16.

Biddle, S.J.H., Fox, K.R. and Edmunds, L. (1994) *Physical Activity Promotion in Primary Health Care in England*. London: Health Education Authority.

Calfas, K.J. and Taylor, W.C. (1994) 'Effect of physical activity on psychological variables in adolescents', *Pediatric Exercise Science*, **6**, 406–23.

Edmunds, L., Fox, K.R. and Biddle, S.J.H. (in review) 'Physical activity profiles of children from three contrasting schools', *Physical Education Review*.

Fox, K.R. (1991) 'Motivating children for physical activity: Towards a healthier future', *Journal of Physical Education, Recreation and Dance*, **62**, 34–8.

Fox, K.R. (1994) 'Understanding young children and their decisions about physical activity', *British Journal of Physical Education*, **25**(1), 15–19.

Fox, K.R. and Biddle, S.J.H. (1988) 'Series: The child's perspective in physical education', *British Journal of Physical Education*, **19**, 34–8, 107–11, 182–5, 247–52.

Gruber, J.J. (1986) 'Physical activity and self-esteem development in children: A meta analysis', *American Academy of Physical Education Papers*, **19**, 30–48.

Harris, J. (1994) 'Health-related exercise in the national curriculum: Results of a pilot study in secondary schools', *British Journal of Physical Education Research Supplement*, **14**, 6–11.

HEA (1994) *Moving on: Symposium Report*. London: Health Education Authority.

Hillman, M. (1993) 'One false move', in Hillman, M. (ed.), *Children, Transport, and the Quality of Life*. London: Policy Studies Institute, pp. 7–18.

Kuh, D.J.L. and Cooper, C. (1992) 'Physical activity at 36 years: patterns and childhood predictors in a longitudinal study', *Journal of Epidemiology and Community Health*, **46**, 114–19.

National Curriculum Council (1992) *Physical Education Non-statutory Guidance*. York: National Curriculum Council.

Powell, K.E. and Dysinger, W. (1987) 'Childhood participation in organised sports and physical education as precursors of adult physical activity', *American Journal of Preventive Medicine*, **3**, 276–81.

Riddoch, C., Mahoney, C., Murphy, N., Boreham, C. and Cran, G. (1991) 'The physical activity patterns of Northern Irish schoolchildren ages 11–16 years', *Pediatric Exercise Science*, **3**, 300–9.

Rosenbaum, M. (1993) 'Independent mobility and children's rights', in Hillman, M. (ed.), *Children, Transport, and the Quality of Life*. London: Policy Studies Institute, pp. 19–27.

Sallis, J.F. (ed.) (1994) 'Physical activity guidelines for adolescents', *Pediatric Exercise Science*, **6**, 19–27.

Sallis, J.F. and Patrick, K. (1994) 'Physical activity guidelines for adolescents: Consensus statement', *Pediatric Exercise Science*, **6**, 299–301.

Seraganian, P. (ed.) (1993) *Exercise Psychology: The Influence of Physical Exercise on Psychological Processes*. New York: Wiley.

Sleap, M. and Warburton, P. (1992) 'Physical activity levels of 5–11 year-old children in England as determined by continuous observation', *Research Quarterly for Exercise and Sport*, **63**, 238–45.

Chapter 9

Curricular Entitlement and Implementation for all Children

David Sugden and Helen Wright

This chapter draws upon several disparate bodies of literature all of which have chronicled changes in their respective subject areas, which in turn reflect ideological and legal developments. We are presenting some of the changes that have occurred in special education over the last fifteen years as well as in PE, because the ideology and legal initiatives in the former have driven practice across a range of subject areas including PE. These twin concepts of ideology and legislation have moved hand in hand to alter our way of thinking about access and entitlement, and it is only when we pause to reflect do we realize how far we have travelled. To illustrate this point, consider the literature sources surrounding special educational needs, particularly in mainstream schools. In 1980, when teaching in-service courses in special needs, it was equally impossible to present a relevant book list of texts from the UK. Now it is virtually impossible to keep abreast of the explosion of literature in the area. These texts reflect an interest in a field of study in which terminology, knowledge, attitudes and, in some cases, practice have changed. This does not mean that all is rosy; it means that the appropriate structures are there to be built upon and all subject areas can draw from this structure for optimal presentation of the curriculum.

DEVELOPMENTS IN SPECIAL EDUCATIONAL NEEDS

Modern special educational needs is usually seen as beginning with the Warnock Report in 1978 which was a government report making a number of recommendations, some of which were taken up by the Education Act (1981), and others which continued to have influence throughout the 1980s. The major recommendations of the Warnock Report included:

1 the abandonment of the distinction between handicapped and non-handicapped;
2 the suggestion as to how many children could be described by the term special education need;
3 special education should, in the first instance, be provided in the mainstream school.

The abandonment of the distinction between handicapped and non-handicapped

We are all handicapped at some time in our lives if adequate support systems are not in place, and so the distinction is difficult if not impossible to maintain. Formal categories such as educational subnormality, maladjusted, physical handicap, etc. were also dropped, and in their place the term 'special educational need' was recommended as it focused on the child's needs not on a child's deficits. This was more than a semantic change, being a change in ideology providing an optimistic model for education because it directed professionals towards providing educational support systems rather than towards medical explanations of deficit. Alongside special educational needs, the term 'learning difficulty' was also proposed indicating that a child had a difficulty in learning over and above same age peers which required additional resources.

How many children could be described by the term 'special educational need'

At any one time, one in six children would have special educational needs, and at some time during their school career this rose to one in five. These figures had great impact because it widened greatly the concept of special education. In England and Wales, only around 2 per cent of children have ever been in special schools and yet here was a report saying that 20 per cent have special educational needs. This meant that 18 per cent were and always had been in mainstream schools, with the implicit assumption that this 18 per cent at best had been ignored and at worst were given a raw deal in terms of resource allocation.

Special education in the mainstream school

Special schools were only recommended for children with severe cognitive, sensory or physical problems, for those with emotional and behavioural problems or those with diverse and complex difficulties. This had a range of implications, the first being that some children who were previously in special schools would now be in mainstream schools. But, more important, it gave a strong message to mainstream schools that they would need to change for the children who had always been in these schools.

Education Act (1981)

The government response to the Warnock Report was the Education Act (1981) which provided a new legislative framework for special educational needs. The Act only addressed a small number of the Warnock recommendations and was at the time widely criticized, but it contained many implications for all teachers in special and mainstream schools, and had an effect on parents, governors, local education authorities (LEAs) and ultimately children with special educational needs. The Act did deal with definitional issues replacing the term 'handicap' with 'special educational need' and 'learning difficulty', and recommended that with certain conditions met, the child with special educational needs should be educated in a mainstream school. These conditions however, did lend themselves to differing interpretations by the various LEAs.

A significant part of the Act involved the identification and assessment of children with special educational needs. The principle of assessment was based upon Warnock recommendations that it should be a continuous process. In some cases, a child's need would be of such a type that a formal Statement is required. The Statement spells out the special educational provision that should be made for the child. Thus the place of schooling, the type of curriculum, the social grouping in which the education is to take place and any other necessary support should be specified in the Statement.

The Act had many critics with complaints about the 'softness' of the legislation leading to variability of interpretation. However, together with the Warnock Report, it led to a number of important changes in practice and in our thinking on special education during the 1980s.

The first change was the high profile that special needs education started to occupy. It had always been the Cinderella of education, but now all schools had to firmly address issues which were previously hidden. The implication was that if 20 per cent of children have special educational needs and 18 per cent of these children are and always have been in mainstream schools, then every teacher ought to be a special needs teacher or at least be aware of the skills and techniques necessary for teaching a broad band of ability ranges. Alongside this increase in visibility and awareness, a group of teachers known as special needs co-ordinators emerged to become a major factor in the provision for children with special educational needs. More children were being brought back into mainstream schools from special schools, there was greater whole school concern for children with special educational needs and the role of the person responsible for them increased. The new era demanded that schools made a systematic approach to special needs education which involved organizing the school from first principles and was not simply an add-on after other areas had been completed. Special needs co-ordinators came upon the scene, some emerging from their previous role as remedial teachers, others coming new into the role. Their job specification varied, but in general it included teaching small groups, teaching classes, providing in-class support to a variety of subject areas, withdrawing other children for support, liaising with the LEA, working with parents and professionals who visited the school, providing information to teachers about the children, providing help in the form of materials, guidance in-service and usually being part of the senior or middle management team in a school. Of particular interest was the move towards more flexible means of support, such as in-class which is a more integrated setting than withdrawal, and which requires great skill in planning and organization such that the teachers concerned can be optimally employed in the same work space. It is noteworthy that a report from Her Majesty's Inspectorate (DES, 1989a) on special educational needs in mainstream schools always found an influential special needs co-ordinator when they observed good practice in special needs education (DES, 1989a; Sugden, 1994; Wedell, 1993).

Special schools too were changing. The benefits special schools had to offer included small classes, expertise of the staff, working with individual programmes, working with other professionals and a total school concern for children with difficulties. However, drawbacks existed and were concentrated in the area of isolation, working in an unrealistic setting, difficulties in providing a broad and balanced curriculum which together with ideological and legal changes placed great demands and strains on special schools. To cope with this some very innovative programmes emerged which involved special schools making links for both staff and pupils with mainstream schools. These links which were quite extensive in some cases appeared to give children the benefits of both worlds that special and mainstream schools could offer.

These changes during the 1980s gave special needs education a prominence never before experienced but, when the Education Reform Act (ERA) (1988) was passed; while not directly addressing special needs education, it contained some major issues which presented the area with threats. The first issue was that of funding: a school's budget was to be determined predominantly by the number and type of pupils they attracted. At the same time, LEAs were required to delegate increasing proportions of their funds to schools thus reducing the amount of central money available within the authority. Community charge capping and the loss of funds allocated to schools which opted out of LEA control further reduced the amount of money available. The threats to special education were obvious with authorities not being able to provide the central resources necessary in such areas as support, and schools with their limited budgets being reluctant to buy in help from outside when they were stretched to meet their own internal costs. In addition, the ERA also introduced the National Curriculum which was to be an entitlement for all children. In general, for special needs education the National Curriculum is a bonus giving rights to children previously denied them. However, it has also caused consternation. In mainstream schools, teachers report that they are having to teach children with a wider range of ability on a set curriculum than ever before, thus diluting the quality of work they are able to offer. In special schools, the problems surround being able to provide the width of specialist teaching that the National Curriculum demands, particularly in areas such as science and modern foreign languages (Sugden, 1994).

The result of this can be seen in a number of telling statistics. The Audit Commission published a report entitled 'Getting in on the Act' (DES, 1992) which described the state of affairs in twelve LEAs which were representative of the country. The following examples from the report illustrate the variability of special needs education across the country. The number of statements in LEAs varied from over 3 per cent of the population in some to less than 1 per cent in others. The percentage of children in special schools ranged from 2 per cent in some authorities to others with less than 1 per cent. This is a crude measure of the integration policies in LEAs, with 2 per cent representing a norm which was prevalent before all the current changes and less than 1 per cent showing a greater tendency towards integration. The third point is a savage indictment of bureaucratic processes involved in special needs education, representing the average length of time it takes for a Statement of Special Educational Needs to be issued. The best authority averaged nine or ten months while in others it was much more, with one authority taking nearly three years to complete the process, a period of time which would allow the child to leave school, start work, and move authorities with nothing happening!

These examples illustrate the variability in provision for children with special educational needs but, hopefully, the Education Act (1993) will put an end to this situation. This Act contains the most powerful implications for children with special educational needs. Most important, a Code of Practice (DFE, 1994) has been published which addresses the issue of identification and assessment. Among others, two important points stood out:

1   Guidelines are given to schools about their assessment procedures which are to follow a five-step model originally proposed by the Warnock Committee, thus placing a duty on a school, procedures with the probable effect of reducing the variability seen in this area.
2   There is a recommendation that the total time for a Statement to be issued should not exceed six months.

Noting the Audit Commission Report that the best LEA took nine or ten months, it is clear that authorities are going to have to radically adjust their procedures. Other documents which we believe will reduce the variability of provision address school policies, provision of support, and the role of special schools.

The one cloud on this now optimistic horizon is the issue of funding and resources. Much of what is described above does have resource implications and there is the danger that an attractive financial option will minimally address the legal issues rather than face them full in spirit. However, looking long-term, the outlook is promising; schools who do take full and responsible action in this area will be models for others, and eventually the implications and consequences for all subject areas including PE will become clearer.

PE, CHILDREN WITH MOVEMENT DIFFICULTIES AND SPECIAL EDUCATIONAL NEEDS

Within this tighter framework of special educational need provision, PE will have to operate, and it is now clear that teachers in mainstream schools will be asked to teach a wider ability range in all subject areas. This is a result of many children returning to mainstream from special schools, and the increasing recognition of the diversity that has always been present in mainstream. Mixed-ability teaching has always been the norm in PE and we have always been faced with children who are experiencing difficulties in this area. This situation is set to become more pronounced.

Children with movement difficulties show a range of abilities: from those who find difficulty combining and co-operating in group situations, through those with moderate co-ordination problems; to those who are barely mobile. In order to place some structure on the needs of these children, it is useful to describe them from two stances which will have important implications for provision:

1   The first group of children have special needs which are primarily described in terms of their movement skills. In some cases, they have a Statement detailing their needs; others with no Statement, still provide challenges for the teacher when movement demands are made. Children with a physical disability such as cerebral palsy are in this group as are so-called 'clumsy' children.
2   The second group of children have special needs in the PE domain, but these are usually secondary to other needs which have been specifically defined. This group of children would include those with learning difficulties, those with sensory difficulties and those with emotional and behavioural difficulties.

Not every child in these two groups will have difficulties in PE; for example, it is perfectly feasible for a child with moderate learning difficulties to be an excellent performer in PE. However, as a group, children with learning difficulties will have needs in PE that are over and above those of their peers. This situation is also true for children with sensory difficulties and those with emotional and behavioural difficulties (Sugden and Keogh, 1990).

Children defined in terms of their movement difficulties

Developmental co-ordination disorder (DCD)

A large group of children arrive at school obviously lacking in the movement skills necessary for them to function effectively in a PE lesson. They have no identifiable neurological disorder and they are not generally delayed, but their movement skills are at a functionally low level. Many terms have been used to describe these children, the most common being 'clumsy' or 'the clumsy child syndrome'. Even though the literature is littered with this term we believe it is not particularly useful because of its lack of specificity and its derogatory connotations. The most recent and formal is developmental co-ordination disorder (DCD) (DSM–IV, 1994) which is becoming more widely recognized (Sugden and Henderson, 1994).

Children with DCD acquire the basic skills of sitting, standing, walking, running, etc., but they may be delayed and they may have difficulty in using them flexibly to adapt to changing environmental demands. They can always perform the skills at a rudimentary level, but they are less skilled than their peers, they have difficulty using the skills in context and often they look awkward. This often leads to a lack of participation in PE lessons and in play and recreational activities at break time. PE is not the only subject in which children with DCD present challenges. In many subject areas, the National Curriculum assumes a basic level of motor competence in tasks like pouring, weighing, cutting, drawing and writing, and children with DCD often have trouble with these (Sugden and Henderson, 1994). A causal relationship between DCD and school achievement has not been established, but there is good evidence to suggest a strong relationship, with Losse *et al.* (1991) showing that they do less well in school than would be predicted from their cognitive ability. This could result from emotional variables like social isolation and lowered self-concept, or could be more direct, like poorly presented work or slowness in finishing tasks.

There is no observable direct cause of DCD which occasionally runs in families. It may be we are simply dealing in the lower end of a normal continuum of motor skill rather than some discrete syndrome. Increasingly, advanced technology has encouraged some clinicians to look for neurological lesions, while others have looked to changes in the developmental progressions that children make. The manner in which children learn has interested other researchers, with an in-depth look at faulty learning characteristics such as deficits in using kinaesthetic and visual information. More recently, researchers have suggested that there is not one global picture of DCD leading to generic management, but several different subtypes which could lead to more specific intervention (Hoare, 1994; Wright and Sugden, submitted for publication).

The reported incidence of DCD varies considerably and it is often linked to the manner of identification. We are presented with incidences ranging from 3 per cent to

15 per cent with the American Psychiatric Association reporting around 6 per cent for children between the ages of 6 and 11. In any average primary school classroom, this would give approximately two children. It is usual though not always for most studies to find more boys than girls with DCD with some studies showing only a slight difference while in others the ratio is as high as 3:1 (Sugden and Henderson, 1994). Again, this often depends on how the children are identified, whether by some form of standardized test, through observation or from teacher reports. All will give different and not entirely consistent incidence figures showing that DCD as a condition is not one which has fixed boundaries and clear characteristics for definitional purposes. Nevertheless, it is clear that, in our primary schools, we have a not insignificant number of children who fall under this definitional umbrella, and who have needs in PE that we should try to meet.

Physiological impairment

A subset of children who are defined in terms of their movement characteristics differ from DCD children in that there is evidence of some physiological impairment. Examples of such children are those with cerebral palsy, spinal bifida and muscular dystrophy, and although it is not our aim to give descriptions of every type of physical disability, we are presenting an overview of one or two as examples of the resources a child will bring to the learning situation, which will have implications for how they are taught.

Cerebral palsy   Cerebral palsy is a condition manifested by poor motor control which is the result of some brain damage. Bax (1964) defines it as 'a nonprogressive disorder of movement and posture due to a defect of the immature brain'. It is not a transient condition, nor does it noticeably deteriorate, although changes do take place, making consistent diagnosis a little unstable. The damage is early in a child's life and the major effect is an impairment of movement. This is not the total picture because about 50 per cent of children with cerebral palsy also show other difficulties. Many have general learning difficulties, and speech and language difficulties are often present. This is not surprising as the brain damage which has led to cerebral palsy may also affect other functions, and the likelihood of this increases with the increasing severity of the cerebral palsy condition.

Cerebral palsy is associated with a number of variables such as birthweight and gestational age together with other biological events occurring during prenatal, perinatal and postnatal time periods. Birthweight is a significant factor and there is a marked increase in the prevalence of cerebral palsy as soon as birthweight falls below 2500 grams. Estimates from a number of epidemiological surveys show that the prevalence of cerebral palsy is around 2.0 per 1000, but this increases to around 10 per 1000 below 2000 grams birthweight and up to 30 or 40 per 1000 below 1500 grams (Sugden and Keogh, 1990).

Cerebral palsy has been classified in a number of ways, and although new methods are being developed, a teacher is most likely to see the following classifications. The simplest is by extent of involvement: the child can be impaired to a mild, moderate or severe degree. This is not the total picture because children are also classified by location of the impairment. Thus we have terms like:

- quadraplegia (all four limbs involved)
- hemiplegia (one side involved or more involved than the other)
- diplegia (legs only or more than arms)
- monoplegia (one limb only) and
- tetraplegia (three limbs).

It becomes more complex with the third classification method which takes the types of movements a child performs. The first type and most common is **spasticity** which involves permanently increased muscle tone, a build-up of tension and releasing movement often described as being akin to a clasp knife. This rigid tonus is not always present, and can vary according to emotional state, and which part of the body is being used. Abnormal reflexes are typical of all types of cerebral palsy and, in spasticity, we see the child having great difficulty in breaking free of the movements imposed upon them by reflexes. This is compounded in voluntary control by the increased hypertonicity which, in some severe cases, can fixate the child's limbs in a few typical postures due to severe co-contractions.

The second major type is **athetosis** which involves unsteady and fluctuating muscle tone which often produces purposeless, uncontrollable and occasionally bizarre movements. These are extraneous involuntary movements and include writhing, squirming, swiping or rotary movements. Fluctuations in muscle control make it difficult for the child to maintain a stable posture, and this is heightened by sudden spasms of flexion or extension. The contraction of one muscle is often not counterbalanced by reciprocal inhibition of the antagonist. The situation is made more complex by athetoid and spastic movements being present in the same child.

Ataxia is characterized by postural instability and problems in balance and co-ordination which becomes apparent when the child begins to sit, walk and stand. There is poor fixation of the head and trunk which promotes a stumbling gait, with voluntary movements being present but appearing clumsy; see Sugden and Keogh, 1990, for a review).

The difficulties of children with cerebral palsy present challenges to the PE teacher whether the child is ambulatory or in a wheelchair. In the next section, we present some of the principles that should underpin working with these children, taking as a starting point the personal resources each child brings to PE lessons. All of the children have neurological problems which involve 'noise' in the motor system which interferes with neural transmission, motor programmes and intrinsic feedback, and which have implications for the tasks we provide and the manner in which they are delivered.

We have used cerebral palsy as an example of the needs of physically disabled children. It is one of the most common physical conditions and the variety of needs that children show present the PE teacher with a range of options and possibilities in his or her lesson. There are several other types of physical disability and we are presenting a brief overview of two or three simply as further examples of the kinds of challenges teachers will be meeting.

Spina bifida is part of a group of conditions in which there is some malformation of the neural tube. Usually the vertebrae have failed to fuse and there is a sac containing cerebrospinal fluid and/or the vertebrae themselves. If the latter is the case, it is referred to as a myelomeningocele and can lead to permanent damage to the spinal cord. The higher the site of the sac, the more disabling the condition. Children with spina bifida have a range of abilities ranging from those who require wheelchairs to those who are ambulant. There may be some fine motor difficulties even if the upper limbs appear to be functioning adequately. They may also be incontinent of bladder or bowel or both which will require organization and preparation.

Muscular dystrophy is part of a subgroup of conditions caused by disorders of the neuromuscular system and characterized by a wasting and progressive weakness of the muscles. It is different to other disabling conditions in that the physical condition of the child deteriorates and therapy may help only to slow down this deterioration. The child becomes increasingly dependent on others and this need requires careful monitoring, planning and emotional support.

Children with **brittle bones** (osteogenesis imperfecta) have a predisposition to bone fracture caused by an abnormality of the protein collagen which gives strength to bones and ligaments. Certainly PE can be a hazardous subject for these children, but it is advised that discussions with parents should take place alongside the child to determine the kind of programme that can be offered.

Other conditions in which the children will have specific needs in PE include **cystic fibrosis, diabetes, asthma, epilepsy** and **haemophilia**. This is not an exclusive list but one which illustrates the diversity of needs a child can present.

Children with movement difficulties as a secondary characteristic

In mainstream, and in special schools, there are groups of children who are not defined as physically disabled, nor classified as clumsy or DCD but they do have substantial movement difficulties which appear to be part of their general profile. If we examine a group of children who would be described as showing moderate learning difficulties, there would be a higher incidence of children with motor difficulties in this group. As the severity of learning difficulties increase, so does the incidence of motor difficulties. If there is no damage to the biological system, establishing control of basic movements may be adequate, but with development their cognitive difficulties may carry over into the motor domain. It must be stressed however that with moderate learning difficulties many children have no motor difficulties and it is only group data that is significant. However, in severe learning difficulties, it is rare to find a child who performs as well as his or her age peers.

Examples of movement limitations in children with learning difficulties are plentiful. For example, Sugden and Wann (1987) tested two groups of children with moderate learning difficulties, one aged 8 and the other 12 years of age. On a test of motor impairment, 50 per cent of the 8-year-olds and 30 per cent of the 12-year-olds were classed as impaired compared to 6 per cent of their chronologically aged matched peers. This is in a group of children with no overt organic impairments. Not only are their motor capabilities lower but children with learning difficulties also show more variability which means that they are less likely to be consistent in giving their best performance. These two general performance findings hold for most movement tasks, particularly as task complexity increases in a changing environment and as the level of learning difficulties increases.

The origins of these performance findings are varied and often speculative, but knowing why a child has particular difficulties goes some way to knowing how to teach. For example, a child with moderate learning difficulties may have problems in taking in sensory information such as vision or kinaesthesis. If this is the case, then modifications to how the task is presented would appear to be a suitable option. On the other hand, another child with difficulty in planning movements may require a simplification of the situation or a step by step procedure to overcome this. A more difficult problem may involve the child having severe delays in basic motor skills. We know, for example, that in children with Down's syndrome early motor milestones such as reaching and grasping and walking are reached later than in non-Down's children; see Sugden and Keogh (1990) for a summary. In this case, the PE teacher may need to liaise with a physiotherapist to determine the kind of activities that would be most appropriate for this child and how the PE lesson can aid in the general motoric functioning of the child.

Children who show **sensory difficulties** in terms of blindness and deafness also as a group have movement difficulties and will be challenging in the PE context. Loss of vision restricts movements by giving the child fewer ways of knowing and organizing spatial information which is so necessary to performing movements in context. As we are emphasizing that movements are context bound, it is not surprising that children with a lack of vision will present different and often poorer movement characteristics.

Early in life, the loss of vision is devastating to a baby and although not many babies are totally without vision, it is a major disability for those affected. Early development of blind babies has been studied primarily in terms of cognitive and social development with classic work from Fraiberg (1977) detailing developmental arrests. Some babies had great difficulty in reaching out into the environment and lack of this activity greatly affects other areas of development. Fraiberg concludes that the movement development of blind babies is greatly constrained by the interactions of personal resources, environmental and personal/social capacities.

The early movements of blind babies is often quite adequate but problems often begin when moving into the environment. Fraiberg (1977) reports on a baby called Toni who achieved the major milestones of sitting, turning over, etc. but who when just starting to crawl, would just spin around instead. It was as if Toni had no place to go and this led Fraiberg to thinking of ways of luring Toni into the environment. Other babies would show different problems leading us to conclude that development is different for blind babies and they have their individual ways of overcoming the development roadblocks that are in their path because of their sensory limitations.

As blind children grow up, a major skill problem is travelling in the environment which is really an extension of their earlier problem of entering the environment. This can involve walking, running or cycling, with skill and confidence two intervening factors for success. Just imagine taking a group of individuals, one or two who are blind, and asking them to run as fast as they can the length of the gymnasium. This would not require a great deal of skill but would involve an awful lot of confidence on the part of the blind persons. Much work has been done on mobility in blind persons usually with an examination of their ability to memorize routes, to detect curvature and gradients, to process information and their spatial maps.

Movement for blind persons is complicated because of their need to use some internal map to represent the environment. Vision is such a rich source of simultaneous spatial information and also for feedback for our movements that a lack or impairment of it leaves the individual at a major disadvantage. However, we have research in the area that tells us how blind children learn, how they are best able to use their resources to acquire skills and our aim must be to translate these into action in the PE lessons not only for them to be full and active participants in the lesson, but also to improve their general mobility for everyday functioning.

Deaf individuals also possess needs that require a modification in the teaching of PE. There is some evidence to show that deaf persons with inner ear problems have some difficulties in balance, and that top-level performers use the noise of a ball against a wall or racquet as cues. However, in general, this is not a major issue and the predominant feature of teaching deaf children surrounds presentation and communication. Various modes of communication are available to teachers working with deaf children. First, there is enhanced hearing through a number of electronic systems such as 'phonic ears' which directly connects the teacher to the child. The child may be learning lip-reading skills, but more likely the child is learning to use British sign language which is the primary language of the deaf population. The onus therefore falls upon the teacher to either be competent in sign language or have some support in the gymnasium/sporting arena from someone who is competent. In those unavoidable situations where support and competencies are absent, it is crucial for the teacher to be particularly vigilant in terms of presentation and feedback including instructions, explanations, directions, demonstrations, reinforcement and corrections of errors.

There are other children with special needs who will present challenges in the PE lesson, but a group which does require special mention is that of **emotional and behavioural difficulties**. This is a group containing a great range of children's needs from those who are withdrawn and reclusive, through those who are overly active and lack attention, to those who appear to be wilfully aggressive, destructive and occasionally violent. The Elton Report (DES, 1989b) reminds us that the main type of emotional and behavioural problems seen in school are of the 'low-intensity–high-frequency' type. This behaviour is not terribly serious but it happens all the time affecting the pupil concerned, the teacher and óther pupils. For these reasons, it is acutely annoying. Behaviour problems are not something seen in isolation; they are always context bound, and we have a great deal of evidence to show that the school is a major force in determining the nature and incidence of problems that are seen. Thus the pupils with these kinds of needs in a PE lesson may or may not be experiencing the kind of total support that comes from a total school behaviour policy. Whether or not this is the case, does not alter the fact that the PE teacher has control of the context in which the pupil is working and is responsible for factors such as rules and procedures, rewards and punishments, the physical layout, dealing with minor issues, getting the year off to a good start, all of which have an effect upon the behaviour of the pupils. We see behaviour problems akin to reading problems in that there are skills to be learned and this learning may take time.

GUIDELINES FOR PROVISION AND SKILL LEARNING

We have always been convinced that PE is not simply education of the physical. It involves much more than that, taking up cognitive, social, language and moral responsibilities as well as the physical. When planning a programme of PE, we rarely sit down and detail how our programme will influence the above abilities. However, with children who have needs over and above those normally present in our classes, it is particularly relevant to take a careful look at the outcomes we are hoping to influence. For example it may be possible to divide our outcomes into two global categories: learning to move, and moving to learn.

Learning to move   Here, we have the traditional outcome from a PE lesson in that movement skills are taught and learned, and are used in a variety of settings. This is a broad area and will include all areas of the National Curriculum. It will also include general physical fitness.

Moving to learn   Here, outcomes come as a result of being in PE and yet are not exclusively concerned with movement. We are looking at rather immediate, specific and observable outcomes – not amorphous claims such as often surrounds a week of outdoor activities. For example, a hyperactive child in the primary school PE lesson may be placed in a situation where he or she is encouraged and rewarded for taking turns, not touching anyone else when they are performing, slowing down, keeping off apparatus when someone else is on it, etc. These are not physical skills but through the unique situations that movement offers, the child may not only acquire these competencies in the PE lesson but, if there is planned follow-up, they may also transfer to other situations. The examples of moving to learn we have presented are all concerned with behaviour, but there are many others such as those involving planning, problem solving, co-operating, explaining, demonstrating, etc.

Although it is not suggested that a detailed analysis of each child is made and a programme planned accordingly, broad desired outcomes for the child can be specified according to the priority of his or her needs. It may be that outcomes change. For example, a child who is hyperactive, may also be quite clumsy. If this is the case, it would seem logical to first plan outcomes which help the child focus their attention, and then move towards improving their physical skills. If both outcomes can be obtained using the same work, then all the better.

What are the major issues in teaching PE to children with special educational needs? The simple answer to this is that the issues are exactly the same as for all children, with special educational needs teaching not being seen as something different and distinct from other forms of teaching, but as an extension of good professional practice. The difference is in the detail and specificity in which the issues are addressed; if the children have special educational needs, it is likely that they have been exposed to a failure situation, and thus the good professional practice will need to be extended.

To deliver the outcomes described earlier, we are dividing the issues into two large sections: those of planning and organization, and those of teaching and learning. Some of these can be done outside of lesson time which will save time and energy in the lesson, while others are an integral part of the lesson.

Planning and organization

When planning and organizing a lesson or programme of work, the starting points are the needs of the child and the situation that already exists. More often than not, it is minor changes in this area which can lead to a substantial change in the accessibility of the curriculum for the child with special educational needs.

An essential feature of teaching children with special educational needs is accurate assessment and diagnosis of their strengths and weaknesses, and this importance is emphasized by the new Code of Practice which gives legal backing to structured assessment. In this, the school is responsible for the first three stages of assessment with Stage 4 being formal assessment procedures and Stage 5 being the Statement of Special Educational Need. Instruments such as the Movement ABC (Henderson and Sugden, 1992) fit neatly into this framework with the ABC check-list being appropriate for Stages 1 and 2, and the ABC test recommended for Stages 3 and 4.

Grouping and support provision   An important issue within any PE lesson is the grouping of children and, alongside of this, the support that is available. A PE lesson is divided into a number of parts which require the children to work on their own, in pairs, in large or small groups, with or without support. Careful thinking about these issues together with minor modifications can make all the difference to accessibility for a child with special educational needs. Our experience in this area leads us to recommend flexible grouping according to the demands of the situation and the resources of the child. For example, a class of 30 primary school children may contain 3 children with developmental co-ordination disorder who are having difficulty in acquiring and performing the motor skills that will allow them to participate adequately in some activities in the PE lesson. For some of the lesson, grouping is not a problem because the children will be working individually and therefore will be choosing their own level of performance. When these children are being asked to work in pairs for skill learning, or sequence building, then decisions have to be made. If the activity is throwing and catching it may be advisable to pair the DCD child with one who is quite competent in these activities. In the first instance, the partner will be a good enough thrower to provide the DCD child with accurate feeding of throws thus facilitating practice and catching. Second, they are competent enough to deal with any wild throws that may come from the DCD child, and this variability of throw will actually be of benefit to the learning of transferable motor skills (Schmidt, 1975). In this case, both children benefit from the pairing. On other occasions, it may be more advantageous to place DCD children or others with special educational needs in pairs or in groups of children with similar ability. For example, the children may be performing a mirror sequence involving a roll, a jump and a balance in a gymnastic lesson. Two children of similar ability will complement each other, will not feel that one is pushing or holding back the other, and can perform to the best of their ability level which should be remarked upon by the teacher. When children are working in larger groups, the nature of the activity and desired outcome will influence the nature of the group. If the children are involved in some form of competition, then random selection of the groups will usually bring parity. If they are involved in skill acquisition practices, then it would seem important to have children in the group who are physically and emotionally supportive of children who have special educational needs. The physical support is evidenced by their skilled feeding in ball activity situations, or their facilitation of agilities, and their emotional support is shown by their constant encouragement, and praise of the child with special educational needs to make them feel that they are an important member of the group. Other examples are available, but they all are guided by the needs of the child coupled with the desired outcome from the activities. These needs are both emotional and physical, and demand that the teacher examines the grouping issue with great thought and then flexibly responds to each situation, rather than stick with some rigid educational dogma.

Support is often an issue that crops up with children showing special educational needs. When a child has a Statement very often some level of support is built into this Statement. For a child showing emotional and behavioural difficulties, the Statement may say that the child requires individual support for 40 per cent of the week; for a group of eight children with severe learning difficulties there may be two support teachers available all of the time; for a class with no individual major problems, but there are mild learning difficulties throughout, a support assistant may be available 25 per cent of the time. In our experience, the only consistent factor surrounding support is the fact that it is never enough! Thus compromises have to be made, and pragmatism takes over. The teacher needs to consider a number of questions: In PE when do(es) the child(ren) require support? Is it all the time or some of the time? Does the child need support in the actual lesson or is it in the preparation of materials, etc.? When support is required in the lessons, is it physical support, planning support, repeating instructions, boosting confidence, suggesting alternatives, simplifying tasks, etc.? Does the support need to be a qualified teacher? Would a special educational needs assistant be required? Would a general teaching assistant be adequate? What about using a volunteer-parent or sixth former? What about using another child in the same class? Can peer tutoring be used in PE the same as it is done in other subject areas like reading? With our limited resources, we have to be specific in what our needs are for various activities, and gear the support to these activities and to the needs of the child. This is not a question of selling the child short; it is about making the optimum use of the 'never-enough' support that is available.

Learning context adaptation and analysis Our emphasis throughout has been on the fact that teaching is an interactive process; it involves the resources of the child, the activities to be learned and the context in which these are learned. Of these three variables, the teacher is in control of the last two. The teacher can arrange the context as we have described above in terms of support and grouping, and can also manipulate the activities. To do this we are concentrating on two related concepts, which are always separated for ease of explanation but in reality merge into each other: task adaptation and task analysis. We actually prefer the terms learning context adaptation and analysis because it helps to focus attention on all the players in the situation not just the task. However, adapting and analysing tasks has come to be a recognized role for teachers when working with children showing special educational needs and they perform two different yet related functions.

Task adaptation involves changing the task, rules of the game, requirements of the activity, modifying equipment and apparatus such that all children can participate in the activity. Entitlement to participation is a fundamental right for all children, and this often requires modifying the activity to meet the resources of the children. Again this does mean that massive changes have to be made. A ball that is more tactile with more 'give' makes catching easier; hitting a ball off a cone takes the parabola out of the ball flight; ensuring that all children in a game situation have to pass the ball before a score can be registered; adjusting the height of equipment for children; having a choice of difficulty in an activity circuit. All of these adaptations facilitate the participation of children in physical activities, and of course increased participation leads to increased learning.

A direct way of facilitating skill learning is to analyse the task to be learned and break it down into its component parts such that it is easier to approach and these parts are wholes in themselves, but also they can be reassembled to make a whole. Here the teacher has to make an interesting decision. There can be no argument with respect to participation; this is a right for every child taking into account his or her needs and resources. With skill learning, it is slightly different. Breaking a skill into its component parts is a complex process, requiring time and effort, and the teacher, parents and child need to be convinced that the child will benefit from obtaining this skill in some tangible manner. When that decision has been made, the process of task analysis is relatively straightforward, although some tasks are much easier than others.

All physical activities are made up of perceptual, cognitive and motor components. Therefore any simplification of activities/tasks involves reducing the demands in one or more of these three areas, for example, in ball catching:

- the perceptual demands can be reduced by having a brightly coloured ball or one with a bell in it for children with visual impairment;
- cognitive components can be reduced by taking out the parabola, by rolling the ball to intercept;
- motor demands can be reduced by slowing the ball down, by using a bigger ball, or by using one that is easier to catch.

All of these processes are progressive in that the first step is to find the level of analysis in which the child is successful, and that is the starting point. Encouragement and praise for this successful completion, followed by a progressive increasing of the task demands moves the child through in small successful stages. We have met many children who will not learn for one reason or another, but we have never met one that cannot learn if the conditions and tasks are appropriate. It is relevant to think thimblefuls not bucketfuls when it comes to progression with some children. There are a number of sources which are useful for providing practical help in the area of task adaptation and analysis (Ainscow and Tweddle, 1984; Brown, 1987; Russell, 1988).

Teaching and learning

The second part of our principles of provision section concerns the actual teaching and learning process itself. Here we are aiming to provide some general guidelines for teaching children with special educational needs and then more specific directives derived from how they learn.

The importance of context   A fundamental principle for all children, but particularly important for children with special educational needs, is that activities should be meaningful to the child; they should understand what is being asked of them and the movements should take place in context. This is often stated and yet equally often forgotten in practice. A powerful example from pathology illustrates this quite clearly. A patient with ideomotor apraxia has some damage to the brain which interferes with translating verbal commands into a symbolic gesture like waving. So if the patient is asked to wave, he or she cannot; when asked to imitate a wave, he or she cannot; but when he or she walks out of the room he or she spontaneously waves goodbye! The movement is now in context; it means something to the patient; it is not some vague abstract action that is being requested but one that is understandable, fits into the patient's repertoire of understanding and is logical. This is a particularly powerful example because if understanding, meaningfulness and context can overcome constitutional damage to promote adequate functioning, the implications for children usually with less severe needs are great. Thus the use of imagery when giving instructions and feedback; that each part of a task analysis be a meaningful movement in itself. The general rule should be that if the child has to abstract meaning from the task or put it in context themselves, there will be a high chance of failure. First, because the child with special educational needs will have difficulty in doing this, and second because it will take attention away from the task in hand. Providing skills practices that have relevance to the child, that are within the child's schema, and which relate to their previous experience is crucial.

Phases of learning

It is well known that when individuals learn skills they go through various phases of learning. It is not simply a question of practising and then the skill is developed, but involves qualitatively different phases. We are presenting a model that has been adapted from an earlier one of Fitts and Posner (1967) and contains four components (Henderson and Sugden, 1992):

1 **Understanding** the skill involves the issue we have just addressed of how to draw the child into the skill in the first instance; how to make them understand what is demanded of them and the resources they have to deal with these demands. This is a crucial part of the learning process and one that is often overlooked; if this part is not right the rest cannot be successful.
2 In **acquiring** and **refining** the skill, the child knows what to do and is now doing the actual physical learning.
3 In **automatizing** the skill, the child is now quite competent and is learning to perform the skill without paying much attention to it.
4 Finally, there is **generalizing** the skill. This does not come at the end but is consistent throughout the other three phases and involves the child using the skills so far learned in situations other than the one in which they were acquired.

Obviously these four phases overlap with each other and it is not useful to try to make definitive distinctions between them. However, observing where the child is in the learning process is always beneficial to the teaching process.

In a PE lesson, the teacher is involved in a number of activities which stimulate the learning process. These involve:

● providing instructions and explanations,
● giving demonstrations,
● providing appropriate practices, and
● giving feedback.

This is not the total sum of the teaching process but these activities do take a substantial proportion of the teacher's time. The issue then becomes how these teaching activities change during the learning phases the child is passing through. We do not possess absolute directions but guidelines are plentiful.

1   When the child is first learning a skill, instructions and explanations should be short and very clear. The object is to draw the child as quickly as possible into the task. Similarly here the feedback should be short and explicit, and any practice should involve a simple unambiguous activity.
2   When the child is acquiring and refining the skill, instructions and feedback become more detailed although still focusing on one or two main points, while practices become more varied, yet still within the same class of movements.
3   If the child ever reaches the autonomous stage, there is a concentration on doing other things at the same time and instructions feedback and practices are geared to this. For example, when bouncing a ball, ask the child to look around the gym at other players, at the equipment, or anything but the ball.
4   Finally, when teaching for generalization, variable practice is a must and the more varied the practice within the same class of movements the better. When teaching for generalization, we are really asking children to be prepared for novel motor situations and thus the larger the schema of movements they have to draw upon, the better chance they have of meeting the demands of this novel situation (Schmidt, 1975).

FROM PRINCIPLES AND GUIDELINES TO PRACTICE

We are presenting three lessons which provide examples of some of the issues we have raised, each one extending good professional practice to allow access for all, and yet not being out of reach for most teachers in most schools.

Example lesson 1

In this first example, we highlight a gymnastic lesson for 7–8-year-olds which includes two children (A and B) with DCD, a group of children often lacking in confidence through a reduced perceived ability when they compare themselves to their peers. This can arise from limited motor experience or a sense of failure because of their movement difficulties. Both causes indicate a need for the child's self-concept to be improved and nurtured in a positive way through their PE experiences before, or running alongside, the more specific motor skills causing them difficulties can be improved. Curriculum gymnastics offers an ideal opportunity for individualized learning to take place where the child can participate despite not performing exactly the same skills as their peers. The opportunities for task adaptation and task simplification to meet the needs of the DCD child are plentiful.

The two DCD children in this example are different from each other despite both finding certain movements difficult to execute and control, and their needs can be accurately specified by the Movement ABC (Henderson and Sugden, 1992). For child A, there is an overall impaired ability across the movement spectrum which has in turn led to a desire to withdraw from PE activities wherever possible. For child B, the problems arise more specifically when the movement environment around them is changing and not directly under their control, e.g. when asked to move in sequence with others or change direction suddenly in a crowded gymnasium with the whole class on the move. Child A needs to be encouraged to participate and become more involved, while child B needs the opportunity to develop control in his or her own time, before tackling the complexities of a changing environment.

Working on a thematic approach to curriculum gymnastics allows the material within the lesson to be challenging and different for each child, if necessary. The theme for the lesson is 'travelling' with the sub-themes being stretching and curling. Each lesson includes a warm-up session, flexibility work specific to the sub-theme of the lesson, skill development, strength work and a slowing-down session. The aim of this lesson is to develop a sequence of different movements on the floor which transport the child using alternate stretching and curling movements.

The warm-up includes a game of 'body parts' in which the children work on their own jogging around the gym and responding to the teacher's instructions to place certain parts of their body on the floor. The game is simple enough for child A to participate in, as long as the teacher paces it appropriately. Similarly, with child B, enough time needs to be given to allow B to stand up and start jogging again. This initial work is safe and encouraging for both children who need to be praised for their success, with the praise being specific to the work and success being attributed to the efforts of the child.

As the lesson progresses, the teacher must ensure that the children know what constitutes stretched and curled positions by introducing simple shapes followed by the opportunity to use those shapes to move from one location to another. Children's own ideas are encouraged. Child A needs constant encouragement, while child B needs space to practise skills without the close presence of others. Choosing their favourite positions, and honing their performance are constant features here. The children are acquiring and refining their skills. From individual work, the children can be put in pairs to learn from each other. Child A needs someone working at a similar level, but who is emotionally supportive. Child B need someone with a good level of control who can act as support and role model. They can teach each other or work on mirror sequences which they can demonstrate to other children if the teacher believes that the children are ready.

For the closing part of the lesson, strength work can be done in pairs with the children partnered in the same manner by partners who complement them in a non-threatening way but who are different to their earlier partners. The cool-down can be done individually using the stretches and curls from the earlier sequence. In this lesson, the major modifications surround the choice of grouping (partners), the emotional support (appropriate praise) by the teacher and the simplification of tasks. No extra help is required and the lesson is a simple yet crucial extension of good professional practice.

Example lesson 2

This example offers guidelines and suggestions for a child with a physical disability in a wheelchair, and one with hearing impairment for participation in a mainstream

basketball lesson for 12-year-olds. All the class must understand rules and procedures for this lesson and must be aware, and supportive, of the needs of the two
children.

For the child with a hearing impairment, the teacher or helper can use sign
language, enhanced hearing technology or the child must be in a position to attempt
lip-reading and must be shown good accurate demonstrations. The role of clear
demonstrations cannot be overemphasized. It may be that if the teacher has no help or
cannot sign effectively, some very simple signs are used for basic instructions. For this,
the teacher must obviously always be in view of the hearing-impaired child. These
signs can be used for encouragement and praise as well as for instructions. The child in
the wheelchair needs extra room to manoeuvre and all the children, at some time, need
to be paired or grouped with this child in order to be able to gauge time and space
required for working.

The aim of this lesson is to use dribbling and passing skills previously taught in a
small-sided game of three versus three to achieve a good position on court for
shooting. Dribbling tag warm-up games can be used as a warm-up which is easily
demonstrated to the hearing-impaired child, and the use of lines can aid the child in a
wheelchair. Little support is required although constant observation is necessary.

Revision work focuses on passing the ball forward and ahead of the team mates in
order to attack the basket area, with children working in threes passing the ball to one
who is slightly ahead of the others. Timing of the pass is crucial and the trailing team
members have to be alert as to their positions in relation to the catcher. A clear
demonstration is essential for the hearing-impaired child and no additional support is
necessary for the child in a wheelchair save for position in the gym, often at the sides
to eliminate potential collisions.

The lesson develops into a conditioned game which highlights certain high
percentage areas of the court for shooting. In each of three areas of the gym are placed
three teams with three or four children in each. Two teams in each group play each
other with the third refereeing and scoring, with these roles rotating. Skittles are used
as targets with different scoring systems for different positions from where the skittle is
knocked over, thus promoting high percentage shooting positions. Again full and
accurate demonstrations are required for the hearing-impaired child, and the game
involving the wheelchair child could include increasing slightly the size of the playing
area and modifying the rules such as not allowing double teaming of this child. A
rotation of teams will allow the children to play against all the other teams. A cooling
session could include ball handling in pairs, requiring control and stretching. As
always, clear unambiguous demonstrations are essential.

The biggest issue with a hearing-impaired child is that of communication, with a
second one of being fully accepted by the children who should understand that the
hearing impairment need not be a barrier to full involvement. Thoughtful
presentation of material in such a way that communication is not impeded for this
child will allow the same inclusion and access to the curriculum as other children.
For the child in a wheelchair, modification of space and, occasionally, rules of the
practices is essential as is an understanding and empathetic attitude by the teacher
and rest of the class. Again, in this lesson, extra help is not a necessity but if present
it should be used specifically and effectively as a result of prior planning and
organization.

Example lesson 3

In this example, a group of visually impaired children from a special school join a lesson with mainstream children. Certain activities are more accessible than others to the visually impaired and can be exploited to bring about an integrated situation with little adaptation. Activities such as gymnastics, bowling, swimming, weight training, skating, rowing, judo, dance and hiking are examples which require little adaptation as long as planning, preparation and teaching are secure and thorough. Appropriate handouts in braille or large print, good lighting, bold colours for balls, clear and comprehensive verbal instructions can all be used to accommodate the children's needs.

At a bowling lesson, two visually impaired children are grouped with two of their sighted peers in a group of four. Four of these groups are present and two teachers are available plus some sixth form help. Children working in pairs introduce themselves (one sighted, one visually impaired) and then walk the distance from the start line to the target area. Usually, the visually impaired child takes the initiative and through holding an arm, only asks for help when needed, not receiving it all the time. Verbal explanations accompany visual demonstrations, and practice of the movement with the teachers and helpers moving around the class giving help, particularly stressing the 'feel' of the movement to the visually impaired children, who may be able to pass this on to their sighted partner. Various workstations are used with different equipment which will involve variability of practice thus encouraging generalization. Throwing large balls at large cones, quoits at a hoop on a wall and medium-sized balls at skittles are all variations on this bowling theme. After a certain degree of mastery is acquired, two versus two games can be introduced thus encouraging competition and co-operation. Feedback, in terms of knowledge of results and knowledge of performance, is given with particular attention being paid to the different noises that the objects make when being thrown, rolled and hit. The cool-down consists of the children gently jogging together with their partner around the teaching area, moving slower and slower until the teacher calls a halt. This lesson has been modified more substantially than the other two and has more support because there are more children with different needs requiring this support.

CONCLUDING COMMENTS

Our overall theme is that presenting a curriculum for all children is an extension of good professional practice. It is not something that is distinct and different with highly specialized techniques. However, it does not come naturally and takes time and effort, but with planning, organization and commitment, it is not only providing equal opportunities for some children who had previously been denied, it also offers enhanced provision and educational opportunities for children without special educational needs. Diversity in the resources children bring to the movement situation should not be looked upon as threatening or even a challenge, but should be viewed as absolutely normal as indeed they are.

REFERENCES

Ainscow, M. and Tweddle, D. (1984) *Early Learning Skills Analysis*. Chichester: J. Wiley.
Bax, M.C.O. (1964) 'Terminology and classification of children with cerebral palsy', *Developmental Medicine and Child Neurology*, **6**, 295–7.

Brown, A. (1987) *Active Games for Children with Movement Problems*. London: Paul Chapman.

DES (1989a) *A Survey of Pupils with Special Educational Needs in Ordinary Schools*. London: DES.

DES (1989b) *Discipline in Schools (The Elton Report)*. London: HMSO.

DES (1992) *Audit Commission: Getting in on the Act*. London: HMSO.

DFE (1994) *Code of Practice on Identification and Assessment of SEN*. London: HMSO.

DSM–IV (1994) *Diagnostic and Statistical Manual of Mental Disorders* (Fourth Edition) Washington, D.C.: American Psychiatric Association.

Fitts, P.M. and Posner, M.I. (1967) *Human Performance*. Belmont: Brooks/Cole.

Fraiberg, S. (1977) *Insights from the Blind*. New York: Basic Books.

Henderson, S.E. and Sugden, D.A. (1992) *Movement Assessment Battery for Children (Manual)*. London: Psychological Corporation.

Hoare, D. (1994) 'Subtypes of developmental coordination disorder', *Adapted Physical Activity Quarterly*, **11**, 158–69.

Losse, A., Henderson, S.E., Elliman, D., Hall, D., Knight, E. and Jongmans, M. (1991) 'Clumsiness in children – do they grow out of it? A 10 year follow up study', *Developmental Medicine and Child Neurology*, **33**, 55–68.

Russell, J.P. (1988) *Graded Activities for Children with Motor Difficulties*. Cambridge: Cambridge University Press.

Schmidt, R.A. (1975) 'A schema theory of discrete motor skill learning', *Psychological Review*, **86**, 415–51.

Sugden, D.A. (1994) 'Moving in the right direction and getting a grip', *University of Leeds Review*, University of Leeds Press, pp. 283–303.

Sugden, D.A. and Henderson, S.E. (1994) 'Help with movement', *Special Children*, **75**(13), 1–8.

Sugden, D.A. and Keogh, J.F. (1990) *Problems in Movement Skill Development*. Columbia: University of South Carolina Press, p. 210.

Sugden, D.A. and Wann, C. (1987) 'The assessment of motor impairment in children with moderate learning difficulties', *British Journal of Educational Psychology*, **57**, 225–36.

Wedell, K. (1993) 'Special needs education: the next 25 years', *National Commission on Education*.

Wright, H.C. and Sugden, D.A. (submitted for publication) 'The prevalence and nature of developmental coordination disorder in Singaporean children aged 6–9 years'.

Chapter 10

Gifted Children and Young People in Physical Education and Sport

Richard Fisher

INTRODUCTION

Giftedness, according to the Concise Oxford Dictionary, is inextricably linked with the concept of talent. In a society wedded to the notion of educing individual potential, the best way of identifying and promoting those who possess talent has long been a legitimate concern for many of our social institutions, including both education and sport. PE is an integral part of the educational process, but recognizing and encouraging pupils with talent for sport is an equally legitimate part of its contribution to the development of children and young people. This was identified clearly in the Interim Report prepared for the National Curriculum for PE (NCPE) (DES, 1991), where opportunities for gifted pupils were outlined, many in partnership with agencies for sport outside the school.

On the other hand, The Sports Council's (1993) policy document on young people and sport provided a clear framework for the network of agencies involved in the development of sport for young people in general, including the gifted, and identified education as a key part of the process. The policy was rooted in The Sports Council's continuum for sport, from foundation to excellence, which itself links well with the developmental thrust of the NCPE.

In many ways the structure of this chapter reiterates the idea of progression. It is concerned with the sporting development of children from a point where thousands may be involved in a mass of sporting opportunities in and out of school, many of whom will show a certain level of ability and work more seriously on their sport. Some will make it to a stage where selection of one sort or another leads to special programmes of training and development. Finally, a very few will reach levels of excellence dreamed of by many but achieved by few. The interlinked, but separate, processes of selection and development, the significance of the progression through the various stages, and the implications for PE and sport are essential matters to be addressed.

However, although the legitimacy of developing the gifted in sport within an educational context is clear, and an increasing number of partnerships between the intertwined, but distinctive, fields of PE and sport is encouraging, there are a number of issues which demand attention. Real talent in sport is not easy to identify, and opinions vary as to the most effective experiences to offer children and young people to promote giftedness, not all of which sit easily with our expressed beliefs for PE. Some serious questions could be asked, for example, about the wisdom of encouraging young people to adopt what can easily become a very lopsided lifestyle, however attractive it might seem to the individual, and however beneficial to school, club and country.

Moreover, it is significant that the National Curriculum has focused on entitlement. Pupils are entitled to receive a particular set of experiences across the whole curriculum and in PE in particular. The concept of entitlement can be extended, though, to encompass some important considerations for those who might be deemed to be gifted. These pupils are also entitled to a childhood and an adolescence during which essential life experiences are encountered, shared with others, and enjoyed in ways chosen mainly by the individuals themselves. It is known that children spend less than one-third of their life at school, and by contrast devote 37 per cent of their waking hours to play of various kinds which occurs at every available opportunity and in every conceivable place (Stephens, 1992). Any responsible consideration of recognizing and developing talent for sport could not ignore the need for such experiences.

Furthermore, Stephens reported an examination of value orientations of children towards sport in Manitoba, Canada, which found that most children viewed fairness as the most important component of playing sport, and winning the least. Skill acquisition was viewed as the next most important component, but significantly less so than fairness. These findings were consistent across all ages and sexes in the study (pupils aged 8–14 years). Indeed, the personal perspectives of PE and sport held by children and young people, including the gifted, their expectations and the personal meaning these experiences have in the totality of their lifestyle are things that we know too little about.

No less important than childhood is the period of adolescence. Brettschneider (1990), has called for a rethinking of adolescent sport and PE and pointed out the importance of regarding the adolescent's world as a coherent whole, in which sport must be viewed as only one element of their general lifestyle through which social values are experienced. He suggested also that sport is not experienced by adolescents as an undifferentiated mass, but as possessing different characteristics in different social groups and situations indicating, therefore, the value of a range of sporting experiences.

If we consider these factors together with the work of Malina (1988) and others, which has focused our minds on such important concepts as 'readiness' for sport, we can appreciate the significance of preserving a balanced lifestyle for children and young people to secure their entitlement to a sensible and meaningful progression to adulthood. If this has been said in other places it does not preclude the necessity, indeed the responsibility, of reiterating it here particularly in view of Swan's (1991, p. 43) observations which relate to the development of young distance runners:

> Most of our elite runners are recruited between the ages of 12 and 15 years. Although this may seem young, in this age of specialization it is not unusual for individual and team

sports, such as basketball, volleyball, soccer and hockey, to have year round programmes for very young athletes. If we are unable to commit an athlete to a running programme at a very young age, we are likely to lose that youngster to another sport.

It must be said, however, that the results of the 1992 Training of Young Athletes (TOYA) study indicate that undue disruption to lifestyle need not be a necessary consequence of involvement in elite sport, although there is still sufficient evidence on the ground to indicate that the problem exists. Similarly, the TOYA study found that dropping out due to medical difficulties or so called 'burn-out' was not a significant problem. Once again, though, there is sufficient evidence outside the carefully monitored confines of this very important and useful project, that the problem both exists and persists.

This chapter then, will look first at the nature of giftedness in sport and the identification and development of gifted children and young people, prior to examining some relevant issues for teachers, parents and coaches, and in so doing will make use of evidence and experience from other countries. In view of the space available, the information and issues selected will of necessity be only a small sample from the vast array available, but one which hopefully will be of interest.

IDENTIFYING GIFTED CHILDREN AND YOUNG PEOPLE

A telephone call to a national athletics coach to discuss this chapter in relation to his sport was met with the response: 'What is gifted?' Further discussion highlighted the comment made by John Monie, previously coach to the Wigan rugby league team, in a television programme about the club and its union counterpart, Orrell: 'The thing about champions is they're different.'

In such simple observations lie a multitude of issues and questions surrounding a misleadingly straightforward task: defining the nature of talent in sport and its development. It is easy enough to observe that we should collate detailed information on the necessary components needed to make a champion as a basis for selection. However, identifying the unique configuration of genetic, personal and environmental characteristics in order to spot future champions in anything like a systematic fashion has proved more difficult. It may be relatively easy to recognize a great player when one performs, and indeed to specify their qualities, but defining exactly what it is they possess, in what measure and how it developed with a view to finding another one is a different matter altogether. Indeed, in many respects outstanding performers in sport often 'break the mould' as it were.

The situation is confounded further by the fact that we are dealing with children and young people, who mature at different ages and who can often fluctuate wildly in the sort of capabilities they demonstrate and the areas of sport in which they demonstrate them. Even with what we might feel are more predictable indicators of performance, such as $\dot{V}O_2$ max for example, Fisher and Borms (1990) cited a comparison of the range of values recorded at elite junior, and elite senior, level in a number of sports, which revealed that the relationship between the scores of the two age groupings in each sport is by no means straightforward or predictable. Indeed such indicators are notoriously unreliable until the growth spurt has passed or until menarche in girls, not to mention the fact that $\dot{V}O_2$ max itself is not without its critics as a true indicator of endurance performance.

In general terms, it is helpful to recognize that in selecting talented children we can identify two main types of models (Fisher and Borms, 1990): systematic and asystematic.

There are two types of **systematic model**:

1 **system-related models**, where private or state bodies actively search for talent in an organized, systematic fashion through testing and/or competition procedures; and
2 **person-related models** where, on the basis of generally available opportunities, an individual might emerge as talented in one sport or another, and structures are available to nurture that talent once it appears. This is what might be described as a fairly traditional model.

In **asystematic models**, children might emerge as talented but the structure and organization is insufficient in most cases to help the realization of potential. Typical of many developing countries, it can also be applied to specific sports in so-called industrialized nations.

The application of precise selection criteria remains a problem, though, particularly at young ages, and for most sports it is still performance in youth competitions which is the major part of the selection process. These results are unreliable in this context since it is well known that the best young performers are not necessarily the best at adult level. Following a study in the late 1980s, an annual survey has been developed of the top six competitors at the English Schools Athletics Championships (McStravick, personal communication), an outstanding festival of youth sport. The pattern remains consistent; few of these champions reach the top at senior level and, if anything, it is more likely that those who finish in the region of fifth or sixth will be the ones to succeed; those who have some ability and interest but have probably not committed themselves to extensive training regimes as yet. It is almost always the case that the top six performers are attached to clubs.

Without reworking a great deal of evidence on the matter, it is possible to move to the obvious conclusion: How can we expect teachers, parents and coaches, generally regarded as the main agents in the selection process, to do an effective job in talent identification if we are unable to give clearer guidelines on what to look for? How many sports have been able to conduct the rigorous analysis necessary to define the essential parameters for success at top level and then ensured that such knowledge is available at grass-roots level? Such evidence has been accumulated in some sports, gymnastics for example, but it is arguably much more difficult in sports involving a rapidly changing environment and direct challenge from an opponent. One is forced to the conclusion that the identification of talent in anything like a comprehensive way can be an extremely complicated, expensive and time-consuming business. Furthermore, we know from the TOYA study that talent identification relies initially very much on parents. While it is true the home is a critical element in talent identification and development (Gardner, 1984), parents are not always capable of viewing the larger picture objectively or their child's position within it.

One of the best known attempts by a governing body in this country to deal with the issue of selection has been developed by the Football Association (FA) School of Excellence at Lilleshall. Often burdened with the expectation of producing the future

England team, the declared intention is to identify, work with, and improve, the quality of young players while protecting their educational and professional future. The potential to be excellent involves a filtering system which starts in 151 centres of excellence licensed by the FA, involves a series of trials and ends with a full medical, educational and personal analysis before admission to the school. Regardless of some of the arguments which have been advanced as to the effectiveness of this scheme, it represents a serious attempt to select in a reasonably comprehensive fashion those youngsters with potential in soccer, together with a declared concern for the welfare and development of the young people concerned. It is interesting to note the observation of a senior FA coach who, in deciding whether to work on elite programmes or on more community-based initiatives, traced back the England teams for the World Cups of 1986 and 1990 to find that only one player, Peter Shilton, had played for England at youth level.

Of particular note here is the development of Champion Coaching, an exciting and well-established initiative by the National Coaching Foundation (NCF). It is based on co-operation between schools, parents and coaches, and opportunities are offered to children who are not already involved in coaching at the performance or excellence levels of the sports continuum. This project has swelled remarkably from 6000 youngsters in 1991 to some 30,000 in 47 schemes in 1992, and in 1994 to some 150,000 in 76 schemes involving around 4000 coaches. The typical child involved is assessed in general terms as likely to be (NCF, 1992):

- in the school team for the chosen sport;
- in the district team for the chosen sport, but probably no higher;
- attending a club where the coaching sessions are mainly at the participation level; and
- playing for a local team without the opportunity for coaching sessions.

The youngsters concerned are in the 11 to 14 years age band and these general criteria are followed by assessment sessions to identify youngsters using more specific criteria for the sport in question. The sessions are planned thoroughly, involving parents, teachers and coaches, and counselling is strongly urged for those who are not chosen. The positive reaction of all concerned gives high hopes for the future. However, there remains the issue of whether this is the best age for youngsters to select individual sports and the extent to which their sporting experience should remain on a broad base in what is a critical period for developing sporting potential – an interesting thought as this scheme gathers pace and evaluates its success.

The available evidence suggests that a graded system of selection is the most effective (Fisher and Borms, 1990). Coarse criteria, such as general ability in sport, give way to finer analysis, such as evidence of ability in particular groups of sports/events and then in a specific position/event. This requires a larger view of the process than individual sports, and so we are led inevitably to arguably the most effective solution to date, the comprehensive filtering system developed in the former Soviet Union and optimized in the former German Democratic Republic (GDR). However we like to analyse success in international sport, it is difficult to deny the efficacy of these two systems of talent promotion. Leaving aside known evidence of use of illegitimate substances in the former GDR, something which cannot be dealt with here and an issue on which few countries can claim an entirely clear conscience anyway, a comprehensive pattern of screening was evolved which made a serious effort to cope with the issues above.

The foundation of excellence was officially PE in schools and mass participation. The better pupils were referred to training centres and the best of these attended one of twenty-five special sports schools. All children in the GDR were screened from as early as the first school year (6 years old), with repeat screenings in the third and fifth years. Twenty years of data collected from the screening of children on basic performance parameters established clear norms for particular ages, which together with the judgements of coaches, the work conducted in the central research institute and the scientific centre (with its specific sport orientations), allowed decisions to be made about who should be supported in what type of sport. With the exception of certain sports, gymnastics for example, specialization theoretically was delayed as late as possible to allow for the effects of maturation and to foster the development of a more rounded 'athlete'. At their peak, the special sports schools had some 10,000 pupils in their charge. More remarkably, one of the best of these schools in Berlin had a pupil–teacher ratio of 2:1, with the overall average standing at 3:1. Indeed, Naul (1992) pointed out that in the system 10,000 coaches were employed (against some 1000 in West Germany), and at the Sports University in Leipzig about 1000 teachers were employed to prepare less than one thousand students to work in the sports system. According to Broom (1991), the centre at Kienbaum in the former GDR cost $4.75 million. Of course, this was part of the overt political strategy of promoting the GDR, but scrutiny of the motives for promoting excellence in other countries also demonstrates a strong concern for national prestige from sport, including the UK.

The ramifications of the GDR experience are most important here. How else do you ensure a genuinely broad view of the development of talent without public or professional bodies of some sort having the power and responsibility for overseeing the process? How far would we go, could we go, in this direction if we felt that national concerns and the welfare of the young people concerned merited such an approach? Furthermore, it is worth noting that around 70 per cent of the youngsters in these special schools returned to general schools (Brettschneider, 1992) in a constant interchange of pupils with the normal education system. Ignoring, due to the pressures of space, arguments about the cultural acceptability of these schools in other social systems, and accusations that pupils were ill-served educationally during their time there, the essential point is that there was a greater attempt to maintain an open access policy for the talented than many of our own projects. Second, third, even fourth chances to return to the system were possible, and in other sports if necessary. This is a critical factor in developing talent since a large number of top-class international performers can either mature late or eventually succeed in a different sport to the one originally attempted. Hemery (1986) has given a number of examples of this phenom-enon, but how many were, and are, lost?

Some of the most important points occur, though, when one looks at the price paid for sporting success in these former communist systems. With regard to the Soviet Union, Riordan (1992) highlighted the general point of distorted priorities by quoting a sports commentator who maintained that they had won Olympic medals while being 'a land of clapped-out motor cars, evergreen tomatoes and totalitarian mendacity'. Both Naul (1992) and Brettschneider (1992) with regard to the GDR, and Riordan (1992) with regard to the former Soviet Union, have shown that not only was success

TALENT IDENTIFICATION   TALENT DEVELOPMENT

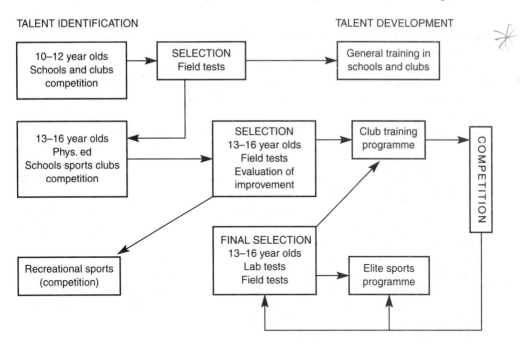

Figure 10.1 *Talent Identification System related to Talent Development and Recreational Sports.*

Source: Pestola (1992), p. 7 (reprinted with permission)

not built upon a broad base of 'sport for all', but in fact sport for the populace was sacrificed in many ways for the needs of the elite. In both systems, and in spite of official ideology, the facilities and resources for PE in schools were poor. The PE curriculum in the GDR was limited and rigid, and facilities for the general population were far less impressive than those reserved for the elite. It is difficult, if not impossible, to justify such an imbalance other than by outstanding results, which were achieved of course. It is another argument altogether as to whether a better distribution of resources would have achieved the same effect and in socially more acceptable ways.

Following this brief review of issues concerned with identification of talented children and young people, a general perspective of the process can be taken from Pestola (1992). His strategy (Figure 10.1) is built upon several key principles:

- the need to tie the early parts of the process to work in schools, both at an early stage and in the second phase at around 13 to 16 years of age;
- the use of general test batteries, such as those identified in Fisher and Borms (1990) and Sobral (1994), as part of a broad profile of physical, personal and training information;
- maintaining the possibility of entering the process at many points.

In a similar vein, Sedlacek *et al.* (1992) pointed out that one of the most important features of the Czecho-Slovakian (CSFR) system of high performance sport, and one which was being developed to adjust to the split into two federal republics, was the huge network of institutions that linked and supported each other. These included sport classes (PE), sport schools, youth training centres, and centres for high-performance sport. Pestola went on to highlight the need for international co-operation to establish data banks on talented young people, particularly with a view to helping so-called developing countries. However, it is now appropriate to address some issues to do with the development of gifted children and young people.

DEVELOPING GIFTED CHILDREN AND YOUNG PEOPLE

There has been much progress in the treatment of apparently talented children and young people during their formative years. Much of this has to do with the greater availability of relevant information and the enormous strides that have taken place in coach education. However, it is by no means clear that, in relation to specific projects and training groups, the interrelated nature of selection and development is acknowledged sufficiently. East German experience confirmed that selection is a multi-level process that interfaces with development involving many possible entrance and exit points for the young people concerned. We have to ask if our procedures and schemes are structured to cope with this and the available evidence would suggest that to a large extent they are not. The TOYA study (1992), admittedly only concerned with four sports, pointed out: 'The talent identification system in this country appears closed, excluding many children from entering sport at a later stage.'

Certainly Champion Coaching has addressed the issue and youngsters have the chance to try again; this may well be one of the most critical developmental aspects of this scheme.

Furthermore, it has been recognized for some years that the type and amount of training provided for young people is crucial to effective development in sport, and for physical and mental welfare in general. In spite of what appears to be a much greater awareness of these matters at national coach and national project level, and of the increasing amount of information available on children in sport in general (Lee, 1993), the evidence on the ground is that much remains to be done. Indeed, perhaps the only important thing to do is to emphasize this particular philosophy–practice gap. In 1992, the FA school of excellence had to ask six out of the final selection group of thirty-two to withdraw because of serious medical problems. All of these were in the top twenty players in the country of those who elected to attend the school. Four or five of the cases involved career-threatening conditions, and the view of the medical experts involved was that none of these were congenital. It has to be said that this was something of an exceptional year in this regard, but evidence over an 8-year period following more than 250 comprehensive medical examinations is that over-exposure to intensive training and competition situations continues to the detriment of many of the youngsters concerned. The last survey of young players of ability showed that something like 100 competitive games each year was not uncommon (Russell, personal communication). This would seem to be confirmed by the latest analyses being undertaken and frequently involves early maturers who look to be physically and psychologically capable of the task, but who clearly are not.

The FA school estimates that for one reason or another something like 10 per cent of the best young players in the country are lost each year, and in track and field athletics Frank Dick, former Chief National Coach, reported in 1992 that 25 per cent of the World Junior Championship team of 1988 were now lost to the sport. Brown's

(1992) analysis of the development of young 5000 metre runners in Europe is another interesting line in this argument, focusing particularly on endurance where the transition to senior ranks in recent years has been particularly poor. He acknowledged some gaps in the information available and the need to interpret statistics carefully, but reported that not one of our 5000 metre medallists at the European Junior Championships had appeared in a European Senior Championships 5000 metre final, or indeed won a medal at any senior championship. Unlike those who did become successful at senior level they specialized in 3000 metres or 5000 metres earlier than their more successful counterparts, and ran significant races at these distances. They also appear to have lacked balance in their training programmes. In the former Soviet Union, Privalova, an outstanding sprinter at the Barcelona Olympic Games and the 1994 World Championships in track and field athletics, had been an outstanding 15-year-old sprinter, but suffered serious setbacks between the ages of 15 and 17 years as a result of intensive training, and only re-emerged at 18 years after a realignment of training loads.

Armstrong and Welsman (1993) have emphasized the need to match exercise prescription to the development of children's physical capabilities, as well as the importance of children understanding the principles underlying fitness and health and how to develop training programmes. This applies to the gifted no less than those with lesser ability. To this can be added the promotion in children of an understanding of what is best for the future in terms of skill, attitudes and training. This is not only possible, but personal experience confirms that it can lead to relatively sophisticated views in children and young people of the development of sporting ability and of their place within it.

However, the sporting environment associated with the development of excellence is predominantly structured, administered and monitored by adults. To succeed requires a child to operate successfully within that system and according to its assumptions. We know well enough the importance of a wide range of general physical experience and of delaying specialization, as strong an argument as one could wish for the place of PE within the process. However, this has yet to be demonstrated widely enough in practice. Andrew Longmore (1992) reviewed a 'weekend of familiar woe' after the national tennis championships in the previous month and referred to the higher expectations several national figures have of children coming through in the sport. The Head of National Training is reported as follows:

> Two coaches have come up to me separately today to tell me how good their 6-year-olds are . . . 6-year-olds? A few years ago, they would have been frightened of being arrested for coaching 6-year-olds. Now the attitude has changed. It's no longer tea and cucumber sandwiches. People are beginning to understand what it takes to be a professional tennis player.

The question is, does it 'take it' at 6-years-old and to what extent is it a valid argument that particular sports need to make much earlier moves than others to promote giftedness? This argument used to be advanced in swimming and proved to be false.

Other factors associated with the development of gifted young people in sport have been identified well by TOYA: medical support, the cost to parents of sustaining a child's pursuit of sport, the personal and financial costs of travel and supervision. There are also ethical issues such as the possible burden for children of being labelled as exceptionally talented, and the danger of discriminating against those who appear to be less able but nonetheless need a meaningful experience in sport, bearing in mind that they may well be the ones who eventually emerge as championship material anyway.

SOME IMPLICATIONS FOR PE AND SPORT

To concern oneself with the extent to which we should consider changing current practice, and the implications of doing so in the light of some of the critical issues highlighted above, is to raise some fairly fundamental issues for PE and sport. Moreover, the political context is not to be denied. At the time of writing, an announcement on a new scheme for sports-oriented secondary schools was reportedly imminent, something that had long been a feature of provision in the former Soviet Union in fact. The pressure for a greater emphasis on traditional competitive team games in the school curriculum, even though they have dominated the curriculum for years, can be seen as a feature of a political context in which tradition, order, stability and accountability are important. Evans (1988) pointed out that while the profession has embarked upon innovative curriculum development, educationally worthy and in the best interests of pupils, the demands from outside the school in the political arena and from parents have been for competition and results. These pressures are part of the reality of teachers' lives and constrain the debate on promoting giftedness in sport; if traditional expectations are not fulfilled, the PE profession is open to criticism, in spite of some fundamental shortcomings in traditional approaches to promoting excellence in sport among young people. This is not to deny a place for competition, or indeed the value of tradition, but is to highlight limitations upon the profession's ability to reorient its thinking on talented children and young people.

Even so, on the basis of what has been presented here and is available elsewhere in cultures such as ours, there can be little doubt as to the fundamental need to provide high-quality PE programmes in schools as a basis for the full realization of individual potential. There is no question that we can find some of the best examples of curriculum PE we have ever had now operating in our schools. If they are not as widespread as we would like then the development of the National Curriculum will be a great help. It must be said, though, that the erosion of time available for the subject, together with changed circumstances in schools and the profession at large, threaten effectiveness in maintaining the base. The European Physical Education Associations survey in 1993 showed that the UK has one of the poorest provisions for PE curriculum time in Europe, and certainly among those with whom we would like to be compared. A fundamentally strong position for the subject in schools must be actively campaigned for, in the interests of the talented and the mediocre alike.

We must also ask who is responsible for the overall picture of the range of demands on children who exhibit talent, particularly when it is evident in a number of areas? Parents are ideally placed but not necessarily knowledgeable or objective enough, and competing demands from school and club sport can easily confuse what is best for the child and, therefore, ultimately sport itself. The GDR had its answer: state planning backed by massive state investment. What is ours? It is sensible, but rather too easy, to call for greater co-operation between interested parties; it needs to be operationalized further. PE is in a good position to contribute, indeed it could be argued to assume this overall responsibility, in which case who will recognize the need for the considerable resources required, time and financial, to cope properly with performing it. The development of networks and partnerships in recent years between schools, the community and sport offer exciting and professionally healthy prospects, but the ultimate responsibility must reside somewhere.

The cost of developing effective programmes for the gifted in sport frequently carries an inherently high resource implication. The provision of quality facilities, available at reasonable hours of the day and for sufficient time cannot be ignored. Traditionally, public bodies such as local authorities have initiated and underpinned many such projects, but their ability to devote sufficient resources is decreasing in spite of a long history of support. Promoting excellence is a costly business and easily prey to competing resources. In the same vein, the need for better data banks on the development of children's abilities, more effective screening procedures and better guidelines for identification requires some substantial research and development: this has been recognized for some years, but although developments are evident in a number of sports, it awaits concerted effort and resources.

In the light of what has been said about youth competitions in sport, PE might do well to examine further the ways in which it promotes school sport in relation to the development of the talented. The balance between providing a broader-based experience of sport and the detailed development of specific sports becomes problematic if it is true that the general promotion of sporting ability is an important contribution that school sport can make to the development of our future champions. Greater emphasis on all-round development at the expense of specialization would serve our educational goals very well and keep a sense of balance in the development of the gifted, but the reaction of agencies outside the school would be very mixed. Sporting achievement, like health and fitness, is a platform which is well and critically understood in society at large, and the most common misconception about the development of the talented in sport is that they need lots of competition in their specialist activity. Furthermore, it is prickly, but relevant, to ask whether PE teachers are well enough equipped in more than one or two sports to promote excellence adequately in specific areas, and whether their strengths with regard to the promotion of talent might actually lie in different directions. In any case, the relationship with sporting agencies at local and national level is confirmed as a critical part of the process.

In terms of club sport, we must ask if the promotion of a broader range of sporting capacity is beyond the capabilities and/or point of acceptance of many coaches working with children and young people. Coach education is making good inroads here, but it requires quite large changes of perspective and expertise to grasp, for example in track and field athletics, the range of experiences children need to be offered in order to take part effectively in multi-event competitions, strongly promoted by national coaches, the advantages of taking this route and the necessity of placing one's own 'special' event in a different, initially less prominent, position in the scheme of things. This can be a threatening situation for local coaches, one that many may be unwilling, if not unable, to accept.

CONCLUSION

In concluding, it is clear that a sufficient number of answers have not been provided, perhaps all the important questions were not raised either. The attempt has been made to provide a perspective on gifted children in PE and sport, in a way which reflects a personal commitment to excellence in sport, but also to the general welfare and education of these and all other pupils. I have no interest in schemes or systems which rest on the sacrifice of the many for the success of the few, only too apparent in certain sports and certain social systems. Moreover, it is clear that the fundamental sense of allowing physical educationalists to retain their important and unique contribution to the development of the gifted in sport, although possibly in other ways, will continue to remain in doubt while the real place of the subject in the curriculum continues to deteriorate. Partnerships with outside agencies are vital for promoting the gifted in sport, but the increasing paucity of curriculum time at school will erode the base if it is not addressed soon, and with authority.

Ultimately, contributing to the successful realization of sporting talent is one of the most uplifting experiences for most PE teachers. An involvement in its promotion is both rewarding and, perhaps most important of all, is appreciated by the people who receive the benefit of it long after they ceased to be either young or excellent.

REFERENCES

Armstrong, N. and Welsman, J. (1993) 'Training young athletes', in Lee, M. (ed.), *Coaching Children in Sport*. London: E and FN Spon, pp. 191–203.

Brettschneider, W.-D. (1992) 'Adolescents, leisure, sport and lifestyle', in Williams, T., Almond, L. and Sparkes, A. (eds), *Sport and Physical Activity*. London: E & FN Spon, pp. 536–50.

Brettschneider, W.-D. (1992) 'Unity of the Nation – Unity in Sport'. Paper presented to International Society of Comparative Physical Education and Sport World Congress, University of Houston, 11–18 June.

Broom, E.F. (1991) 'Lifestyles of aspiring high performance athletes: a comparison of national models', *Journal of Comparative Physical Education and Sport*, 8(2), 24–55.

Brown, M. (1992) 'The development of young 5,000 metre runners', *Athletics Coach*, 26(2), 10–14.

DES (1991) *National Curriculum, The Interim Report of The Physical Education Working Group*. London: Department of Education and Science.

Dick, F. (1992) *The Times*, Monday, 2 November, p. 23.

European Physical Education Associations. *1993 Annual Report*, (held by the Physical Education Association of the United Kingdom).

Evans, J. (1988) *Teachers, Teaching and Control in Physical Education*. London: Falmer Press.

Fisher, R. and Borms, J. (1990) *The Search for Sporting Excellence*. ICSSPE Sport Science Studies, Volume 3. Schorndorf: Verlag Karl Hoffman.

Gardner, H. (1984) *Frames of Mind*. New York: Basic Books.

Hemery, D. (1986) *Sporting Excellence*. London: Willow Books.

Lee, M. (1993) *Coaching Children in Sport*. London: E & FN Spon.

Longmore, A. (1992) *The Times*, Monday, 9 November, p. 25.

Malina, R. (1988) *Young Athletes*. Champaign, Illinois: Human Kinetics.

Naul, R. (1992) 'Changes in sport and PE in East Germany', in Fisher, R. (ed.), *The Changing Face of Physical Education and Sport in Europe*. Proceedings of a seminar held at St Mary's College, London, 29 February, pp. 32–42.

NCF (1992) *Champion Coaching. Working with coaches*. Leeds: National Coaching Foundation.

Pestola, E. (1992) 'Overview: Talent identification', *IAAF Magazine*, **7**(3), 7–12.

Riordan, J. (1992) 'Soviet style sport in eastern Europe: the end of an era', in Fisher, R. (ed.), *The Changing Face of Physical Education and Sport in Europe*. Proceedings of a seminar held at St Mary's College, London, 29 February, pp. 1–18.

Sedlacek, J., Matousek, R., Holcek, R. and Moravec, R. (1992) 'The influence of the political changes on the high performance sport organisation in Czecho-Slovakia'. Paper presented at The International Council for Health Physical Education and Recreation S.D. (Europe) Congress, Prague, 15–19 July.

Sobral, F. (1994) *Desporto Infantil – Juvenil: prontidao e talento*. Lisbon: Livros Horizonte.

Sports Council, The (1993) *Young People and Sport: Policy and Frameworks for Action*. London: The Sports Council.

Stephens, K. (1992) 'Central Issues in Children's Play', in Williams, T., Almond, L. and Sparkes, A. (eds), *Sport and Physical Activity*. London: E & FN Spon, pp. 591–6.

Swan, G. (1991) 'Developing young distance runners', *IAAF Magazine*, **6**(4), 43–50.

Training of Young Athletes Study (1992) *Identification of Talent*. London: The Sports Council.

Chapter 11

Physical Education: Beyond the Curriculum

Rod Thorpe

INTRODUCTION

Curriculum time is insufficient for 'physical education' of the child. This has always been the case, and few would deny that there is a real need to extend physical activity beyond the curriculum. Few would dispute that the quantity and quality of PE in the curriculum is variable, perhaps more so in the primary sector, where the degree of specialist knowledge can be minimal. But there are sport opportunities beyond the curriculum (Youth Sport Trust, 1994, p. 2):

> Sport plays a vital role in the education and development of children. Taking part in sport helps children develop positive attitudes and skills. It also promotes a healthy active lifestyle and encourages lifelong participation.

Some schools encourage 'active' playtimes, others do not; some schools offer extra-curricular programmes, others do not; some local authorities run sports programmes, others do not; some communities are well served by sports clubs, others are not. It is little wonder that the 'physical education' our children receive is largely a matter of chance.

In some localities, there are very active 'outside agencies' providing relevant sport and activity experiences for children. Sometimes, these agencies can provide a valuable resource to integrate with the curriculum, but it must be said there are dangers if these agencies, however well meaning, begin to replace, rather than supplement, existing provision for children.

Readers may find it useful to frame the discussion that follows against the five models; 'substitution', 'versus', 'reinforcement', 'sequence' and 'integration', described by Murdoch (1990) to show possible relationships between PE and sport.

There is no intention in this chapter to separate child-directed play from formalized, controlled, rule-bound sport. Some 'play' schemes employ coaches who direct procedures, while some 'tots' gymnastic clubs are very playful. One youth worker might allow a 'kick-about', while another might organize a mini-soccer tournament. Retaining the essence of 'play', within a safe and structured environment might be an aim for many working with the younger child. The term sport is used in the broadest sense.

It is not the intention of this chapter to quantify the amount of sport which goes on beyond the curriculum. There has been much ill-informed debate, hitherto (Sports Council, 1991, p. 14):

During the last decade increasing concern has been expressed about a perceived decline in the provision of Physical Education and in school aged sport. Often this concern has been misplaced and has often been related to a decline in participation in the traditional team games – overlooking the fact that in many sports providing opportunities for individual participation, numbers have remained stable or have increased.

Even so a recent survey of some 898 Nottinghamshire schoolchildren between the ages of 5 and 18, revealed that (Clough *et al.*, 1994, p. 8):

Seven out of ten of the young people indicated they would play more if there was freedom for them to play when they wanted to and there was a competition available in one of their favourite sports in which they could do well.

There is also evidence that some children are exposed to too much of an inappropriate sport experience (Allen, cited in Nelson, 1994, p. 10):

Sports injuries among children were practically unheard of but now about 10 per cent of our caseload are youngsters. . . . We see a lot of running injuries from training sessions, rather than youngsters hurt actually playing sport.

The case will be made that there are many exciting opportunities for children beyond the curriculum, but much needs to be done to take some of the chance out of this provision. Inevitably, with so many diverse schemes throughout the country, any attempt to provide any more than a personal perspective is doomed to failure.

SUPPLEMENTING THE PE CURRICULUM

While accepting that children need more activity and broader learning opportunities than those provided by school curriculum time, there has always been a tacit understanding that the teaching profession has been the guardian of this experience, the pillar around which other initiatives revolve. Of course, there is ample logic for such an approach; school curriculum time is still the only place in which children are guaranteed a physical education. There is no compunction to take part in physically active pastimes at break or lunch, and often no opportunity. Similarly, not all children will have access to community-based sport.

The curriculum time could be carefully planned so that children move through a logical programme from 5 to 16. Few would want a heavily prescribed curriculum and the very different nature of facilities, staff expertise, community culture, etc., in our schools would ensure such a prescribed curriculum would meet fierce resistance. But, it is my experience that teachers, particularly non-specialists, would welcome resources which are easy to use, logical, not bound in educational dogma and verbiage. I find teachers can happily make links to National Curriculum requirements, where they need help is with the very nature of the activity.

While the PE profession creeps towards a logical curriculum, examining how best to achieve National Curriculum guidelines, a number of sports are making significant attempts to provide logical development programmes for children. These logical programmes are being 'presented' to schools with the professed intention of extending the child's physical experience but, in reality, at primary level at least, these sport-generated programmes often provide a resource which the teacher sees as highly valuable in the curriculum. In many cases, the teachers are able to 'see' some very practical solutions to their 'organizational' problems, solved *in situ*.

On the one hand, a more appropriate sport input would be excellent, as our curriculum work would be supported by experiences that are quite in keeping with the needs of children. But, of course, the PE profession is concerned for two reasons. First, the PE curriculum is not strong, particularly in the primary sector, and second the resources to hand for sport, or some sports, are clearly so great, that there is a perceived danger that sport, or even a single sport, will dominate the curriculum. Many would argue that, as the structured support for teachers from PE has constricted, with the reduction of PE advisers and advisory teachers, so the support from 'sport' has expanded with the increase of Sports Development Officers.

It would, however, be quite erroneous to suggest that there is a strong PE 'versus' sport divide. There are numerous examples of attempts to work together, for example the British Council of Physical Education (BCPE), National Coaching Foundation and Sports Council liaison with National Governing Bodies, which led, with the support of two experienced physical educators respected in the sport world, to a resource for primary schools (Read and Edwards, 1992). At the same time, many sports are alerting their coaches and development officers to national curriculum issues.

While some physical educators look with suspicion and perhaps a little envy at the growth of the sporting lobby, it is important to accept that 'sport' has made a strong commitment to the school-aged child in a number of quite obvious ways.

- The Sports Councils have placed young people to the fore in their strategy.
- Many National Governing Bodies have moved some way toward the development of good content and more appropriate delivery systems for children.
- The National Vocational Qualifications for Coaching identify children as a 'special' group.
- The Children's Act has identified requirements for the many people offering sport in leisure centres, etc.
- There are an increasing number of commercial ventures supporting, perhaps even targeting, children's sport.
- The Prime Minister extols the virtues of team games.
- At the time of writing, a Youth Sport Trust is being piloted in an attempt to better co-ordinate, improve and extend the opportunities for children playing sport (Youth Sport Trust, 1994):

    The Youth Sport Trust is a new charity which will help to bring sport to life for all children in the UK. Our mission is to develop quality sporting programmes for young people aged 4 to 18 years which will be co-ordinated nationally and delivered locally.

SOME RELEVANT PARALLELS: AUSSIE SPORT AND KIWISPORT

As so many organizations increase the attention given to children's sport, one begins to ask if a co-ordination of these initiatives, as proposed by the Youth Sport Trust, might produce a 'dynamic' in which children's sport gains a higher profile. Such a situation has occurred in Australia and New Zealand and there are lessons we can learn. (For a fuller appraisal of these programmes, see Thorpe, 1993.) Programmes operating under the sport banner, such as Aussie Sport and KiwiSport, with a significant (controlling) input from the Australian and New Zealand (Hillary) Sports Commissions are providing youngsters with sport experiences which, research findings would suggest, are very appropriate and very well received. (For an excellent review of the Australian programme, see Traill and Clough, 1993.)

If we look at the original aims of the Aussie Sports programmes for the mid-1980s, as reported by Traill and Clough (1993, p. 1) they were:

1   to improve the quality, quantity and variety of sporting activities available to Australian children;
2   to provide all children with the opportunity to participate in appropriate sporting activities;
3   to encourage participation and skill development in a variety of sports;
4   to reduce the emphasis on 'win at all costs' and promote enjoyment and good competition through participation in sport;
5   to promote the principles of good sporting behaviour; and
6   to improve the quality of sports instruction available to Australian children.

In the early 1990s these were re-stated as follows (Traill and Clough, 1993, p. 1):

- The promotion of the importance of sport as an option for an active lifestyle
- The improvement of the place of sports education in the education curriculum
- An improved and integrated structure/organization of sport for young people (delivery)
- Development of appropriate levels of sport competition and fair play attitudes
- Greater local community responsibility for enhancing sports delivery
- The development of participants sports-related skills
- Greater equality of opportunity and access to sports activities
- The development of leadership activities through sport
- Increased numbers of educated sports instructors
- Enhancement of volunteerism in sport.

'Aussie Sports', had become synonymous with the modified sports programme and so a new title 'Aussie Sport' was introduced to embrace a range of progressive programmes aimed at different ages:

- Sportstart (It's all about play)
- Sport It (A sporting start)
- Sport for Kids (Games just my size)
- Active Girls Campaign (Sport everyone's game)
- Sports Search (What sport's for me?)
- Sports Fun (Learning to lead)
- CAPS (It's more than just play).

In the aims of the current programmes, the British reader will recognize phrases like 'lifestyle', 'community responsibility' and 'equality of opportunity', and would I am sure sympathize with the sentiments expressed throughout. Perhaps the phrase 'improve the place of sport education within the education curriculum' should be noted. The value of a sport education, which is somehow separate from PE, in the curriculum is not a new one, indeed the 'games' afternoon is still common practice in the independent sector in the UK. It may be that the idea of allocating additional time in the day for team sports, which has been proposed, is in some way a similar, if less balanced attempt to increase children's sport. Certainly in Australia and New Zealand one sensed real efforts, by the Sports Commissions, to overcome the 'substitution' and 'versus' issues, and a simple way was to remain somewhat separate[1] from the PE curriculum, but 'reinforcing' it.

That the original aims and the more recent modifications of Aussie Sport reflect, in the main, attitudes to sport with which PE teachers can empathize, should not be a surprise. Both the Commissions in Australia and New Zealand do much to embrace the expertise of physical educators. In Australia, I was impressed to find PE teachers and community workers, seconded to 'work up' programmes, sitting alongside the Sports Commission Officers responsible for the strategic overview and the national implementation. In New Zealand, the Hillary Commission made available a very experienced and well respected PE adviser to work with the Sport Associations (NGBs), so that, while the sport owned the package, the philosophy of KiwiSport was maintained. In both programmes, the realization that there needed to be a balance between officers with a physical education, a community and/or a sport training, seemed well founded.

The effect of these schemes is perhaps best illustrated by personal 'anecdotal' information. On visiting Australia and New Zealand in 1992 (on a Winston Churchill Travelling Fellowship), my first contacts were probably the most telling. As I passed through immigration in Australia, I was asked the purpose of my trip. On replying 'to see Aussie Sport', I was given a brief résumé on the values of the programme from the immigration officer. When a more detailed treatise on KiwiSport was provided at my first hotel in New Zealand, I began to realize that these programmes were having a significant effect on the general population. The high profile achieved by both programmes was apparent throughout my ten-week stay. I became increasingly impressed by the way key messages like 'fairplay', 'no "angry" parents', 'width of experience', 'equity', were so clearly identified with the schemes. In my opinion, a major reason for this public awareness was the fact that the philosophy was being delivered simultaneously in the schools, on the recreation 'ovals' and in the sports clubs.

In Australia, Level O (Orientation) coaches (perhaps equivalent to sport specific leaders in the UK) are made aware of the Aussie Sport programmes and their underlying principles, as they become accredited through the Australian Coaching Council. I have to say that this made me wonder whether the decision made by the National Coaching Foundation (NCF) – to provide coach education which National Governing Bodies could, if they wished, embrace – was really as good as a centralized compulsory accreditation scheme. How many teachers or coaches in the UK are aware of the NCFs 'Play the Game' booklet produced in 1986? A similar leaflet is central to the Level O input in Australia. Perhaps the National Vocational Qualification, 'Coaching Children' will rectify this to some extent, but this will not affect the many volunteers coming in to sport. I could gain no accurate figures for the number of Level O coaches trained each year, there were so many.

One still has to ask how the key messages become so widespread. I think the answer is simple. The Aussie Sport and the KiwiSport programmes are promoted as a whole. Some of the more 'powerful' sports feel that they could do more in their own sport if the money came directly to them, but in supporting a corporate children's sport approach, the key messages pass through more clearly. Civic advertising slots on television help.

If this gives the impression that here are two perfect 'sport for children schemes', a word of caution: Observation of the programmes in the field raised a wide variety of interesting points:

- the problem of dealing with skill development with inexperienced teachers and coaches;
- the challenge of the talented children, particularly at 9 or 10 years of age, when the children 'know they are good' and 'know the teacher is not';
- the appropriateness of producing a host of girls who love 'socceroo' (mini-soccer) but who, after 11, face the lack of structures to develop, thereby accentuating inequality, but in so doing producing a 'dissonance' which might lead to change;
- the need to ensure the quality of instruction given to the teachers/coaches by sport specific officers; and
- the difficulty of promoting development programmes in organizations which have a legacy of highly structured junior competitive programmes, and see success at junior level as an end in itself.

RELATIONSHIP BETWEEN PE AND SPORTS PROGRAMMES

At the time of my visit in 1992, New Zealand had proponents suggesting that PE be 'thematically based' and sport should play little part; others felt that PE should be 'daily exercise', and yet others were extolling the value of 'sport education'. There was considerable condemnation of some sport images, often those associated with aggression, particularly in rugby. Higher education institutions, in moving to the supposed academic respectability in sports science, had, in the opinion of some teachers, reneged on PE. It all sounded very familiar. Not surprisingly, with some real confusion as to the nature of PE and a dearth of specialist knowledge at primary level, a coherent child-friendly programme like KiwiSport filled the void. In some primary and intermediate schools, KiwiSport had become the PE programme. It is important to note that the agencies providing the modified sport experience normally associated with KiwiSport were producing a range of other programmes related to PE, e.g. Kiwidex (a movement/exercise programme). The regional Sports Trusts, who house the KiwiSport Officers, were, in some cases, becoming very influential even, in educational establishments.

At the secondary level, a Hillary Commission programme, Sportfit, 'pump-primed' schools to provide a 'co-ordinator' of the extra-curricular sport programme to work alongside the PE teachers. In separating the two roles, it seemed to me, that the curriculum subject PE, and the responsibilities of the PE teacher could be identified the more clearly. Most similar positions in the UK assume a community sport, rather than, a school sport development.

In Australia, the PE curriculum looked at one stage, in 1992, to be subsumed (or perhaps overwhelmed) within the health curriculum at the national level. Subsequently, with the help of the sport lobby, PE has regained its identity with a national statement and profile being developed in health and PE. Few historians of PE will be unaware of the South Australian PE programme, with excellent written resources and a network of support advisers. I am sad to say they are no more. Similar political pressures to those apparent in the UK have, according to many people I interviewed, stripped the support mechanisms from PE in schools. While Aussie Sport is intended to supplement and extend PE with a sport education, it is often the only PE the child receives.

Further parallels with the UK are obvious. The primary teacher is usually female, with an average age in the mid-40s, having had less than ideal PE and sport experiences as a child. This can be coupled with a very limited ITT, particularly in class management in the PE situation, as well as content which leant more to 'education theory', than to the practicalities of 'taking' a class of thirty children. Not surprisingly, we have teachers lacking confidence, crying out for content that works and the support of experts. Sport is, whether the PE profession likes it or not, providing both content that works and expertise.

SPORT CONTENT

Clearly this is the most important factor. If the activity is interesting, exciting, motivating, etc., children will play, and probably improve, despite the teacher. In this respect, the Aussie Sport and KiwiSport programmes go a long way to meeting this need. It is my own contention that in presenting excellent modified sports, the teachers and coaches gain confidence. However, in then expecting the teacher to teach skills in a rather 'direct way', the teachers inadequacies are brought to the surface. It is my opinion that the teacher needs more 'progressive' games and more guidance on how to cope with different abilities, etc. Of course, a bias toward 'teaching games for understanding' (Bunker and Thorpe, 1982) would lead me to suggest that teachers, lacking physical ability, could help the children think about their intentions in the game, albeit at a simple level.

Between 1991 and 1994, together with a research assistant Ben Tan, and with the help of several colleagues, I amassed a whole host of games in a number of sports, which we felt would be suitable for 7 to 12-year-olds. While information from abroad was used, many sports and many individuals in the UK have numerous activities which meet the needs of children. Certain 'games' were then selected, adapted and presented in a form that we hoped would allow very inexperienced parents, leaders, teachers, youth workers, etc., to offer progressive 'games' to children. We tried to design the games and the instruction cards so that children would merely take the card and relevant equipment and 'start playing the game', thereby reducing the management problems for the person in charge. The games described on the front of the cards were 'fair', e.g. batters had an equal number of hits. Questions designed to encourage children to be involved in a broader range of roles – organizer, coach, scorer, player – were included. Written instructions were reduced to a minimum and the 'exciting' picture, which filled most of the A3 card, was to contain most of the information. On the back of the card, management advice was given: equipment needed, safety considerations, modifying the game for skill and/or age differences, ideas for people with particular impairments, how to adapt it for the confident and competitive, e.g. batters might be out first ball, etc.

Built into the system was cross-referencing to other types of activity, to encourage a variety of experience across sports, as well as 'Where to next?' information to ensure development within a given sport.

The intention was to capture the essence of the activity, but remove those demands better met by specialists, e.g. coaches and teachers. Doing this, and overcoming group management problems, we hoped would convince more people that they could contribute to children's sport.

This programme, first called 'Playsport' and supported by the Sports Council – East Midlands Region, has been piloted in the region. It is, at the time of writing, being piloted as 'TOP sport' in each Sports Council Region in England, under the auspices of the Youth Sport Trust. Throughout, the intention was to extend the curriculum, using break times, after school, Brownie meets, play schemes, etc. In addition, it was hoped that sport specific clubs might see the value of fun games from other sports that might add variety to sessions, reduce repetitive loads on certain body parts, but for the ardent coach might be justified for the cross-training effect. It will be no surprise that the few teachers who have seen the resource have used the games in their PE programmes – they are designed to overcome the very problems of lack of knowledge and lack of confidence that many primary teachers express.

> Many students and teachers lack confidence in their ability to teach PE properly. They often express feelings of inadequacy in this area of the curriculum, they may be excellent teachers in other respects (Thomas, 1988, p. 7).

SPORT EXPERTS

Both the Australians and the New Zealanders reported that, while they felt the materials provided for Aussie and KiwiSport were good and schools had purchased them, the appointment of Aussie Sports and KiwiSport officers/co-ordinators in each state, territory, region or district had been the catalyst that had ensured the materials were used. In some cases, the Aussie/KiwiSport officer took demonstration sessions themselves, but more usually the Aussie/KiwiSport officers have recruited the services of National Governing Body personnel. With inexperienced 'deliverers', the 'trainer' who arrives to 'show' the activity is a very powerful model. While the Aussie and KiwiSport officers were extremely aware of the sensitivities of the sport and PE links and could see how important the 'presentation of the activity' was to the overall scheme, the sport specific coaches/development officers they employed to present the activities varied, in my opinion, from excellent to abysmal. The Aussie/KiwiSport officers are still dependent on the sport and, in some cases, sport development officers are appointed for reasons other than to develop young people's sport. Under these circumstances, it is not surprising that some of the presentations were poor. Most worrying, but not surprising, some of the less-experienced teachers could not recognize the poor input.

This point should be noted when assessing the research on Aussie Sport, pre-dominantly by Clough and Traill – see Traill and Clough (1993), which finds very positive results for the programmes. There is little doubt that the programmes are meeting a need and satisfying both the children and the adults working with them, but some might argue that such is not difficult with the younger primary-aged children and inexperienced teachers.

As children reach 9 or 10 years of age they begin to make comparative judgements on ability. It is at this age that the inexperience of the teacher becomes critical and if the expectations of the teacher, e.g. to demonstrate and improve skill, are not met, in that the teacher can neither demonstrate nor explain the skill required, all credibility is lost.

YOUNG PEOPLE'S SPORT IN THE UNITED KINGDOM

In contrast to Australia and New Zealand, where there is a central focus for young people's sport, the UK has been, in the early 1990s, typified by a whole host of excellent initiatives, between a confusing range of partners. The most obvious factor is that in the 'United' Kingdom, sport is rarely united.

For example, all four home countries have 'leadership' schemes. Occasional exchange of ideas occurs by intent, but more often by hearsay. The Northern Irish have traditionally linked their Leadership quite strongly to the Sport Bodies. The Welsh have built their programme upon the Sports Development Officer network, extending it into other community-based organizations with care. The Scots tied their Leadership programme into an education framework, well before National Vocational Qualifications. The Central Council of Physical Recreation (CCPR) aimed at the community but achieved a stronger base in the education system, perhaps because of the poor working links with parts of the Sports Council during the 1980s, who, at regional level could have readily tapped the sports development network (Thorpe, 1988).

Some sports have a 'British' identity; others are closely associated with national pride. Few would dare to suggest that the Welsh Rugby Football Union should lose the identity of Dragon Rugby for their mini-game. The children's game can be the start of a national sport identity; other examples spring to mind: Socceroo in Australia, Leprechaun Rugby in Ireland. It might surprise a number of readers to realize that some of the states and territories in Australia are as fervent about their rights to determine the future of sport in their area as the four home nations are here. States and territories have Ministers of Sport and Ministers of Education. Until relatively recently, educational certificates were not comparable. The Aussie Sport programmes have had to overcome some of the sorts of issues that would face a co-ordinated approach to children's sport in the UK. Even so, few would deny that the nationally co-ordinated, multi-sport approach has done much to help children to gain a better sport experience.

SOME SPECIFIC EXAMPLES

As mentioned earlier, in my opinion, one of the greatest strengths of the Aussie and KiwiSport organizations is that they bring ideas developed locally into the national scheme. In contrast, children's sport in the UK is almost characterized by the wealth of excellent developments at a local level, or within a single sport or organization, which rarely reach national awareness, never mind become implemented. Of course, the Sports Council with its demonstration projects, but a budget constraint and a philosophy that implied 'we've shown you it works, now you get on and do it', has not helped the process. Even if one concentrates on the English situation, to avoid the 'national' issues, the plethora of partners one could be involved with in children's sport is confusing. At the local level, if one can find a Sports Development Officer, this person has been trained to utilize the sport network, and will clarify the situation, but not every District Authority has a Sports Development Officer!

The wealthier sports have extensive networks, but still seek partnerships which extend their influence. The Games Assistant Service, which is just a part of The Football Association Coaching and Education Scheme – Community Programme, was set up with the support and approval of The Physical Education Association of Great Britain and Northern Ireland (PEA) (for an initial period).

This was a direct response to the NCPE reference to 'partnerships' and is designed 'to provide football coaches, paid on an hourly basis, to assist school physical education programmes' (Football Association, 1993).

The quality control would be achieved in the following ways. The Games Assistant should have:

- previous experience with young people;
- knowledge of health and safety in their activity;
- organizational skills;
- National Governing Body qualifications; and
- knowledge of the NCPE.

According to the Football Association (1993, p. 2):

All coaches selected will have had experience coaching mixed ability, mixed gender children in the age range required . . . All coaches as Games Assistants will be required to hold The Football Association's Preliminary Coaching Award and have successfully completed the training programme provided by The Physical Education Association of Great Britain and Northern Ireland to meet the National Curriculum criteria.

Clearly, some might question the wisdom of focusing an input like this in the curriculum, in that it might well de-skill teachers and, if extended to other sports, could be seen as justification for a reduction in permanent PE staff.

The fact that the FA are writing curriculum resources, e.g. The World Cup Pack (1994) which cross curricular boundaries, is to be commended. Many staff interested in PE and sport have tried to make cross-curricular links, but the resources available to a wealthy governing body ensure a quality of production far beyond that normally found in education.

The wealthier sports have extensive 'professional' sports development networks. The Lawn Tennis Association (LTA) reorganized their regional structure in 1994, to include eight Area Development Managers and seven National Training Coaches, clearly identifying a 'development role' for the Managers. There are County Coaching and Development Officers, Tennis Development Officers in the new indoor centres, and yet others linked to LEAs and they are all targeting children.

Recognizing the problems some teachers have in using tennis in the National Curriculum, the LTA have designed a course for teachers. Whereas, in the past, the course was a modified coaching course, now the course is produced by people better informed about the National Curriculum than most of the teachers on the course. Couple this with a child-sensitive 'tennis leaders' course, award schemes aimed at children in and out of school, national schools team tournaments and the influence of the National Governing Body becomes apparent. In some areas of the country, schools have this expertise on their doorstep.

Some statements from the City of Nottingham Schools Tennis Programme might indicate how tennis moves from national ideas to local implementation:

> Diamond Cable Communications have pledged £15,000 to fund the City of Nottingham Schools Tennis Development Programme. This figure has been matched under the Government's Sports Match Scheme, creating a total sponsorship package worth £30,000. This innovative project will target all secondary schools and 15 primary schools in the City. Specially trained Lawn Tennis Association qualified coaches will visit the schools to undertake coaching clinics and stimulate tennis activity. (City of Nottingham, 1994a)

Just as the FA have additional training for their Games Assistants, so the City of Nottingham run a workshop to ensure their coaches are prepared to go into schools. The training of the coaches who visit the schools will be done by the North Midland Area Development Manager and will cover (City of Nottingham, 1994b):

- National Curriculum
- Nottinghamshire Schools LTA
- British Schools LTA
- other schools initiatives, e.g. Midland Bank
- mixed ability groups
- integrating children with a disability
- use of equipment.

Once again the National Governing Body seems to be well aware of the current issues facing teachers, e.g. the National Curriculum and differentiation, and are attempting to direct the coaches to these. It remains to be seen whether the coaches will 'skill' or 'de-skill' the teachers they work with. Even so, as PE teachers have always leant heavily on sport, particularly games, it should be gratifying that resources are to hand that match curriculum requirements.

Both soccer and tennis would be classed as 'wealthy' and professional. While quite dissimilar in many ways, with a very different 'community' base, both have the resources to produce a coherent support system for schools. Other sports, e.g. Rugby Union, are similar, but there are many sports who rely heavily on Sports Council support for development initiatives, consequently some sport schemes are more modest and are dependent upon regional, or even local, support.

In Australia and New Zealand, it is probably the 'smaller' sports, and of course the children, that have gained the most from the corporate approach to children's sport. The Youth Sport Trust has, in embracing the developing programmes 'TOP play' and 'TOP sport', derivatives of 'Playsport' (described earlier), and the well-established Champion Coaching initiative, have programmes aimed at various points on the Sports Development Continuum. A fourth programme 'TOP club' is also being developed.

For many 'casual' play is not enough. To achieve maximum enjoyment from participating in sport, we need the friendship of fellow club members, the opportunity to compete and quality coaching in a club environment (Axford in Youth Sport Trust, 1994, p. 4).

Perhaps 'Champion Coaching' best illustrates the lessons to be learnt by a more co-ordinated cross-sport approach to children's sport. The purpose of Champion Coaching is (National Coaching Foundation, 1993, p. 8):

to help local communities provide quality-assured youth sport coaching for the per-formance-motivated child within a co-ordinated community structure.

In attempting to provide a quality controlled coaching input for children, Champion Coaching has to work with the National Governing Body, the schools and the community agencies. The realization that much of the success of a given scheme is dependent on the Youth Sports Manager raises interesting issues. According to the National Coaching Foundation (1993, p. 12):

No other single factor contributes to the success of a Champion Coaching scheme as much as the commitment of the Youth Sport Manager.

Similarly, the fact that the scheme actually causes the organizations contributing to become more focused and often better structured, is also worthy of note. Both points would support my overall conclusions about the success of the Aussie and KiwiSport programmes, i.e. that some measure of national guidance and control around a clearly identified programme, developed against a background of informed opinion, is essential. The programme must be flexible enough to suit individual needs, as it will be delivered in slightly different community settings. Quality assurance comes both from the content and key personnel within the system.

Individual National Governing Bodies, particularly the wealthier ones, might say that they have the organization to develop the resources necessary for their sport and certainly one would expect this to be so. There seems, however, an increasing realiza-tion that these developments might be more pertinent within a balanced programme of sport experiences. If 'communities' (including schools) can more readily tap into this balanced sport programme, then it seems that we may well achieve a PE beyond the curriculum.

At the curriculum level, Murdoch (1990, p. 75) in moving our thinking to an integrated model, suggested, amongst other things, that,

The preparation of teachers both in the primary and secondary schools will need to develop and change. . . . A joint in-service provision is called for so that teachers, coaches and leaders can work from a common base in relation to meeting children's needs.

In my opinion, conflicts about sport and PE arise when people are ill-informed and/or insecure. Until we overcome the problems of 'confidence', particularly in our primary teachers, then we are unlikely to make progress. It seems to me that some parts of 'sport' are more child aware, more curriculum aware, and more ready to work to the teachers' agenda. The National Curriculum has given some clear guidance as to the nature of PE. There has never been a better time to resolve issues of sport within the PE curriculum, while recognizing and promoting those aspects of sport which extend the education 'beyond the curriculum'.

NOTE

1. At the time of my visit, sport education was normally seen as separate from PE. The concept of sport education as part of PE was the central theme of the Australian Sports Commission Publication – Aussie Sport Action, Summer 1994.

REFERENCES

Bunker, D.J. and Thorpe, R.D. (1982) 'A model for the teaching of games in the secondary school', *Bulletin of Physical Education*, **10**, 9–16.

City of Nottingham (1994a) 'Diamond Cable Schools Tennis Programme', promotional pamphlet.

City of Nottingham (1994b) 'Coaches Training Day', promotional pamphlet.

Clough, J.R., Thorpe, R.D. and Traill, R.D. (1994) 'A Mapping of Participation Rates in Junior Sport in Nottinghamshire', a report for the Sports Council East Midlands and Nottinghamshire County Council.

Football Association (1993) *Games Assistant Service*. Pamphlet, London: FA Publications.

Murdoch, E.B. (1990) 'Physical Education and sport: the Interface', in Armstrong, N. (ed.), *New Directions in Physical Education Vol 1*. Leeds: Human Kinetics, pp. 63–72.

National Coaching Foundation (1993) *Champion Coaching 1993. More recipes for action*. Leeds: White Line Publications.

Nelson, B. (1994) 'Young victims in sports injuries', *Leicester Mercury*, 2 November, p. 10.

Read, B. and Edwards, P. (1992) *Teaching Children to Play Games. A Resource for Primary Teachers 5–11*. Leeds: White Line Publications.

Sports Council (1991) *Coaching Matters*. London: Sports Council.

Thomas, P. (1988) 'Initial teacher training: Meeting the demands: Perceptions from the schools', in *Conference Proceedings of the Standing Conference on Physical Education in Teacher Education*. Loughborough: Standing Conference on Physical Education in Teacher Education, pp. 7–9.

Thorpe, R.D. (1988) 'Sports Leadership – A review of the current situation and suggested ways forward', unpublished report, London: Sports Council.

Thorpe, R.D. (1993) 'The deliverers of young people's sport experience in Australia and New Zealand with particular reference to Aussie and Kiwi-sport', unpublished report, London: Winston Churchill Memorial Trust.

Traill, R.D. and Clough, J.R. (1993) *Aussie Sport since 1986. A Brief Review*. Canberra: Australian Sports Commission.

Youth Sports Trust (1994) 'Youth Sports Trust introduces TOP play, TOP sport, Champion Coaching and TOP club', promotional pamphlet.

Chapter 12

Physical Education Teachers and the Search for Self: Two Cases of Structured Denial

Andrew Sparkes

INTRODUCTION

> As every pupil knows, teachers are not people. Yet people become teachers. Evidently therefore teaching as a profession robs men and women of their individuality, even their identity. . . . The separation of person from occupation is theoretically and practically unsound, since both personal and teacher behaviour are determined by the individual's concept of him/herself. (Nias, 1985, p. 3)

For interactionists such as Nias (1985, 1989) and Woods (1983, 1990, 1993) the 'self' is intimately associated with, and expressed through, the personal dimensions of teaching. Woods (1984) notes that, 'individuals can and do chart their own courses, and can engage with the curriculum at a deep personal level' (p. 260). Both of these authors draw upon the work of Ball (1972) to acknowledge the self as multiple in terms of there being 'situational' and 'substantial' selves. For Nias (1989) the latter is an inner self or core which is persistently defended and highly resistant to change since it comprises the most highly prized aspects of our self-concept and the attitudes and values which are salient to them. Nias suggests that the personal concerns of teachers are those preoccupations and interests which relate to the definition and maintenance of their 'substantial' selves, that apparent changes in these concerns reflect a long drawn out search for congruence between their view of themselves as persons and as teachers and that in default of such a match, they pursue sequential or parallel careers. These developments are accompanied and supported by changes in significant others.

Similarly, P. Woods (1990) talks of a preferred self but notes how individuals adopt different guises in different situations as a way of coping with the world, and particularly institutional, depersonalized life. He points out that a number of these situational selves may be contradictory and difficult to resolve. Of interest here is the manner in which teachers develop strategies that strive to maintain the integrity of the self in various situations, often against the odds. As Sikes *et al.* (1985) suggest, the idea of a coping strategy makes it necessary to specify what it is that has to be coped with (the external constraint, problem, expectation), as well as the creative act of coping that individual teachers create and develop. To gain insights into these strategies requires that great importance is given to the teachers' own views, both of the nature of the problem, and their ways of coping with it.

Drawing upon these concepts I want to focus in this chapter upon moments from the lives of two PE teachers. Jessica (a pseudonym) is a lesbian PE teacher and Alexander is a gay male PE teacher.[1] The moments from Jessica's life are based upon an ongoing series of life history interviews (Sparkes, 1994a, b). In contrast, the moments from the life of Alexander are part of an ethnographic fiction I have created in the spirit of critical storytelling (Barone, 1992; Tierney, 1993).[2] Their stories are used to illustrate how both are forced to deny their substantial sense of self on a daily basis due to the ideologies of homophobia[3] and heterosexism[4] that pervade society in general, and schools in particular. The strategies that Jessica and Alexander adopt to survive in schools are illuminated by drawing upon the analytical framework developed by Griffin (1991) who outlines a continuum of identity management strategies used by lesbian and gay educators. These range from being totally closeted to being publicly out.

Totally closeted strategies   Being totally closeted involves being out to no one in school and to very few in the community beyond school (this can include parents and close friends).

Passing strategies   Passing is a strategy that leads others to believe that the individual is heterosexual. This strategy has active and passive forms. The former involves intentionally doing or saying something that leads others to believe that the individual is heterosexual, for example, wearing clothes that signify heterosexuality, lying to colleagues that one has a girl/boyfriend, or changing gendered pronouns when talking partners (male partners become 'she', female partners become 'he'). The latter involves allowing the assumption that the individual is heterosexual to go unchallenged.

Covering strategies   Covering strategies include an important difference from passing. When covering the individual is not trying to be perceived as heterosexual but is attempting to hide their gay or lesbian identity. Here, individuals censor what they share about themselves with students and colleagues and this is defined as a step towards greater self-integrity. Included in covering strategies are the avoidance of settings in which discussions of personal life are likely to occur (e.g. the staff room); only attending obligatory school events and then going alone; declining voluntary invitations to socialize with colleagues out of school; and the use of non-gendered language in which personal pronouns are omitted to become, for example, 'my friend'.

Coming out   Implicitly coming out to someone means that while the individual does not directly disclose her or his identity, it is assumed that the other person(s) know the individual is lesbian or gay. Here, individuals decide to stop passing or covering and openly share information about their personal lives and their partner using the appropriate gender, but without using the words lesbian or gay. This non-confirmation of their identity is the key distinction between being implicitly and explicitly out. Finally, in explicitly coming out individuals disclose their lesbian or gay identity by using the words 'lesbian' or 'gay'.

Each of these strategies carries risks and rewards at both a personal and a professional level. For example, choosing to pass means maintaining a strict separation between personal and professional identities. This negates the possibility of self-integration while at the same time protecting the individual from discrimination with regard to career advancement. In contrast, being explicitly out enables a greater integration of personal and professional identities but carries with it the professional risk of a blocked career. These are dilemmas that Jessica and Alexander struggle with on a daily basis. By relating aspects of their lives to Griffin's (1991) framework, I hope to indicate the manner in which the structural constraints that homophobia and heterosexism impose, and reinforce, are not uniform and that they vary between contexts and individuals in ways that impact powerfully on the ability of lesbian and gay teachers to freely express themselves and develop an integration of self and situation in a work context.[5] That Jessica and Alexander in their jobs as PE teachers are unable to negotiate such an integration, and have constantly to maintain a split between their personal and professional life for fear of losing their jobs, highlights the manner in which heterosexism and homophobia operates to oppress each of them and many other teachers like them. With these points in mind, the following are some moments from the lives of Jessica and Alexander.

MOMENTS FROM JESSICA'S STORY[6]

Jessica is in her late twenties. She had her first lesbian experience during her teens and during this period, by accident (her mother found a copy of Gay News under her bed), she came out to her parents and sisters. All of whom have been fully supportive of her since then and have welcomed her partners into their homes. Being explicitly out within her family enabled Jessica to experience self-integration and this positive affirmation of her lesbian identity formed a solid foundation for her views regarding 'being out and being me' as she encountered less supportive situations in the future:

> It wasn't a major problem or a tragedy for me and I hadn't been kicked out of the house. I had a very sort of middle class family from suburbia who were totally supportive and liked my girlfriend. It gave them a positive image about it.

However, having come out to her family Jessica was also learning to maintain a separation of selves in different contexts since she was was totally closeted at school:

> I didn't ever tell anybody at school . . . I wasn't wearing badges or shouting from the rooftops that I was a lesbian but at the same time I was doing what I could in a way that I felt comfortable.

This issue of feeling 'comfortable' with herself in relation to the forms of social interactions undertaken were to become increasingly important to Jessica. From these early days, it was clear that, in terms of her integration of self and situation, she was not prepared to adopt passing strategies and that covering was the baseline strategy she could feel comfortable with. Having said this, there was already an implicit acceptance of a separation of self and situation that depended upon the context where Jessica was 'out and me' at home (private life) but was denying her substantial self during school hours (public life).

During her time in school Jessica excelled at sports and having gained her 'A' levels she left home to study for a degree in sports science. When she moved to another part of the country to start her course Jessica was in a secure long-term relationship, felt comfortable with her sexuality, and was seeking to express her lesbian identity on a daily basis and be herself:

> Well, I'm away from home. I'm not going to affect anybody that I care about in a negative way. It's me and if people can't accept it then that's their problem.

Feeling the need to find some form of self-expression within an organizational framework Jessica joined the Women's Group on her arrival. As part of this group, she was involved in organizing a public meeting on the topic of sexuality. It was well attended and included some students from her course. Jessica remembers:

> So I can remember seeing it filling up with all these faces that I didn't recognize. I then realized that I was actually coming out, kind of, *en masse*.

In this incident, Jessica explicitly came out and used the term lesbian to define her identity in front of a large number of students. However, she was not sure if this revelation had filtered through to the staff who lectured on her course where she continued to be implicitly out or used covering strategies for fear of discrimination. These perceptions of hostility added to her growing sense of alienation from the course so that she increasingly directed her energies into life outside the academic domain where she felt secure within a small but supportive lesbian network.

> I wasn't going to get anywhere with anybody and that drove me away from studying to prove anything, to myself even, which I feel is a regret now . . . I submerged myself into socializing and going out. Living a gay existence, if you like, in a way that I wasn't able to do as part of my course . . . having what became a social group became fun, exciting, expressive and comfortable. We had a few houses where we all used to live. We became a bit immune, because we grew in numbers and we became immune to any derogatory attitudes.

At polytechnic, Jessica's ability to be 'out and be me' was best met in the company of her friends who offered each other support. These feelings of security and integration need to be contrasted to the context, as she perceived it, on her course in terms of her interactions with staff and PE students where, at best, she could only be implicitly out or covering. Having to adopt these strategies clearly negated her sense of self and fractured any integration between the two contexts.

For a variety of reasons Jessica decided not to go into teaching on completing her degree. She took several years out to work in a range of jobs both here and abroad. Eventually she decided to do a PGCE year with PE as her main subject. When she arrived at the university she was struck by the conservative climate that prevailed:

> To come here and find people even more conservative and even more closeted [than when I was a student] was quite a shock. I thought people would be much more relaxed and open about it, even if they weren't necessarily out in all aspects of their life as students.

She quickly became aware that few of the lesbian PE students she met were explicitly out for fear of harassment. The majority were adopting passing strategies, even to the extent of dating male students in order to keep up appearances of heterosexuality. Jessica found these passing strategies unacceptable:

> I can't do it [passing]. I find that really offensive almost. You are saying a lot of things by doing that. You're saying that you are not happy or not proud about your sexuality. That

can then have repercussions for your partner, like feelings of doubt and insecurity . . . I find that very hard to cope with. It hurts a lot emotionally.

However, there were times on her main teaching practice in a large secondary school when Jessica was forced to adopt passing and covering strategies to defend her sense of self, and survive. For example, it was during this teaching practice that Jessica was questioned for the first time by a group of children regarding her sexual identity. She remembers:

> There was this little group of about four or five who started saying things like, 'Miss, how do you spell lesbian?', and were really being difficult, they'd sussed me out basically . . . It was really hard for me, really hard. I didn't know how to react.

Jessica wanted to discuss the issue with them but knew that this would not be deemed appropriate behaviour for a student teacher.

> I didn't feel I had any power to do that. I don't know whether it was right or not anyway. Everything around me told me it was wrong . . . I wanted to . . . not necessarily making it personal but making it an issue and talking about it. I just had to ignore it. I felt awful. I felt horrible. It was really difficult because I guess I didn't want them to know, I didn't want them to guess. I didn't want them to say things. I felt like I was being attacked in a way.

The threatening nature of this incident emphasized to Jessica the need eventually to seek employment in a school where she might be able to explicitly come out to a few colleagues and thereby have their support:

> Ideally I'd like to think that there would be a few members of staff that I'd be able to build up relationships with, where we got to the stage where they did know. Where I had a few people I could turn towards. But that's very ideal. I don't know, it depends. The strain could be unbearable if the kids get onto me and I didn't feel I had any support from anybody.

With a view to gaining some integration of self and situation Jessica opted to apply for teaching posts in or near London. This location would also assure her of a stable network of friends and guaranteed Jessica a certain level of anonymity in her private life.

Jessica gained a post in London and began her job as PE teacher with a sense of optimism. However, she gradually became disillusioned. Her professional and social life were increasingly fragmented and distanced from one another. In describing a typical week she comments:

> At the weekend I'm in London with my friends. That's kind of almost reinforcing this need to get out of one life and into another because I'm geographically picking myself up and moving. Spending time with different people at the weekends and having a social life with my friends. Then back home, it's back here . . . That's reinforcing that split . . . It's a conscious decision. I feel I almost need it. I need to be able to relax, to be me.

Other incidents also reinforced this fragmentation and illustrate how fears of exposure to her work colleagues acted as a constraint on her life outside of school. For example, Jessica regularly participated in the annual Gay Pride march held in London. However, this year she was not sure about going.

> I was suddenly faced with the decision of whether I risked going and possibly being seen by somebody . . . Even though you rationalize that those chances are very remote, there's still a pressure that hadn't been there until I started the job.

Eventually, Jessica decided to go on the march but remained nervous throughout in case someone saw her, or her face appeared on the TV screen and was noticed by her teaching colleagues or parents of pupils.

Towards the latter part of her first year in teaching Jessica explicitly came out to one other female teacher in the school. This incident highlights the sense of isolation and loneliness that Jessica was experiencing plus the need she felt for, at least, the support of one colleague that she could relax with in a professional context.

> I came out to her. I was actually quite conscious of the burden, of relief, a sensation of 'at least I've told one person'. I mean, one is so many more than none. Sadly enough, she's now left the school and she's got another job somewhere else. So I'm back to square one in those terms . . . You see, Allison [a pseudonym] was really the only person that I'd spoken to socially, that I would talk to about my life outside of school . . . Just that there was somebody else on the staff that knew. I think it was almost, at least somebody else knows, at least somebody could be on my side if anything was to happen.

These 'happenings' included a fear of discrimination from colleagues, pupils and parents along with an awareness that this might lead to her eventual dismissal from her teaching post. As Jessica commented when asked what the reactions of parents might be if they knew she was a lesbian: 'It just doesn't bear thinking about.' Informal conversations with teaching colleagues, several of whom expressed homophobic views, made Jessica far from convinced that she could count on their support in the event of her sexual identity becoming public knowledge. Such conversations confirmed Jessica's feeling that the teaching profession had a negative view of lesbian women and gay men in that there was:

> Still a lot of fear, derision and prejudice. There are still a lot of people I think who hold the views that anybody of a different sexual orientation is a child molester, which is totally laughable . . . There are a lot of dangerous myths still around and still in teaching, maybe more than other areas of work because we're dealing with children.

These concerns, coupled with the fact that the one person she had explicitly come out to and looked to for support had left the school, acted literally to silence Jessica on several occasions. For example, an INSET day during her second year of teaching highlighted the tensions of having constantly to suppress her substantial sense of self and beliefs in the school context. Part of the day focused on the counselling role of the teacher when dealing with sensitive issues in the classroom. During seminar sessions child abuse and sexual abuse were mentioned. Jessica wanted to raise the issue of sexual identity as a relevant topic, but didn't. She remembers:

> I was aware, I was tense the whole time thinking, 'I want to say something. This issue needs to be raised.' But I just didn't feel I could do it. I felt that as soon as I stood up and opened my mouth that I would either just reinforce what people thought already or suspected, or it would just be incriminating myself. I just couldn't get that thought out of my mind . . . I just felt the incrimination so much I couldn't do it. I was thinking on the way here this morning: If there had been one other person, say Allison who I had come out to before, I'd have built up a relationship with her by now to have actually said to her at coffee break, 'Mention this', and she would have done because she wouldn't have that fear. It wouldn't have been the same kind of issue for her . . . I just felt horrible. I felt like a coward and I'd let myself down. I felt really strongly about it. I got home in a hell of a mood. I just felt like: 'Here's me sort of purporting all this stuff about bringing the issue out in other ways, and when I get the chance to professionally, I don't do it . . . I really

feel so isolated . . . I didn't have the confidence because I didn't know what the reaction would be.'

The issue of self-denial was also becoming increasingly important with regard to her relationships with pupils and the maintenance of her self-integrity. Jessica remained unsure how she would react if a pupil made a derogatory remark about lesbianism to her or at her:

> It worries me because I know what's going to happen, I'm going to get very uptight and want to say something. But I know also that I might think that would give me away if I do. But if I don't, I'm almost condoning it so I wouldn't be able to deal with that either.

However, on the increasingly numerous occasions when Jessica gets asked by pupils about her personal life she has opted for covering strategies to cope with the situation. Recalling a situation when she was transporting a school team to a match, Jessica commented:

> It was, 'Miss, I'm not being funny right, but Suzanne said that if you wear rings on your little fingers it means that you are a lesbian.' I was thinking: 'I'm glad I'm looking forwards and I'm glad that they can't see any kind of expression that might have crossed my face, or changes in the colour of my skin.' I just turned around and said: 'Oh, that's interesting. I wonder how she knows that?' I laughed and played for time. Coping strategies coming in . . . I was dying really. I kept thinking: 'They know. They've sussed, and they are just looking for confirmation.' I get asked about boyfriends all the time. Am I married? Am I engaged? Am I going to have kids? All that kind of stuff. I evade it all the time. I joke with them, I don't cut them off, I don't get funny with them. I just say: 'Oh, I don't know. What do you reckon?' Throw it back at them.

These kinds of situations along with those where pupils make homophobic remarks are very threatening to Jessica and reinforce a sense of denial that she is increasingly finding difficult to cope with. Jessica remains unsure about how to deal with such situations and how far it would be possible for her to have a 'balanced' conversation with the pupils about the issue of sexual identity.

> There's going to be some that disagree and some that do agree, and you can have a nice chat and you can agree to differ. Well, I know that is no way for me. It's not up for discussion as far as I'm concerned. It's not an issue that is discussed, there are facts about it. That makes me sound totally extreme, or even radical, or narrow even on it. But as far as I'm concerned I can't accept that there are some people who are going to disagree with it. Disagree with me, how can I allow someone to disagree with the essence of me? It doesn't bear thinking about.

At the moment, Jessica is not explicitly out to any colleague in her school and is employing covering strategies to cope with the situation. There is a sense of daily denial. She still feels that she has some ideals left in relation to realizing her educational philosophy as a PE teacher coupled with being out and being herself with more people in a school situation. However, the ongoing dislocation and forced separation of her professional and personal life are exacting a heavy emotional toll on her. Jessica is keenly aware that for her to approximate her ideals will require a change of job in the immediate future in the hope of finding greater integration of self and situation.

> People don't have a positive image of a gay person at all. There are no positive role models. All the stereotypes tend to be negative. If you are talking about PE, there is only one stereotype that people are familiar with and that's the butch, dyke type. I don't think

they even contemplate a gay male PE teacher. They would probably convince themselves that they don't exist . . . I feel invisible on a lot of counts actually. I feel invisible sure, in terms of what I basically am in terms of my sexuality. I also feel invisible in as much that I haven't been able to make the contacts, either socially or professionally, that would give people a rounded idea of me.

MOMENTS FROM ALEXANDER'S STORY

Alexander is also in his late twenties. He is six feet tall, and weighs about fourteen stones. His muscular physique bears testimony to many years of hard training coupled with the blessings of good 'mesomorphic' genetics. Alexander excels at a range of sports but has been particularly successful in rugby which he has played at first-class level. As a teacher, Alexander, just like Jessica, is dynamic, articulate and outgoing. He gives a lot to the students he teaches in terms of energy and time. They, in turn, think highly of him. So do his fellow teachers who find him a committed and supportive colleague to work with; someone who gives a great deal to the life of the school and has developed the PE programme extensively in terms of, for example, developing health-related exercise modules. In many ways, Alexander has all the characteristics of the 'good' male PE teacher. All the characteristics except one that is. Alexander is gay. He has only recently explicitly come out to his mother following the early death of his father. The pain of losing his father, a man he idolized in many ways, also acted as a release and a stimulus for Alex to 'name' himself and take a new direction in his own life. What follows are some moments from his life in his own words.

> Growing up thinking you are gay in a strong working class family isn't my idea of fun. My Dad had a tough upbringing and sport, especially football, played a big part in his life. In fact, he almost turned professional but it didn't quite work out. He was a real 'man's man', a hard man. When I say that, he was hard but fair. But I think he found it very difficult to show his emotions. I can't ever remember him hugging me a lot as a child, not unless I made the first move. He would still get embarrassed when I gave him a hug in public sometimes when I went home for a visit. I think he was simply like many men of his generation.
>
> Sport was our connection, our bonding. He got me playing football for local teams as soon as I could walk and I was clearly talented. Then, when I was eleven I had the chance to get a scholarship to a direct grant school, but it played rugby. It was a quandary for my Dad for a while but to him, and my Mum, getting a good education and 'getting out' of the kinds of jobs they were locked into was all important. So I went and, lo and behold, I took to rugby easily. Again, without being big-headed, it was clear that I was talented in sport and the teachers recognized this. Mum came to watch when she could but she had a Saturday job. My Dad would come and watch every match and I knew he got a buzz from it when I played well. I remember when I played my first game of top-class rugby and I scored my first try. As I ran back I looked over into the crowd at him and you could feel the pride oozing out of him. He just wanted to shout: 'That's my son!' Funnily enough, even in those situations he found it difficult to show his emotions. After the game he just said: 'You did well out there today Alex, a pity about that missed tackle!' He would always deflect any compliment with humour. But that was my Dad.
>
> I miss my Dad like mad. His death has left a big hole in my life. It's difficult to say how much he meant to me. His death was a turning point for me in many ways. You see, although I love him and I know he loved me there was one thing we could never discuss,

and that was sexuality. I could never tell him I was gay. He just couldn't have coped with it. You see, in my Dad's world, and particularly in his world of work, the pub and sport, men were always 'real' men. That is, they were straight [heterosexual]. As I grew up I learnt from the jokes he would tell his mates, and later to me when I started playing rugby, that 'queers', 'faggots' and 'poofters' were a source of ridicule, something to be despised.

Other than the jokes we never spoke about gay men directly, that is as a topic in itself, but his views slipped out sometimes. I remember when one of the Fashanu brothers, Justin I think it was, 'came out' and said he was gay. I thought my old man was going to have a fit. There it was all over the sports page of the Sunday paper. He just could not believe that a professional footballer could be gay. When he did have to believe it because Fashanu confirmed it on the TV, his reaction was hostile. Something along the lines of: 'He should be banned. I wouldn't want to have a shower next to a queer. No thank you!' The AIDS issue has also brought out the worst in him. When Freddie Mercury [lead singer with Queen] died he just said: 'Good riddance to bad rubbish. That AIDS stuff will sort all those queers out.' Only a few years ago, I remember taking him and Mum out for a meal and my Dad got it into his head that the waiter was gay. Just from the way he talked, my Dad said he was gay. This made him nervous because, in my Dad's head, gay meant AIDS, and AIDS can be passed on by someone touching a plate that you eat off! Honestly, it really got to him. How do you fight that kind of ignorance when it's your own Dad? I tried to put him straight on some of the facts about AIDS but without much success I'm afraid.

Now all this kind of stuff was being reinforced by the sports I was involved in, and especially the rugby. At school, the big insult you gave another boy was to call him a 'queer' or a 'gay boy'. It was a standard form of put down in the school rugby team: 'What are you, queer or something?' And we would all laugh. I would laugh too but inside I felt very uneasy about it all. As I moved up the ranks in rugby the joking went on but I saw another side to all this, a violent side. We had played a game in London and after we had eaten and what have you, some of the guys in the third team who had travelled with us put out a general announcement that they were going to some bars for a bit of 'queer bashing'. I remember feeling my blood go cold as I watched five big drunken men set off to intimidate physically, perhaps harm, someone they had never met but were going to have a go at just because they were gay. By the time they got back to the coach to leave they were in a drunken stupor. But they remembered enough to tell us that they had taunted and roughed up a young guy coming out of a gay club. I sat there thinking how they would react if they knew I was gay.

And so on it went. I was trying to sort my life out with all this hatred going on around me. I began to feel I was different during adolescence. I learnt the game of going out with girls but I didn't feel right about it. I guess my emotional connections wanted to be made with men but first, I didn't know how to make the connections and second, I was scared to admit to myself that I was gay. I was so difficult to get a fix on. I could hardly go up to my Dad and say: 'Hey Dad, I think I'm queer. Can we have a chat about it?' You must be bloody joking! You couldn't talk to the teachers. I got on well with the PE teacher but he was married with kids, clearly straight, and he had never stopped negative comments or jokes being made about gays when we travelled with the rugby team or in the PE lessons, so nothing there for me. Also, I just didn't know anybody who was gay and who was 'out'. I had no reference points, nobody to talk things over with. It was a bad period in my life in that sense despite all the success I was getting elsewhere on the sports field.

As 'A' levels loomed I was asked by the PE teacher what I planned to do when I left. As usual I didn't have a bloody clue. So he suggested doing a degree in sports science or something like that as it would allow me to continue with my sport and get a qualification as well. As they say: 'It seemed like a good idea at the time.' So I applied, got the grades and got in. It was good being away from home. I missed my Mum a lot, I missed my Dad. But, again, I knew that me 'their son' going to university to get a degree made them as proud as hell. In fact, university was a Godsend. It gave me a bit of space away from my family to get to know myself. It wasn't all hunky dory though. I was still locked into the sports culture, or the jock culture I should say. As usual, I heard nothing positive said about gays and the underlying feelings of hostility clearly were still there. For example, at the Freshers' Bazaar where you can join all the clubs some of the big guys from the rugby club 'minced over' and joined the Lesbian and Gay Society but gave names of their friends in the rugby team. It was a source of great amusement in the bar later. I laughed about it while at the same time wishing I had the guts to go and join the society for real. Having said that, at the bazaar it was the one stand that I kept well clear of. Almost fear by association if you like. I guess I had to be more straight than straight to protect myself, to keep the front going.

A couple of months later I was in a pub and I saw one of the guys who was on the stand of the Lesbian and Gay Society. I scanned the pub to make sure that there was nobody there that I knew and then went over to talk to him. He was really great and made me feel at ease immediately. He was a very good listener. I guess he had to be because I spilled it all out, there and then in that pub. It was the first time I had ever talked to another person about myself being gay. It was a big weight off my shoulders. Mark was also good because he knew the kind of culture I was living in, he knew how jocks viewed lesbian and gay issues. So his advice was sensible. He didn't advocate some dramatic 'coming out' to the jocks or the rugby team as the consequences would be too severe. I remember laughing and saying that death would be a simpler alternative! No, he simply said it was about time I began to get to know myself and feel good about who I was. So we worked within the framework I was living in. He introduced me to some gay friends and gave me the addresses of gay support groups and some gay clubs. It was all new to me. I was excited and scared at the same time. Eventually, I met Gavin and it all happened. When it did it just felt so natural, so good, so right for me. I had said hello to myself. I wasn't afraid any more. I knew who I was.

Knowing I was gay and feeling good about my sexuality didn't help me much on a daily basis at university. I never came out to anyone on my sports science course, the PGCE course, or in the rugby team. You see, jock culture is based on the notion of straight sex. It's male dominated, and its about screwing women who are basically seen as objects for the pleasure of the lads. That may sound a bit harsh, but deep down inside that's how it works. I simply played my part when I had to. Most of the time I managed to detach myself from things more than most, that made them see me as 'serious' and a bit too much into academic work. But I also had all the right credentials. I could do all the sports well and I was a first team player in rugby, that counts for a lot. So when I went to a disco or a club I would dance the night away and leave with a girl to walk her home. The assumption was then made by the rest of the lads that I would, by definition, sleep with her. I never did and simply walked them home. When I felt that the women expected something more from me I made some lame excuse to get me out of the situation. But the point is the boys assumed I had done it. Like, next day they would say 'Have a good night Alex?', with a big grin on their faces. I would simply grin back and say 'Yes thanks'. I wasn't lying to them. I did have a good night, but not in the way they meant. So I got by. The rugby set up was a bit claustrophobic but I used the space that the travel away to rugby games gave me to visit gay clubs in some of the larger cities where I felt nobody would recognize me. I told the lads that I was going to stay with a friend in the city and made my way back to university on my own the next day.

Splitting my life in two carried on when I began teaching. I went in knowing that I would have to stay in the closet as far as teaching PE was concerned. All that has been confirmed by my experiences in this school. Even more so now that Clause 28 is around. Anyone who comes out now is dead professionally, they wouldn't last ten minutes before the governors got them out on some technicality or other. I remember the boss [headteacher] last year asked me about one of the candidates for a job in another subject because he had put down some qualifications that meant he could help with games. The boss said, only in passing, that the guy was 40-years-old and not married which wasn't a good 'sign', and that they had to be careful recruiting these days, especially if it was anything to do with kids in PE, not to get the 'wrong kind of person'. He meant gay of course. Single, male, 40, therefore possibly gay. Result, no interview. So can you imagine the headlines in the *Sun* if they found out that I was a full-time PE teacher and a full-time gay, 'Gay PE teacher watches children in showers.' Tell me about it!

Having said all that, because I look the part, and because of the rugby and so on, everyone just assumes I'm straight. Nobody has every asked me, kids or staff, if I'm gay. My masculinity has never been questioned. I've got all the right 'visible' credentials. Quite simply, they don't even conceptualize that a gay male PE teacher could exist. They just can't get their heads around that one. Can you imagine it, PE the bastion of masculinity, the makers of real men, has gays in their midst! So I just pass as straight because the question is never raised about whether I'm gay or not. I just let the assumption ride and never challenge it. For example, I flirt with some of the women teachers and we get on well, we have a great laugh. When there is a staff do I usually invite one of my female friends who I've met through the rugby club or the gym I use. We all have a good time and no questions asked. So in that sense being gay has not been a problem for me. I play the game.

In the last few years, I've become more and more dissatisfied about remaining in the closet at school and leading this double life. You see, two years ago I met Andy and we have been together ever since. I'm getting sick of denying his existence and talking at school about going off to see my 'girlfriend' at the weekend when I'm going to see him. We want to make a go of it and live together. Now clearly, if he moved up here with me that could cause some problems. It wouldn't take too long perhaps before something got back to the school and I would live in fear of that. But that issue won't arise. Andy has his own business and he has to stay put. That means I have to move. So what with my Dad's death, meeting Andy and all that goes with that I have had to come to some crucial decisions about the direction I'm going to go in from now on. I'm getting close to thirty now. My rugby is becoming less and less important to me and I've got into lots of other activities, gym work, just keeping fit basically and I really enjoy it. If I stay in teaching, particularly PE teaching, I don't think I will ever be able to come out publicly and I'll spend my professional life in the closet living a lie. I just don't want that any more.

I don't want to go and work as an employee in Andy's business as I feel the other staff might feel I have an unfair advantage over them. He's out. They know he is gay. So what I've done is got a job with a large sports marketing company in the same city. That way we can be together but I still maintain my independence in a financial sense, that's important to me. I suppose I could have got a job teaching in the area but what would have been the point, it would not be any different from here really. My Mum's been great about it all. She's met Andy and likes him a lot. I feel so good that she knows about me and accepts things as they are even though I don't think she really understands all the implications of me coming out. I still wonder what would have happened if I'd told my Dad. I guess I'll never know. Perhaps it's best that way. So that's it. I'm going to be out as far as you can in today's society, and I'm going to leave teaching at the end of this term. Scary, isn't it?

REFLECTIONS ON MOMENTS

These moments from the real life of Jessica and the fictional life of Alexander have been presented not with a view to being predictive or claiming that their experiences can be generalized to all lesbian and gay teachers in schools, but rather to present a view of schooling from a particular standpoint that for the most part has been repressed.[7] I have also attempted, via the use of their stories, to indicate how Alexander as a gay male PE teacher experiences school life in ways that differ from Jessica as a lesbian PE teacher. As Squirrell (1989b) makes clear from her own work with lesbian and gay teachers, there are clearly a number of differences in their experiences: 'Lesbians are liable to harassment for both their sexuality and their gender.' Consequently, as Rich (1980) argues, lesbian existence should not be viewed as a mirror image of either heterosexual or gay male relationships. Likewise, Faraday (1981) emphasizes, that lesbians should not be seen as the direct counterparts of the gay male. 'It is essential that notions of the lesbian are reconceptualized within the context of her oppressed social position as a woman and not as a "female homosexual"' (p. 112). In relation to this, Woods (1992) argues that while all lesbian and gay teachers are targets of homophobia, those who teach subjects that are not consistent with traditional gender roles are particularly vulnerable to homophobic accusations.

> The lesbian physical educator is perhaps the most vulnerable target of all. She (and all other female physical educators) is frequently assumed to be lesbian whether or not she publicly discloses her sexual orientation . . . Within the firmly entrenched male domain of sport and physical education there is an assumed relationship between traditional gender roles and sexuality . . . To put it more simply, to be athletic is to be equated with masculinity and masculine women are labelled as lesbian. Therefore, athletic women are stereotyped as lesbian . . . Allegations of lesbianism are used to intimidate and harass women in physical education and sport. (p. 91)

Having acknowledged these differences, it is important to recognize how both Jessica and Alexander experience educational institutions and how they relate these experiences to other moments in their lives. The strategies they are forced to adopt to cope with specific situations provide important insights into a reality that is oppositional to the taken-for-granted reality of the dominant and privileged sexual class in schools, that is, heterosexuals. In commenting upon the benefits of adopting a lesbian standpoint Harding (1991) comments:

> In identifying what one can see with the help of a lesbian standpoint, I do not point exclusively to insights about lesbians. The standpoint epistemologies have a different logic. Just as the research and scholarship that begin from the standpoint of women more generally is not exclusively about women, so these insights are not exclusively about lesbians. The point is that starting from the (many different) daily activities of lesbians enables us to see things that might otherwise have been invisible to us, not just about those lives but about heterosexual women's lives and men's lives, straight as well as gay. (p. 252)

Bensimon (1992) also acknowledges that viewing the public sphere (structured by the discourse of compulsory heterosexuality) from the position of those in the margins can provide a different vision of the academy. This vision can expand the unidimensional and partial story of those situated in the centre by provoking a different understanding of their own situation as well as of the situation they create for others. Therefore, by presenting the struggles that Jessica and Alexander face on a daily basis to construct their lives and maintain their sense of self in the public spaces that the school provides, my intention has been to provide insights into how schools, as patriarchal institutions that are ideologically and culturally heterosexual, create and maintain a set of inequitable circumstances that exercise a level of control over the 'private' lives of lesbian and gay teachers. My intention has also been to illustrate how these circumstances lead these teachers to experience 'public' school life in ways that are hard to imagine for those (the majority) who are the beneficiaries of the privileges of heterosexuality. Finally, by focusing upon the enforced split both Jessica and Alexander have to make between their public (professional) and private (personal) lives, along with the identity management strategies they are compelled to draw upon to cope in specific situations, I have attempted to illuminate how their experiences as a lesbian and a gay PE teacher are structured and shaped by existing sets of social relationships that are oppressive. To briefly illustrate this point I want to focus upon the public–private divide as a common feature of an oppressive mechanism that operates in the lives of both Jessica and Alexander.

THE PUBLIC–PRIVATE DIVIDE

Jessica's and Alexander's silence and invisibility, along with the identity management strategies they are forced to adopt, are structured by a heterosexual hegemony that for Burrell and Hearn (1989), 'tends to construct lesbians and gay men as isolated exceptions, so that they and their sexuality come to be seen, by many heterosexuals, at least, as private and individual, even as personal "problems"' (p. 23). To highlight this issue, I want to focus on one of the strategies that Jessica and Alexander have adopted to protect their substantial sense of self which involved maintaining a split between their public (work) life and their private (personal) life. This strategy was evident in the study by Woods (1992) who worked with North American lesbian PE teachers.

> The participants justified their personal/professional split in many ways, describing it as a norm for all teachers, as an individual right, as a necessity, or as a given for lesbians. All experienced conflict around separating their lesbian identity from their teacher identity. This conflict took the form of both resentment and fear: resentment because there was no overlap between their two worlds, and fear because there was. Many of the participants described making this separation as a choice, but in various ways, their words and experiences contradicted this description. As lesbians, they believed disclosure of their sexual orientation would cost them their jobs, and as female physical educators, they assumed they were already stereotyped as lesbians. Both these assumptions shaped the way they experienced being a lesbian physical educator. From their perspective, the only real choices were to conceal their sexual orientation to stay in teaching or to leave teaching altogether. (p. 102)

The strategy of splitting the private and public, the personal and the professional, has been seen to operate in the lives of other lesbian and gay teachers in schools and other forms of organization (Hall, 1989; Squirrell, 1989a, b). Of course, this is not to suggest that heterosexual teachers do not draw upon this and other coping strategies (Nias, 1989; Pollard, 1982; Woods, 1979). However, due to their positioning as heterosexuals their experiences of this private/public split differ dramatically from those of Jessica and Alexander. Equally, the consequences, as described earlier, of not rigorously maintaining this split are very different for lesbian and gay teachers when compared to their heterosexual colleagues. For example, one likely consequence of not maintaining this split for lesbian and gay teachers is that they would face discrimination on the basis of their sexual identity in applying for jobs or gaining promotion within schools. Therefore, paradoxically, while the private/public split offers a form of protection against discrimination, it also obscures the inequities experienced by lesbian and gay teachers in the public sphere of the school.

Jessica and Alexander's identity management strategies are framed within the 'professional' expectation, held by many of their colleagues, that one's private home life should be kept separate from one's public work life. In particular, issues of sexual identity are commonly assumed to be 'private' affairs that should not be brought into the public and professional world of work. Kitzinger (1987) suggests this view is informed by a liberal humanist ideology that is a fundamental faith for many middle-class Western intellectuals, which means questions are rarely asked about how this value system can 'serve the interests of patriarchy in ensuring the continuing oppression of women' (p. 192). However, Kitzinger, and others (Bensimon, 1992; Hearn, 1987; Khayatt, 1992; Walby, 1989) have revealed the deceptiveness of this distinction between public and private spheres and how, in fact, this dualism is very much rooted in the ideology of patriarchy and the key sets of patriarchal practices that relate to compulsory heterosexuality. In this sense, due to his membership of the social category of 'male', Alexander clearly experiences this forced divide in relation to life in school differently than Jessica in that he is the beneficiary of some of the privileges that go with being a male in a patriarchal culture. He also feels less threatened because during his educational career his masculinity and sexuality has never been openly questioned. Having said this, for both Alexander and Jessica the private/public distinction is partial, distorting, and perverse. As Bensimon (1992, p. 99) argues:

> It is partial because . . . the public/private distinction is derived from a vision of the public that takes into account only the reality of the dominant sexual class. It is distorting because . . . it normalizes sexuality as heterosexuality. And it is perverse, because . . . the public/private distinction provides a distinction for not bringing about change. (I use the term perverse to convey the terrible wrong that is committed when an argument is based on a logic that has the capacity of making an oppressive situation appear rational.)

The work of Shilling (1991) on the spatial dimensions of social interaction and reproduction in schools is extremely useful in highlighting the partial and distorting nature of the private/public divide. For Shilling, space is no longer seen just as an environment in which interaction takes place, but is taken to be deeply implicated in the production of individual identities and social inequalities. Drawing on Giddens' (1984) theory of structuration, Shilling focuses attention on the concepts of 'locale' and 'regionalization' to illustrate how social space is implicated in the production of gender inequalities in schools. In particular, he points to the staffroom as a gendered locale:

> This locale is also regionalised on the basis of gender and while the staffroom may be a 'haven' for some, it is also used as an area where male teachers exert their dominance over women . . . Consequently, while the staffroom may be a place for men to relax, unwind, and escape from the pressures of classroom teaching, it may not offer the same benefits to many women. Furthermore, men not only draw on patriarchal cultural rules (i.e. sexist humour) to exert control over women in the specific locale of the staffroom; they may also organise resources within the staffroom itself to symbolically reflect their position of dominance. . . . The patriarchal cultural rules and resources drawn upon by male teachers make this part of the school an area embedded with different meanings for women and men. (pp. 38–9)

The patriarchal cultural rules and resources that shape interactions in the staffroom are also laden with different meanings for lesbian teachers who experience further inequalities associated with their sexual identity in this locale. For Jessica, the staffroom and other supposed back regions such as staff socials and informal gatherings in the pub, are certainly not places where she can relax, repair her sense of identity and disclose aspects of her self. Indeed, in these 'back' regions for others, Jessica is in a 'front' situation where she is 'on guard' and has to deny her sense of self and identity in ways that can cause emotional stress rather than bring about emotional repair. Alexander feels a similar pressure to protect his sexual identity, for example, he talks about visiting his 'girlfriend'. However, he experiences less tension in social gatherings in school than Jessica simply because male PE teachers are assumed to be heterosexual. Therefore, heterosexual women and men may be able to openly disclose aspects of themselves and their lives to others if they so choose in terms of, for example, mentioning what they did over the weekend with their husbands/wives/ partners or families. However, this option is not available to Jessica or Alexander who, feeling themselves to be under surveillance and being conscious of constant assessment from the vantage point of heterosexuality, carefully edit their conversations with other teachers, even in back regions, so as not to reveal their lesbian and gay identities. As Khayatt (1992, p. 72) comments:

> What this means in the everyday life of a lesbian teacher is that she may not take her lover to staff functions, may not wear a ring or labrys or give any indication of her sexuality. She cannot talk openly about her weekend activities – in short, her life must remain invisible. This is in contrast to her heterosexual sister, who notes her attachment to a man by wearing a wedding (or engagement) band, who is encouraged to talk endlessly about her relationship, and whose pregnancy is celebrated as proof of his virility and her fertility.

In the front regions when they are teaching and interacting with children, Jessica and Alexander feel similar pressures. Therefore, in front and back stage regions both are denied an essential freedom involving the freedom to interact in the public space, without having to hide their sexual identity, and construct their lives in school according to the prescribed script of assumed heterosexuality (Bensimon, 1992). This right is systematically granted to heterosexual teachers but systematically denied to Jessica and Alexander in a way that legitimizes the partial and distorting nature of the public/private dichotomy.

The partiality of the public/private dichotomy is further revealed when we consider how, for Jessica and Alexander, these two spheres are not mutually exclusive but interactive. For example, the public sphere is able to impact significantly upon their private lives in terms of where they spend their spare time with their partners. Similarly, Jessica's choice to live away from the catchment area of the school was informed by her concern to protect her lesbian identity from pupils, other teachers and parents. Even though Jessica lives close to a major city and Alexander lives in a large city that provides them with spaces to 'escape' to, their concerns to guard against exposure give a real sense of what Burrell and Hearn (1989) call 'institutional closure'. According to them this, 'brings into play a particular, and sometimes very powerful, set of organizational controls over time and space, over sexual time and sexual bodies' (p. 22).

The distorting nature of the public/private dichotomy is also evident in the manner in which this dichotomy reduces being lesbian and gay to sexuality. Here, the common assumption is that being a lesbian or gay is simply an issue of what a person wants to do in private and with whom. However, as the moments from Jessica and Alexander's life reveal, their lesbian and gay identity is central to their very being as a person and shapes the way they relate to the world as a whole. Yet, in the ideologically heterosexual school environment, their sexual identity is denied and their public life is dominated by a range of strategies that are designed to conceal from others what

Jessica called the 'essence' of herself. Therefore, the pressures to keep their sexual identity a private and invisible matter forces Jessica and Alexander to restrict their public interactions with both children and other teachers. That is, the private impacts upon the public.

Finally, Bensimon (1992) comments that the public/private distinction is perverse, 'because it sets up a situation which, in effect delegitimizes complaints about inequalities in the public sphere that arise from the personal choices one makes in and about the private sphere' (pp. 107–8). Woods (1992) also comments on how defining sexual identity as a personal and private matter acts to deflect institutions from developing non-discrimination policies on the basis of sexual identity, 'When sexual orientation is viewed from this perspective, the institutional forces that shape and define oppression are not questioned . . . The onus of change is placed on the individual and not the system. One consequence of a person-change perspective is person-blame' (pp. 114–15). This stance allows heterosexual teachers and administrators to appear liberal and tolerant with regard to lesbian and gay issues without having to recognize and address both the personalized, sociopolitical and institutionalized aspects of homophobia and heterosexism that renders many of their lesbian and gay colleagues invisible. Essentially, as Bensimon (1992, p. 101) argues:

> The public/private distinction universalizes sexuality as heterosexuality, blinding those who belong to the dominant sexual class – women and men – to the very specific ways in which they impose invisible and intolerable existences on lesbian faculty. The invisibility of lesbian faculty is maintained by the public/private distinction.

Having focused upon the public/private distinction and the manner in which it operates to enforce the silence that Jessica and Alexander experience in their school life, it is important to note that my intention has not been to portray either of them as a passive 'victim'. As Woods (1992, p. 112) notes regarding the lesbian PE teachers she interviewed:

> Individually as lesbians in physical education, the participants challenged the under-pinnings of their oppression. As women, they defied stereotypical definitions of femininity and as athletes, assumed roles that women historically have been barred or discouraged from assuming. As physical educators, they broke new ground for young girls and boys, teaching and modelling the athletic potential of females. As lesbians, they silently, but visibly rejected women's dependence upon men for economic support and emotional validation. Consequently, their presence alone challenged the foundations upon which homophobia, sexism and heterosexism are built.

In this regard, it would seem that Jessica, more so than Alexander, has actively resisted compulsory heterosexuality and challenged it in the public sphere. Good examples of this include her joining the Women's Group at her polytechnic and giving a public talk on sexuality. Likewise, her regular participation in the London Gay Pride march, her selective coming out to a colleague at school, and her reluctance to adopt passing strategies to conceal her sexual identity, are all acts of resistance that carry a number of risks for Jessica that should not be underestimated. Indeed, it needs to be recognized that even when Jessica and Alexander opt to be silent about their sexual identity this can be seen as a form of resistance. As Bensimon (1992) argues, this form of resistance is grounded in the refusal to be a victim and is a source of power to deprive heterosexuals of the satisfaction inherent, 'in the act of being understanding and tolerant of the "negative" other without conceding how their heterosexual privilege and advantage contribute to the heterosexist structures that make lesbian existence oppressive' (p. 109). Therefore, when Jessica and Alexander choose to remain silent this provides them with a form of resistance in which the conscious refusal to be defined as a victim provides them with a sense of agency. It also resists the final irony for many lesbian and gay persons who decide to come out explicitly only to find themselves 'tokenized' by their colleagues. Commenting on this paradoxical situation for many lesbians Hall (1989, p. 135) notes:

> Stylized out of existence, she forfeits her private mutinies, cannot mobilize the resistance necessary to shield her individuality from engulfment by the collective purpose of the organization. Homogenized, the token corporate lesbian becomes the consummate 'organization (wo)man'.

CLOSING COMMENTS

Having recognized the complexities of the dilemmas that Jessica and Alexander face, it is important to emphasize that with regard to their own invisibility, silence and daily denial of self, they feel that in the present cultural climate their situation is likely to worsen rather than improve. This is particularly so given contemporary new right agendas on sexuality and education in which a significant moment was the 1988 Local Government (Amendment) Act.[8] This Act included Section 28 which has contributed to an atmosphere of fear and uncertainty regarding discussions of sexuality. As Kelly (1992, p. 23) argues:

> While . . . most legal opinions view it [Section 28] as an extremely poorly drafted piece of legislation, it has nonetheless been a powerful brake on attempts to challenge heterosexism in schools in particular, and society in general.

Given this cultural climate, both Jessica's and Alexander's pessimism about the possibilities of finding congruence between their sense of self and the school context may be well founded. However, this is not to suggest that nothing can be done and there has been mounting resistance to Section 28 along with the social injustices perpetuated by homophobia and heterosexism from a variety of sources (Epstein, 1994; Kelly, 1992; Stop the Clause Education Group, 1989). While challenges can, and should, be mounted against national policies, Jessica's and Alexander's stories, by bringing into sharp relief the consequences of heterosexual privilege that so many take for granted, emphasizes the need for teachers in schools and institutes of higher education to reflect upon their own implicit support for, and acceptance of, homophobia and heterosexism in their places of work and begin to challenge actively these oppressive ideologies (Dewar, 1990; Flintoff, 1993; La Salle, 1992; Scraton, 1993). In relation to this Griffin (1992b, p. 263) comments:

> In the same way that it is important for white people to speak out against racism and for men to speak out against sexism, it is important for heterosexual people to object to antigay harassment, discrimination and prejudice. It isn't enough to provide silent, private support for lesbian friends. To remain silent signals consent.

Consequently, Griffin and Genasci (1990) argue that taking action against homophobia and heterosexism is the responsibility of all teachers regardless of sexual identity. Their own work provides some important guidelines that can assist teachers to recognize, and change, their own homophobic and heterosexist attitudes and actions. These include, systematically monitoring the school curriculum and institutional policy for homophobic and heterosexist bias, so that a safe and affirming climate is developed which is based on an acceptance, and celebration of difference, for all members of the educational community. In such a climate, Jessica and Alexander would no longer be intimidated and fearful. They would not need to deny their sense of self on a daily basis nor lead a 'double life'. They could be explicitly out if they chose this option and, like their other lesbian and gay colleagues, would then be able to enrich the life of the school in so many ways.

NOTES

1. I have chosen not to use the word 'homosexual' throughout this paper as it is gender neutral and is frequently used in relation to gay men's experiences, which are then assumed to be representative of lesbian experiences. This not only renders lesbians invisible but also makes invisible the sexism that exists in both the heterosexual and gay communities (Frye, 1983; Kitzinger, 1987). While the term 'homosexual' does appear in the gay and lesbian literature, I have felt it more appropriate to use the more cumbersome terms lesbian and gay (for men) so that it is clear that there are indeed differences both within and between these communities.

    Similarly, I have chosen to use the term sexual identity rather than sexual orientation. Identity implies more than the choice of same sex partners; it recognizes that being a lesbian or gay man is about developing an identity and (for some) a politics of resistance to patriarchal heterosexual hegemony. It further suggests that lesbians and gay men make active choices to develop their identities and that these are different in more than 'orientation' to the identities developed by heterosexual men and women. The term identity also allows for the existence of different lesbian and gay identities which recognizes the complexities and differences that exist in the lives of lesbian and gay men in terms of, for example, race, ethnicity, social class, ableness, linguistic and religious affiliations, and politics. My thanks to Alison Dewar for clarifying these issues for me.

2. It needs to be emphasized that I have created the character of Alexander. He is a fiction constructed from my own positioning as a white, heterosexual male. This creation was necessary because I have never met a gay male PE teacher who was explictly out. This kind of writing has been used elsewhere to good effect in the services of a critical agenda. For example, disenchanted with traditional portrayals of organizational life, Tierney (1993) used ethnographic fiction to highlight the background and personalities involved in significant changes undertaken in one university where a sexual orientation clause was added to its statement of non-discrimination. In terms of evaluating ethnographic fictions, Tierney suggested the reader might like to ask the following questions: What is learned from the text? Are the characters believable? Are there lessons to be learned from the text for my own life? Is the situation plausible? Where does the author fit in the formation of the text? And finally, has the text enabled me to reflect on my own life and work? I hope the reader will judge Alexander's story in relation to these questions. For a further consideration of ethnographic fiction in relation to other ways of writing and representing lives, see Sparkes (in press).

3. Homophobia, according to Lorde (1984, p. 45), is 'the fear of feelings of love for members of one's own sex and therefore the hatred of those feelings in others'. This fear and hatred often leads to name calling, threats of violence and, even more dangerously, acts of violence against lesbian and gay people. That is, homophobia is expressed by people through overt, deliberate and harmful language and behaviour. However, as Lenskyj (1991) notes, this term should not be understood in purely individual or psychological terms since homophobic violence is not confined to random, individual acts. She suggests that institutions such as the

church, the courts and the educational system are responsible for homophobic violence when, for example, they bar lesbians and gay men from holding office, or deny them custody of their children, or fail to include sexual identity as prohibited grounds for discrimination.

4. Closely associated with homophobia is heterosexism which Lenskyj (1991) argues remains the dominant perspective of a patriarchal culture. According to Harris (1990), heterosexism is a set of beliefs, attitudes and practices which presents and promotes heterosexual social/ sexual relationships and lifestyles as the norm. It therefore sees such relationships and life cycles as being superior to any others and, in extreme cases, considers such alternatives as unacceptable and unnatural. Inherent in such beliefs is the right of dominance of one group over others whereby a variety of privileges and opportunities are denied to non-heterosexual people.

5. It needs to be acknowledged that while my attention is given primarily to the impact of heterosexism and homophobia in, and on, the life of Jessica, that these intersect and operate in combination with a range of other forms of oppression relating to, for example, social class, gender, race, ethnicity, ableness and age. Consequently, my focus on heterosexism and homophobia is not intended to privilege these forms of oppression and domination over other forms that also need to be challenged.

6. Further moments from Jessica's life are considered by Sparkes (1994a). The ethical and methodological dilemmas and tensions associated with my collaborative research relationship with Jessica from my position as a male heterosexual, the problematic nature of voice in life history work, issues or representation, and the potential for producing social change in this kind of research are considered by Sparkes (1994b). This work is part of a larger life history project that focuses on the lives of PE teachers (Schempp *et al.*, 1993; Sparkes, 1992; Sparkes and Templin, 1992; Sparkes *et al.*, 1990, 1993; Templin *et al.*, 1991, 1994).

7. Few studies have focused on the experiences of lesbian, bisexual and gay teachers. For some exceptions see Epstein (1994), Griffin (1991, 1992a, b), Harbeck (1992), Olsen (1987), Squirrell (1989a, b). In recent years, radical feminist scholars, in particular, have begun to analyse the experiences of lesbians in sport (Dewar, 1993; Griffin, 1992b; Lenskyj, 1986, 1990, 1991; Palzkill, 1990). Some insights have also been provided into the sports experiences of gay men (Pronger, 1990a, b; Rotella and Murray, 1991). However, studies that have specifically considered the experiences of lesbian, gay and bisexual PE teachers in the context of schooling are very scarce (Grossman, 1992). There are rare exceptions. For example, the phenomenological investigations informed by oppression theory of S. Woods (1990, 1992) reveal how homophobia and heterosexism envelop the world of lesbian physical educators. On the experiences of gay male PE teachers, there is nothing.

8. For more detailed discussions of Section 28 see Epstein (1994), Kelly (1992), Saunders and Spraggs (1989), and Stop the Clause Education Group (1989). Also see Harris (1990) who points out the following provisions of Section 28 as relevant: (1) A local authority shall not (a) intentionally promote homosexuality or publish material with the intention of promoting homosexuality; (b) promote the teaching in any maintained school of the acceptability of homosexuality as a pretended family relationship. (2) Nothing in subsection (1) above shall be taken to prohibit the doing of anything for the purpose of treating or preventing the spread of disease. For full details of Section 28, see DES (1988); see also Porter and Weeks (1991).

REFERENCES

Ball, S. (1972) 'Self and identity in the context of deviance: The case of criminal abortion', in Scott, R. and Douglas, J. (eds), *Theoretical Perspectives on Deviance*. New York: Basic Books, pp. 173–89.

Barone, T. (1992) 'Beyond theory and method: a case of critical storytelling', *Theory Into Practice*, **XXXI**(2), 142–6.

Bensimon, E. (1992) 'Lesbian existence and the challenge to normative constructions of the academy', *Journal of Education*, **174**(3), 98–113.

Burrell, G. and Hearn, J. (1989) 'The sexuality of organization', in Hearn, J., Sheppard, D., Tancred-Sheriff, P. and Burrell, G. (eds), *The Sexuality of Organization*. London: Sage, pp. 1–27.

DES (1988) *Local Government Act 1988: Section 28: DES Circular 88/90*. London: Department of Education and Science.

Dewar, A. (1990) 'Oppression and privilege in physical education teacher education: Struggles in the negotiation of gender in a university programme', in Kirk, D. and Tinning, R. (eds), *Physical Education, Curriculum and Culture: Critical Issues in the Contemporary Crisis*. Lewes: Falmer Press, 67–99.

Dewar, A. (1993) 'Will all the generic women in sport please stand up? Challenges facing feminist sport sociology', *Quest*, **45**, 211–29.

Epstein, D. (1994) *Challenging Lesbian and Gay Inequalities in Education*. Milton Keynes: Open University Press.

Faraday, A. (1981) 'Liberating lesbian research', in Plummer, K. (ed.), *The Making of the Modern Homosexual*. London: Hutchinson, pp. 53–67.

Flintoff, A. (1993) 'Gender, physical education and initial teacher education', in Evans, J. (ed.) *Equality, Education and Physical Education*. Lewes: Falmer Press, pp. 184–204.

Frye, M. (1983) *The Politics of Reality: Essays in Feminist Theory*. New York: The Crossing Press.

Giddens, A. (1984) *The Constitution of Society*. Cambridge: Polity Press.

Griffin, P. (1991) 'Identity management strategies among lesbian and gay educators', *International Journal of Qualitative Studies in Education*, **4**(3), 189–202.

Griffin, P. (1992a) 'Lesbian and gay educators: opening the classroom closet', *Empathy*, **3**(1), 25–8.

Griffin, P. (1992b) 'Changing the game: homophobia, sexism, and lesbians in sport', *Quest*, **44**(2), 251–65.

Griffin, P. and Genasci, J. (1990) 'Addressing homophobia in physical education: responsibilities for teachers', in Messner, M. and Sabo, D. (eds), *Sport, Men and the Gender Order: Critical Feminist Perspectives*. Champaign, IL: Human Kinetics Press, pp. 211–21.

Grossman, A. (1992) 'Inclusion, not exclusion: regulation service delivery to lesbian, gay and bisexual youth', *Journal of Physical Education, Recreation and Dance*, April, pp. 16–19.

Hall, M. (1989) 'Private experiences in the public domain: Lesbians in organizations', in Hearn, J., Sheppard, D., Tancred-Sheriff, P. and Burrell, G. (eds), *The Sexuality of Organization*. London: Sage, pp. 125–38.

Harbeck, K. (ed.) (1992) *Coming Out of the Classroom Closet: Gay and Lesbian Students, Teachers and Curricula*. New York: Harrington Park Press.

Harding, S. (1991) *Whose Science? Whose Knowledge?* Milton Keynes: Open University Press.

Harris, S. (1990) *Lesbian and Gay Issues in the English Classroom: The Importance of Being Honest*. Milton Keynes: Open University Press.

Hearn, J. (1987) *The Gender of Oppression*. Brighton: Harvester Wheatsheaf.

Kelly, L. (1992) 'Not in front of the children: responding to right wing agendas on sexuality and education', in Arnot, M. and Barton, L. (eds), *Voicing Concerns: Sociological Perspectives on Contemporary Educational Reforms*. Oxford: Triangle Books, pp. 21–40.

Khayatt, M. (1992) *Lesbian Teachers: An Invisible Presence*. New York: State University, New York Press.

Kitzinger, C. (1987) *The Social Construction of Lesbianism*. London: Sage.

La Salle, L. (1992) 'Exploring campus intolerance: A textual analysis of comments concerning lesbian, gay, and bisexual people'. Paper presented at the annual meeting of the American Educational Research Association, San Francisco, April.

Lenskyj, H. (1986) *Out of Bounds: Women, Sport and Sexuality*. Ontario: The Women's Press.

Lenskyj, H. (1990) 'Power and play: Gender and sexuality issues in sport and physical activity', *International Review for the Sociology of Sport*, **25**(3), 235–43.

Lenskyj, H. (1991) 'Combating homophobia in sport and physical education', *Sociology of Sport Journal*, **8**, 61–9.

Lorde, A. (1984) *Sister Outsider*. Trumansberg, NY: Crossing Press.

Nias, J. (1985) 'A more distant drummer: teacher development as the development of the self', in Barton, L. and Walker, S. (eds), *Education and Social Change*. London: Croom Helm, pp. 3–28.

Nias, J. (1989) *Primary Teachers Talking*. London: Routledge.

Olsen, M. (1987) 'A study of gay and lesbian teachers', *Journal of Homosexuality*, 13(4), 73–81.

Palzkill, B. (1990) 'Between gym shoes and high-heels – the development of a lesbian identity and existence in top class sport', *International Review for the Sociology of Sport*, 25(3), 221–33.

Pollard, A. (1982) 'A model of classroom coping strategies', *British Journal of Sociology of Education*, 3, 19–37.

Porter, K. and Weeks, J. (eds) (1991) *Between the Acts*. London: Routledge.

Pronger, B. (1990a) 'Gay jocks: A phenomenology of gay men in athletics', in Messner, M. and Sabo, D. (eds), *Sport, Men and the Gender Order: Critical Feminist Perspectives*. Champaign, Ill.: Human Kinetics Press, pp. 141–52.

Pronger, B. (1990b) *The Arena of Masculinity: Sports, Homosexuality and the Meaning of Sex*. London: GMP Publishers.

Rich, A. (1980) 'Compulsory heterosexuality and lesbian existence', *Signs*, 5(4), 631–60.

Rotella, R. and Murray, M. (1991) 'Homophobia, the world of sport, and sport psychology consulting', *The Sport Psychologist*, 5(4), 255–369.

Saunders, S. and Spraggs, G. (1989) 'Section 28 and education', in Jones, C. and Mahoney, P. (eds), *Learning Our Lines*. London: The Women's Press, pp. 79–128.

Schempp, P., Sparkes, A. and Templin, T. (1993) 'The micropolitics of teacher induction', *American Educational Research Journal*, 30(3), 447–72.

Scraton, S. (1993) 'Equality, coeducation and physical education in secondary schooling', in Evans, J. (ed.), *Equality, Education and Physical Education*. Lewes: Falmer Press, pp. 139–53.

Shilling, C. (1991) 'Social space, gender inequalities and educational differentiation', *British Journal of Sociology of Education*, 12(1), 23–44.

Sikes, P., Measor, L. and Woods, P. (1985) *Teachers' Careers: Crises and Continuities*. Lewes: Falmer Press.

Sparkes, A. (1992) 'The changing nature of teachers' work: School governors and curriculum control in physical education', in Armstrong, N. (ed.), *New Directions in Physical Education (Volume 2): Towards a National Curriculum*. Champaign, Ill.: Human Kinetics Press, pp. 1–31.

Sparkes, A. (1994a) 'Self, silence and invisibility as a beginning teacher: A life history of lesbian experience', *British Journal of Sociology of Education*, 15(1), 93–118.

Sparkes, A. (1994b) 'Life histories and the issue of voice: Reflections on an emerging relationship', *International Journal of Qualitative Studies in Education*, 7(2), 165–83.

Sparkes, A. (1995) 'Writing people: The dual crises of representation and legitimation in qualitative inquiry', *Quest*, 47, 158–95.

Sparkes A. and Templin, T. (1992) 'Life histories and physical education teachers: exploring the meanings of marginality', in Sparkes, A. (ed.), *Research in Physical Education and Sport: Exploring Alternative Visions*. Lewes: Falmer Press, pp. 118–45.

Sparkes, A., Templin, T. and Schempp, P. (1990) 'The problematic nature of a career in a marginal subject: Some implications for teacher education programmes', *Journal of Education for Teaching*, 16(1), 3–28.

Sparkes, A., Templin, T. and Schempp, P. (1993) 'Exploring dimensions of marginality: reflecting on the life histories of physical education teachers', *Journal of Teaching in Physical Education*, 12(4), 386–98.

Squirrell, G. (1989a) 'In passing . . . teachers and sexual orientation', in Acker, S. (ed.), *Teachers, Gender and Careers*. Lewes: Falmer Press, pp. 87–106.

Squirrell, G. (1989b) 'Teachers and issues of sexual orientation', *Gender and Education*, 1(1), 17–34.

Stop the Clause Education Group (1989) *Section 28: A Guide for Schools, Teachers and Governors*. London: ALTARF.

Templin, T., Sparkes, A. and Schempp, P. (1991) 'The professional life cycle of a retired physical education teacher: a tale of bitter disengagement', *Physical Education Review*, **14**(2), 143–56.

Templin, T., Sparkes, A., Grant, B. and Schempp, P. (1994) 'Matching the self: The paradoxical case and life history of a late career teacher/coach', *Journal of Teaching in Physical Education*, **13**(3), 274–94.

Tierney, W. (1993) 'The cedar closet', *International Journal of Qualitative Studies in Education*, **6**(4), 313–14.

Walby, S. (1989) 'Theorising patriarchy', *Sociology*, **23**(2), 213–34.

Woods, P. (1979) *The Divided School*. London: Routledge and Kegan Paul.

Woods, P. (1983) *Sociology and the School: An Interactionist Viewpoint*. London: Routledge and Kegan Paul.

Woods, P. (1984) 'Teacher, self and curriculum', in Goodson, I. and Ball, S. (eds), *Defining the Curriculum*. Lewes: Falmer Press, pp. 239–61.

Woods, P. (1990) *Teacher Skills and Strategies*. Lewes: Falmer Press.

Woods, P. (1993) 'Managing marginality: Teacher development through grounded life history', *British Educational Research Journal*, **19**(5), 447–65.

Woods, S. (1990) 'The Contextual Realities of Being a Lesbian Physical Education Teacher: Living in Two Worlds', doctoral dissertation, University of Massachusetts at Amherst. *Dissertation Abstracts International*, **51**(3), 788. (Order No. ADG 90-22761).

Woods, S. (1992) 'Describing the experience of lesbian physical educators: a phenomenological study', in Sparkes, A. (ed.), *Research In Physical Education and Sport: Exploring Alternative Visions*. Lewes: Falmer Press, pp. 90–117.

Chapter 13

New Directions for Physical Education Teacher Education in England and Wales

Chris Laws

INTRODUCTION

It has become a truism to say that the only permanent thing in this world is change and teacher education in England and Wales is no exception to this observation.

Even before the publication of the proposals for reform of initial teacher training (ITT) in September 1993 (DFE, 1993) and the criteria established in *DFE Circular 9/92* that all secondary teacher education programmes had to meet by September 1994, the past few years have seen an unprecedented number of attacks on conventional approaches to the training of teachers. These attacks on teacher education, largely from the new right and government policy makers want to see the removal of teacher education from higher education and for it to be unambiguously located in schools, where it can be linked to the 'theory-free' development of practical skills. Meanwhile, various attempts have been made to find new ways of training teachers. Conventional four-year BEd courses and one-year postgraduate certificate of education (PGCE) courses have been joined by shortened courses, conversion courses, part-time courses and the relatively new Articled Teacher and Licensed Teacher Schemes.

The discussion contained in this chapter does not contain a defence of current practice in higher education teacher education programmes. However, it does provide a rationale for a continuing role for higher education while at the same time endorsing a move towards more experientially based professional learning. In doing so, the intention is to transcend the polar opposites that the new right and the present Conservative government want to couch the current debate in. On the one hand, we have a theory-based and impractical form of training emanating from higher education and, on the other hand, we want a more realistic practically based form of training, based in schools.

Implicit in this chapter will be the argument that the practice of teaching is neither a matter of applying ideas derived from theory rather than experience nor simply a matter of applying instrumental technical skills, learned on the job, to produce standardized and measurable end-products. Rather the stance will be taken that teaching is best viewed as a practical science in which the relationship between theory and practice is interactive. Practical skills are not simply technical in character. They are structured by values and understandings of how to act consistently with them. Such values and understandings constitute 'practical educational theories' which inform practice with varying degrees of explicitness.

To give these arguments more context the nature of teacher education as a whole will be discussed. To do this data from the Modes of Teacher Education (MOTE) research project (Barrett *et al.*, 1992), Her Majesty's Inspectors (HMI) *Report of Initial Teacher Training in England and Wales* (DFE, 1991), and recent Standing Conference on the Education and Training of Teachers (SCETT, 1991) reports are drawn upon. Some of the key issues of the reform criteria and will then be teased out together with their potential consequences for PE. Some of these comments will be speculative because we do need to separate out 'what will be', from 'what may be' that is the consequence of legislation from pragmatic considerations and our ideological beliefs on how teachers should be prepared.

TEACHER EDUCATION RECRUITMENT

Teacher education in England and Wales is a large and complex 'industry'. In 1993–4 there were 90 institutions offering over 300 courses to about 24,000 annually enrolled student teachers (HEFC, 1993).

There are a variety of 'routes' to obtain 'qualified teacher status' (QTS), from which the 24,000 or so students who enter ITT each year at present can choose. The two that have dominated are the one-year PGCE, normally a one-year programme following a three-year subject study undergraduate degree. The second is the four-year concurrent teacher education degree, BEd, BA/BSc (QTS) with subject study and professional study in equal proportions.

In 1993–4, there were 186 postgraduate ITT courses on offer, 105 (56 per cent) of which were secondary (11–18 yrs) ITT courses and 132 undergraduate ITT courses, of which 64 (48 per cent) were secondary ITT courses. Total ITT student numbers were almost equally divided between undergraduate and postgraduate courses, with postgraduate courses recruiting slightly more students (52 per cent) than the undergraduate routes. Almost 60 per cent of all ITT students in 1992–3 were training for the primary phase qualification (5–11 yrs). There are differences in the pattern of undergraduate and postgraduate secondary age phase subject specialisms as Table 13.1 illustrates.

Table 13.1   *Most commonly offered postgraduate and undergraduate secondary specialist subjects (1993–4)*

Rank order	Postgraduate	Undergraduate
1	Maths	Maths
2	French	PE
3	Physics	Physics
4	Biology	Design Technology
5	English	Business Education
6	Chemistry	Biology
7	German	Music
8	PE	Chemistry
9	Religious Studies	Religious Studies
10	General Science	General Science

Mathematics is the most commonly available subject on both routes but the pattern of availability of PE is quite markedly different. This may have particular implications for the nature of knowledge between the two routes for PE. In England and Wales, there is no undergraduate PE programme at present that does not have qualified teacher status. Students enrolling for the PGCE would normally have followed a three-year Sports Studies, Sports Science, Leisure and Recreation, or similar three-year undergraduate programme. Students can therefore enter the teaching profession in PE with quite a distinct difference in their knowledge of subject study.

REFORMS OF TEACHER EDUCATION

Since 1989, it has been possible to categorize Government reform of teacher education into six policy tactics as follows:

1   to set up a competitive market in the training of new teachers and to break the monopoly of higher education in providing ITT;
2   to establish ITT in the form of wholly or substantially school-based courses, with little or no time spent in higher education;
3   to recruit new student teachers into teaching by means of targeting new sectors of the population (from business and armed forces, *inter alia* and 'mothers');
4   to destroy the all-graduate entry to the teaching profession and to lower the academic and theoretical status of teaching;
5   to relate a great proportion of time in existing BEd (or equivalent) and PGCE courses into schools, away from higher education;
6   to control far more rigorously, stipulate, regulate, and conform the curriculum content of BEd and PGCE courses – thereby, also exercise greater control over curriculum pedagogy and the hidden curriculum of ITT.

It is beyond the scope of this chapter to examine the origins and the consequences of all of these policy tactics. Specific focus will be given to requirements and criteria that have to be met by all secondary ITT courses by September 1994. These criteria will be overlaid with examples of the current situation to assess how far teacher education may have to travel to meet the new requirements.

There are three main principles to the Department for Education *Circular 9/92* (DFE, 1992):

1   schools should play a much larger part in ITT as full partners of higher education institutions;
2   the accreditation criteria for ITT courses should require higher education institutions (HEIs), schools and students to focus on the competences of teaching; and
3   institutions, rather than individual courses, should be accredited for ITT.

In addition the main intentions of the reform proposals published in September 1993 (DFE, 1993) were to:

1   establish a Teacher Training Agency with a statutory responsibility for the central funding of all courses of ITT – this was established by the Education Act (1994);

2   establish new criteria for the accreditation of teacher training courses which will favour an increase in schools running their own courses rather than institutions;
3   encourage the growth of diversity of routes into teaching including three-year undergraduate teacher education degrees; and
4   transfer more responsibility for the training of teachers to schools.

The Government's criteria require that students on ITT courses spend a specified minimum amount of time in schools. On secondary PGCE courses, this amount of time was 75 days in 1990/91, on four-year undergraduate secondary courses the minimum time was 100 days in school-based training in 1990/91.

The new criteria increased the requirement for school-based training on the one-year full-time secondary PGCE course to 24 weeks (or 120 days) while for the four-year secondary undergraduate courses the school-based element was increased to 32 weeks (or 160 days).

According to the MOTE survey, SCETT documentation and HMI evidence in 1990/91, no one-year PGCE course provided students with as much as 120 days although all courses provided more than the minimum levels. The shortfall between the current provision and the new proposals was even more marked in the four-year undergraduate courses. If students are to be provided with the pattern of training that had been proposed by the Government in England and Wales, it clearly involved a radical overhaul of existing course structures.

The new criteria are intended to enhance the role of schools in the training of teachers as well as proposing a significant increase in the amount of time that must be spent in school-based training on secondary courses.

It was envisaged that schools and teachers will be 'in the lead in the whole of the training process, from the initial design of a course through to the assessment of the performance of the individual student' (DFE, 1992).

Such proposals are altering the relationship between many higher education providers and their local schools, leading to changes in the roles and responsibilities of college-based tutors and school-based teachers, and altering the ways in which the 'partnership' between schools and higher education is managed.

The HMI report on school-based training states that (DFE, 1991, p. 6):

> The idea of partnership is crucial to the concept of school-based training. The extent to which a course is school-based cannot be determined adequately just by counting the hours students spend in school; the more influential role for teachers implied by the criteria needs to be evident too.

The MOTE survey (Barrett *et al.*, 1992) collected data about the role of teachers in the planning, supervision and assessment of the various elements of ITT courses. The findings revealed that on all aspects of ITT courses, teachers were more likely to be involved in teaching and supervising students, or in planning courses, than in student assessment. Although recognizing that there are many partnership arrangements between higher education programmes and schools in many areas, the data suggested that only a quarter of courses made any payments to teachers or schools for their role in training. In only a few cases was this found to be more than token payments.

Furlong *et al.* (1988) have drawn attention to the significance of the levels of training that can be provided and added to an already extensive list of attempts to resolve the theory/practice issue in training when investigating the role of the school and ITT. Tomlinson (1989) summarized the findings and noted that four levels or forms of training had been distinguished. These were to be categorized as follows (Tomlinson, 1989, p. 236):

Level 1 Direct practice: in the classroom
Level 2 Indirect practice: practical training in classes and workshops within the training institution
Level 3 Practical principles: critical study of the principles of practice and their use
Level 4 Disciplinary theory: critical study of practice in the light of theory and research

Furlong *et al.* (1988) argue that completely school-based training would not presently be possible at Levels 3 and 4.

Mentors in schools

One possibly beneficial result of the debate concerning school-based ITT is that it has at last highlighted the significance of the quality of the trainer and/or mentor in schools. The HMI Report (DES, 1991, p. 4) *Perspectives on Teacher Education: Other Trainers' Views* (Introduction, XV) stated:

> The teacher trainers in schools were not specifically trained to be trainers. The school teachers who supervised the students' school experience, normally had no training in supervision and those who ran the training course were not automatically given management training.

The view of one industrial trainer who contributed to the report was that, '(work in school) the key stone of the training process is based on the goodwill of an untrained, (for supervision), unaccountable, unrewarded and overly busy classroom teacher'. The Report also found that the partnership between training institutions and schools was, in resource terms, a fragile structure which compared poorly with some other training arrangements.

The present moves to school-based training (and indeed the improvement of standards and quality for induction, teaching practice experience and appraisal for professional development) suggest that 'mentors' should have more responsibility for the training at Levels 3 and 4 (Furlong *et al.*, 1988) what they refer to as 'skills in the sophisticated analysis of teaching and skills in the training of students which are widely considered to form quite distinct areas of professional expertise' (as quoted by Tomlinson, 1989).

Experience from pilot school-based programmes such as the Articled Teacher and Licensed Teacher Schemes suggest that it was expensive and complex, and demanding on teacher time. Understandably, schools need reassurance about proper resourcing. A good deal of current practice is undertaken on goodwill. Schools can handle this because students are in school for a pre-determined period of time. In 1993, there were 200 Articled Teachers registered. The prospect of 24,000 student teachers being in schools for between 120 and 160 days does present quite a different scale of operation. Recent reforms within schools in England and Wales have created a different climate in schools and understandably different attitudes towards student teachers. Greater partnership is to be welcomed but the balance does need to be fair on schools.

The results of a national survey conducted by the Standing Conference of Principals (SCOP), January 1994 into the views of 2000 headteachers concerning the training of student teachers appears to contradict assumptions underlying government policy. In contrast to the impression created by policy makers, the majority of headteachers claim not to want a major training role. Responses revealed a 90 per cent reluctance to accept major responsibility for students, most preferring a partnership model in which schools share with HEIs the different tasks involved in preparing new teachers. Of headteachers, 75 per cent were interested in providing only minimal input on course design, in maintaining course quality and in providing subject knowledge. Only 12 out of the entire sample wanted a major role in designing programmes and setting course objectives. Almost 50 per cent of respondents wanted a key role in the assessment of practical skills and saw this as the essential element of the school's contribution. The other half preferred that this task be shared with HEIs, some expressing reluctance totally.

Mentorship training is obviously a key factor in preparing schools for the increase in school-based training. However, this training in itself has to be quite substantial if teachers are to undertake a role which involves much more than guiding a student teacher through a list of competences. Many involved in teacher education are being forced to question their own traditional role and responsibilities including colleagues teaching PE in schools.

Student teacher competences

One of the Government's reforms requires higher education, schools and students to focus on defined competences of teaching emphasizing the pre-specification and standardization of job functional skills. These competences include specific reference to:

- subject knowledge
- subject application
- class management
- assessment and recording, and
- further professional development.

Teaching as an intellectually rigorous activity is in danger of being reduced to a check-list of behaviour objectives if it is not underpinned by a philosophy of teaching and learning and a sound model of the teacher. Instrumental competences ignore a range of the qualities, understandings and abilities by a teacher, not least an appreciation of how young people learn.

It may be possible to view these competences not purely as instrumental but within the framework of three knowledge-based fields:

1   Subject/technical knowledge
2   Process/application knowledge, and
3   contextual knowledge.

It is then possible to locate the required competences within these three fields of knowledge.

Subject/technical knowledge Subject/technical knowledge is the knowledge required for the understanding of the knowledge, concepts and skills of the specialist subject in the school curriculum, together with a breadth and depth of subject knowledge which extends beyond Programmes of Study and examination syllabuses in schools.

Process/application knowledge Process/application knowledge is the knowledge required to:

- employ a range of teaching strategies appropriate to the age, ability and level of pupils;
- produce coherent lessons plans and schemes of work which take account of school policies;
- ensure continuity and progression within and between classes;
- set appropriately demanding expectations for all pupils;
- present subject content in a clear and stimulating manner;
- recognize diversity of talent including that of gifted pupils;
- identify, assess and provide for special educational needs learning difficulties;
- diagnose and evaluate pupil learning, including a recognition of the effects on that learning of teacher expectations, and discuss with significant others pupils' performance.

Contextual knowledge Contextual knowledge includes both the generic context of education across all Key Stages of compulsory education from 5 to 16 years, together with specific contexts in which the specialist subject appears in schools and the community. This would for example include knowledge of and specific reference to:

- National Curriculum developments together with concomitant themes and dimensions;
- curriculum developments such as personal and social education, the nature of academic and vocational qualifications;
- the evolving nature of subject specialisms and their application within the school and community.

The conceptual model shown in Figure 13.1 serves to illustrate how these fields might be encapsulated within role definitions for partnership arrangements between higher education and schools in preparing teachers for the future.

Schulman (1986) outlines a similar conceptual model when referring to content knowledge. He refers to three types of content knowledge:

1 subject matter content;
2 pedagogical content knowledge;
3 curriculum content knowledge.

Subject matter content knowledge Subject matter content knowledge includes the structures which define the field of the subject. In PE, this includes practical knowledge

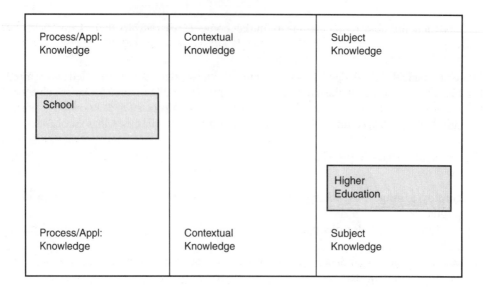

Figure 13.1 *Conceptual model*

in the various activities which represent the scope of the school curriculum. It also includes theoretical knowledge which has been claimed to represent the foundation disciplines on which the study of PE is based.

Pedagogical content knowledge Pedagogical content knowledge is concerned with how to teach the subject matter content knowledge. It includes the most useful forms of representation, analogies, example, illustrations, explanations, demonstrations of the subject matter content knowledge. It is obviously possible to possess theoretical knowledge about how to teach PE and so Schulman also refers to two forms of pedagogical content knowledge as with subject matter content knowledge.

Curriculum content knowledge Curriculum content knowledge focuses on curriculum programmes, their organization and structure and to some extent matches what I referred to earlier as contextual knowledge.

In viewing competences derived from subject knowledge in either model, we would do well to remember the findings of Sparkes *et al.* (1990). Sparkes and his co-authors found that our PE teacher education programmes at present contained a considerable amount of time on physical activity. Students they found not surprisingly, learn the rules, principles and tactics of a range of games, they learn how to support safely in gymnastics and they learn the correct technique for the arm action in the front crawl and the teaching points to correct any deviations. They also learn a great deal about how the body works in courses that deal with physiology, biomechanics, and psychology of exercise and motor performance. Some time is also given to the history and sociology of sport and PE. However, it is the sciences that have dominated PE throughout its development as an area of study for teacher education in higher education. Sparkes suggests that it is a technocratic or instrumental rationality that tends to dominate the teacher education programmes in this country.

Such programmes have tended to be concerned with method and efficiency rather than with purposes. Instrumental rationality limits itself to 'How to do it?' questions rather than 'Why to do it?', or 'Where are we going?' questions.

There is a potential danger that the new reform of teacher education could support Sparkes' concerns with regard to an overtly technical performance by the teacher if competences continue to be viewed as purely check-lists of behaviour objectives. The emphasis on performance-outcomes rather than theoretical understanding ignores the importance of theoretical knowledge as a foundation for intelligent professional practice and judgement.

Final thoughts

Given the discussion and issues raised in this chapter so far, it could be possible to argue that the period of renaissance in PE teacher education is yet to come, but the golden years have passed by. This statement is intended to reflect both optimism and reality as to the future of PE. The challenges inherent in the reforms of teacher education can be viewed as 'threats' or 'opportunities'. The psychology of the two conditions can impact dramatically differently on action, direction and progress towards a destination. Obviously to 'circle the wagons' to meet a threat, which is one alternative, is to stand still or reduce oneself to travelling in a circle. A second alternative is to do nothing, out of indecision, or in the hope that the threat will pass. Earl Zeigler (1986) describes this irresolution as 'decidophobia'.

To view these current issues or challenges as opportunities, however, is to commit to action and to set about the task of defining strategies to make the best of each opportunity to improve the field of PE operation and interests. The PE profession in England and Wales has vacillated for some years on these issues or perceived threats. Little of real consequence has resulted. It could be argued that PE teacher education cannot escape from the criticism, that apart from tinkering with some of the super-structure, little has changed over the past twenty years or so and it has been rather conservative in nature and even design. Some cynics may go even further and express the view that far from adapting to changing circumstances attempts have been made to resist or arrest change, and to build a wall around how PE operates and what happens.

The need for student teachers to be more adaptable to fit their future roles is evidently clear. PE teacher education needs to reflect the fact that student teachers should be encouraged to develop intellectual skills which will enable them to become better informed, to be active in their own learning, to challenge, to analyse and to evaluate rather than simply absorb and imitate; when introduced to research they should learn to recognize what counts as evidence, how to develop an argument and to distinguish rationality from prejudice and doctrine. In addition, the PE teachers that are trained now and in the future should have the ability to introduce children to local clubs, facilities and community provision, and the ability to encourage children to participate in their running and decision making. These teachers should be able to cultivate ability in those who can and want to excel but not at the expense of those whose motive for participation is enjoyment and recreation. A change of mission is being required of PE more than a change of content to give pupils greater satisfaction, community involvement and relevance.

In reality, teacher education and PE teacher education finds itself in a 'Catch 22' position. To encourage substantive change, change agents are needed. But many teacher educators are products of their own curricula and educational processes – the very things under scrutiny and in need of change and reform. Higher education seems to be faced with the twin demands of not only anticipating but also delivering the future.

It seems self-evident that institutions in England and Wales must undertake rapid adaptations. Failure to respond could prove catastrophic; inevitable results could include loss of control of their future and perhaps elimination of their programmes of preparation.

This chapter has tried to indicate that the new directions for teacher education involve selecting the most appropriate option and taking deliberate, planned action to cause this choice to occur. It should be recognized that despite government tactics, the future is there, at least in part, to be made not simply received, but that action is required. This action constitutes the will to be anticipatory and pro-active rather than 'decidophobic' and simply reactive. To a large extent, the reform of ITT education has provided many in England and Wales with a catalyst to concentrate their minds as to what is and will be the future of teacher education.

REFERENCES

Barrett, E., Barton, L. and Whitty, G. (1992) 'Initial teacher education in England and Wales: A topography', Modes of Teacher Education Research Project, Economic and Social Science Research Council, Goldsmiths' College and Institute of Education, University of London.

DFE (1991) *Perspectives on Teacher Education – Other Trainers' Views*. HMI Report, London: HMSO.

DFE (1992) *The Accreditation of Initial Teacher Training Under Circular 9/92*. London: HMSO.

DFE (1993) *The Government's Proposals for the Reform of Initial Teacher Training*. London: HMSO.

Furlong, V.J., Wilkins, M. and Wilcocks, S. (1988) *Initial Teacher Training and the Role of the School*. Milton Keynes: Open University Press.

HEFC (1993) *Initial Teacher Training Allocations for 1993–94, Circular 37/93*. Bristol: Higher Education Funding Council.

SCETT (1991) *Teacher Education – Policy For The 1990s*. London: Standing Committee for Education and Training of Teachers.

Schulman, L. (1986) 'Those who understand: Knowledge growth in teaching', *Educational Researcher*, **15**, 4–14.

SCOP (1994) *School Based Teacher Training, What the Headteachers Say*. London: Standing Conference of Principals.

Sparkes, A., Templin, T. and Schempp, P. (1990) 'The problematic nature of career in a marginal subject: Some implications for teacher education programmes', *Journal of Education for Teaching*, **16**(1), 19.

Tomlinson, J. (1989) 'The Enigma of theory v. practice', *Education*, 10 March, p. 236.

Zeigler, E. (1986) *Assessing Sport and Physical Education: Diagnosis and Projection*. Ontario: Stipes 1.

Chapter 14

A New Vision for Physical Education

Len Almond

INTRODUCTION

The National Curriculum for Physical Education (NCPE) has been revised and a slimmer version presented to the profession. We have been promised no more changes for the next five years. Does this mean time for consolidation and relief from the numerous changes of recent years? Or does it give us the opportunity to reflect critically on the aspirations that guide our actions in schools and attempt to match them with the reality of current practice. I believe it is time to do the latter because the practical concerns of the past few years have dominated our thoughts and left us bereft of a clear direction in which to pursue the richness and potential of PE for every child.

In this chapter, I shall attempt to sketch out a direction – a vision of PE which represents a coherent set of ideals and aspirations that informs this vision – that I believe the profession should pursue. This vision needs to be translated into a set of strategies which illustrate a process of delivery on how to achieve these aspirations. However, such a strategy must be able to generate a set of practices which never lose sight of the long-term aspirations enshrined in the vision and which exemplify real guides to action and practice. This is a very tall order: therefore, in this chapter, my sketch represents a framework for discussion to enable us to clarify the variety of interpretations which I hope this chapter can generate and which will lead to real guides to practice.

A VISION OF PE

First of all my framework for a vision of PE consists of three central ideas which represent a useful heuristic to focus our attention on the kinds of ideas and aspirations that can guide our actions:

1 active living
2 cultural practices of significance
3 physicality.

They represent three central aspects of PE which are interrelated and symbiotic with each other. What do they involve?

Active living

Active living is a term much used in health promotion but, for me, it represents an idea that is important to PE. Our PE programmes in schools should be concerned with promoting physical activity in the sense that they represent purposeful pursuits that can enrich lives and enable young people to flourish as persons because they can find joy in being active and learn to love it. As teachers, we are attempting to help young people to acquire both a commitment to being active and a new perspective on life informed by the satisfactions generated in the pursuit of purposeful physical activity of the kind provided by schools.

Cultural practices of significance[1]

My second element – cultural practices of significance – is directly linked to the first. Sport, dance and adventure pursuits are human practices of great significance and value that affect people in a very pervasive manner and have become a fundamental and important part of human heritage and cultural life. Such activities take up a great deal of media coverage and, at certain times, international festivals of sporting excellence arouse a great deal of interest generating also considerable political and social debate. In the same way, sport, dance and adventure activities have inspired the art world to create works that have contributed to a deeper understanding of these cultural forms. These activities have the power to enrich and transform lives, become an absorbing interest which rewards and fulfils, and also provide avenues for the enhancement of human capacities and qualities and the pursuit of excellence.

It has been argued most cogently by Lawton (1975) and Skilbeck (1984) that one of the tasks of schools is to provide access to, and engagement in, cultural forms and practices so that young people can become acquainted with important and significant features of cultural life. Schools provide the means by which young people can become initiated into sport, dance and adventure activities which contain rich traditions and exemplify the very best of human endeavour. Coming to understand this scope and recognizing their significance within our culture and tradition is an important aspect of school life.

Finally, purposeful physical activity can promote the corporate life of a school by stimulating morale and providing opportunities for teachers, pupils and ancillary staff to find mutual satisfaction in individual and team successes. When schools place a high value on purposeful physical activity it can promote further participation beyond the school.

Physicality

The third element in my framework – physicality - is not an easy term because our language does not allow me to express it more clearly. Physicality does not mean 'taming the body' or 'schooling the body' in the sense that PE is engaged in conditioning the body, submitting to a form of regimentation or attempting to perfect the body; nor is it a form of curbing the body.

It is more an attitude of mind than any kind of activity area. People want to seek out and face personal challenges in which they can push themselves, are physically challenged and go beyond accepted boundaries in which they push back personal limits in the process of overcoming odds, barriers or fears. It represents an adventure in exploring personal boundaries and potential.

At one level, it represents a desire to sail single-handed round the world or walk to the centre of Antarctica. At another level, it represents a need to run, swim or cycle a certain distance and, for some people, in a particular time; or perhaps it represents the need to run, or cycle on one's own, to be solitary, and simply enjoy the satisfaction of being physically active. I am well aware that this brief sketch does not do justice to this idea but I hope to persuade the reader that this element deserves our critical appraisal and exploration of its possibilities. I am simply identifying an aspect of PE that can easily be overlooked yet it represents an important dimension – it is this aspect of PE that excites, it creates a personal challenge to be faced and the thrill of trying to master it. There are a number of possibilities which could enlarge our understanding of this dimension of PE.

The educational role of PE

But these central features that I am claiming represent elements of a vision for PE cannot be made available at any time. There must be good reasons why they are included in the education of young people in schools. These central features of PE need to be made available to the unformed and uninformed minds of young people whose life plans are in the process of unfolding and whose ability to evaluate is not yet well-developed. It is for this reason that there is a need to consider the 'educational' role of PE. This represents a feature of PE that we tend to forget or ignore yet it is an important dimension that cannot be overlooked.

PE in schools contributes to the overall education of young people by helping them to learn how to lead full and valuable lives by engaging in purposeful physical activities such as sport, dance or adventure. It is these activities that can lead to an improvement in the quality of people's lives. They learn to value these activities in a rich and fundamental way of coming to care about them. Schools provide the opportunity for young people to make sense of their situation, to illuminate their understanding of what to do with their lives and help them to make informed choices in terms of how they choose to spend their lives.

Thus, I would argue that this 'educational' role of PE is important because there is much to learn. Young people need to learn how to:

- lead full and valuable lives;
- make informed decisions about what to do in their lives;
- acquire power to make choices of a certain kind (informed and rational) and arrived at in a certain way (i.e. non-coercive, non-indoctrinatory); and
- become activity independent.

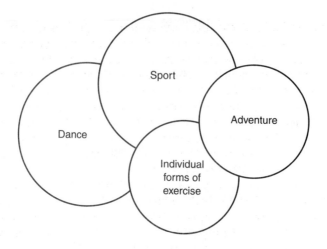

Figure 14.1   *The content of PE.*

This is best achieved in the context of schools (anywhere is simply not good enough) with teachers whose professional responsibility it is to make available what is best in PE and to help young people to make informed decisions and to acquire the power to implement them.

THE CONTENT OF PE

So far I have elaborated three distinctive features of PE and located them within the need to consider our educational role. But what are the activities of PE – the content of what we teach? In one sense, this is straightforward: PE consists of a family of activities grouped within four areas – sport, dance, adventure and other individual forms of exercise which are not covered by the previous three areas, e.g. tai chi. These are represented in Figure 14.1.

They are areas of experience that have their own distinctive form which makes them different and illustrates something of the richness of PE. Sport is concerned with competitive activities whereas dance is concerned with expressiveness in which artistic and aesthetic criteria are employed. These two areas offer qualitatively different experiences and therefore they represent opportunities to explore different dimensions of being physically active.

In this chapter, I cannot explore all these areas in any sort of depth. Therefore I propose to take one aspect – sport – and attempt to illustrate something of what it can offer. However, it is necessary first to point out that these distinctive areas of PE have something in common. I believe they represent disciplined forms of activity in the sense that there is a great deal to learn in each area which requires practice and refinement. To accomplish anything, commitment, dedication and real effort is involved. At the same time, pursuing these activities generates satisfactions that motivate further participation.

However, sport as a disciplined form of physical activity – as one of three areas: sport, dance or adventure – needs to be represented to young people in a form that is acceptable to their level of understanding and maturation. This is important because I am not advocating that we introduce sport in this form to very young children. It is much more important to recognize that sport can be translated into a play form which makes it much more developmentally appropriate to children at Key Stages 1 and 2. Thus, I am proposing that sport as play and sport as a disciplined activity need to be acknowledged as mutually separate, independent aspects of sport which need different approaches and challenges, but they are closely related. The PE and coaching world have recognized this, and progress has been made in developing ideas which need time to permeate through the profession and become part of established practice. When this happens children will benefit, but so will sport.

How should we present sport to young people? I would like to propose that one strong feature of sport in schools should centre on the idea of sport education. Space does not allow me to illustrate a more complete picture of what sport could look like in schools therefore I shall confine myself to one aspect that needs to be developed in schools. The task for teachers is twofold, we need:

1   to initiate young people into a range of sporting activities which illustrate their significance as important aspects of cultural life; and
2   to demonstrate how engagement in sporting activities can enrich people's lives and improve its quality so that young people are able to illuminate their understanding of what to do with their lives and how to spend their time.

Simply presenting a range of sports to young people is not good enough. We have to go beyond this and present sport as an opportunity to

1   maintain an active interest in sport,
2   engage in a sport because it represents an absorbing activity, or
3   pursue excellence.

This is an enormous task for any teacher.

But, what is 'sport education'? In addition to the mastery of techniques and skills which are fundamental to all sporting achievements, there are four other important aspects of learning about sport and its traditions and practices:

1   Celebrating sporting endeavour through festivals
2   Learning roles and responsibilities in sport participation:
    ● performer
    ● official
    ● leader/coach.
    In addition, educational institutions need to recognize the value of helping young people to become:
    ● informed and intelligent spectators
    ● intelligent students of sport.
3   Learning to compete and identifying what constitutes competition:
    ● the role of rules in competition – structure, equality, protection, conduct
    ● what makes a 'good' competition
    ● acquiring morally acceptable attitudes in sporting behaviour.
4   Learning to prepare for taking part in sports events as festivals:
    ● fitness (conditioning)

- developing tactics, skills and technical competence
- affiliation to one's team
- planning and organization for culminating event/festival
- making plans and setting targets.

These four components have been described in more detail in Almond (1989); therefore I do not wish to elaborate any further. However, these four components set out a comprehensive framework that will make great demands on any teacher of PE because they go beyond the simple teaching of techniques and the presentation of sport as a series of blocks of different sporting activities with little continuity or progression. They place the learning of sporting skills in context and make sport a much more important aspect of PE.

THE CONTEXT OF PE

Sport education as I have presented it, even as a simplified sketch, is a personal encounter in which young people learn to recognize the need for mastery in sport to enhance the satisfactions derived from engagement in such a purposeful physical activity. However, Strike (1990) makes an important point when he writes: 'These activities are not only the means for realising the goods of accomplishment; they are also the context for friendships and community' (p. 217). Thus, PE should not be merely concerned with its content; there is another important aspect that is often neglected, forgotten or even ignored – this is the context in which there are opportunities for interpersonal competencies to be acquired, appreciated and shaped as a result of interactions with others, and in this process enable one to achieve an understanding of their relevance. Within the context of PE two distinct aspects emerge:

1 Social learning and relationships:
   - learning to mix with others
   - establishing relationships
   - co-operating on a task
   - sharing the learning process
   - caring, consideration of others, unselfishness
   - trust and respect for others
   - fairness and tolerance
   - sensitivity to others.
2 Learning to cope with feelings and emotions about participation in purposeful physical activities:
   - frustration in one's attempts to practise
   - the process of competition
   - tension in competition or presenting a performance
   - success in competition
   - recognition of (a) one's limitations and (b) barriers or constraints to one's performance
   - the pressure of preparing (or performing) well and meeting expectations
   - fear in gymnastics or adventure activities or about one's future performance in any activity

In each of these aspects of the context of PE there are important interpersonal dispositions to be acquired, shaped and appreciated. There is much learning that needs to be accomplished and PE can provide significant opportunities for identifying oneself as a person through personal encounters with the 'goods of accomplishment' as well as 'goods' that can be generated in interaction with others.

DEVELOPING A COMMUNITY TO SUPPORT LEARNING

Though the content (the physical activities that pupils engage in) and context (the situations in which pupils encounter and engage in physical activities) of PE can generate significant opportunities for promoting a person's well-being, this can only be achieved by creating a community (in this case within a school) in which this can unfold. This is an important condition for ensuring that both the content and context of PE can bring about real learning.

Just as teachers plan a scheme of work to establish continuity, development and coherence across a Key Stage, I would argue that teachers need to plan in the same way and consider how they can create a suitable school structure to generate a sense of community (a sense of shared committed experience).

Such a community is centred on a belief that it is necessary to generate a set of common purposes and shared understandings about the enterprise of creating a learning environment and adopting appropriate teaching approaches. In this sense, the community is attempting to create procedures which lead to successful common action in which it should follow that a pedagogy of care needs to inform our practices.

This process entails a shared commitment in which every individual (teachers and pupils) must be allowed and enabled to contribute to the community. Donald Soper claims that 'you change society to make people better, not the other way round' (*Guardian*, 21 January 1993). There is a great deal of insight in this statement and it has particular relevance for the idea of a caring community. You can only (or you are more likely to) behave responsibly or learn to care about others if the environment permits it or encourages it.

Strike (1990) points out that caring is a central good and lies at the root of many others and he proposes that 'no coherent view of a desirable human life can simply reject it' (p. 215), and goes on to say: 'Many of the goods of relationships are highly dependent on the goods of accomplishment for their realisation.' This reinforces the point made earlier that, in addition to the content of PE, the context can be a powerful tool for learning. Thus, in schools where teachers deal with many young people at the same time, it is necessary to have also a concern for justice, for the distribution of scarce goods, in the sense that there is competition for the teacher's time. This is a point well made.

To move towards a community which:

- values all individuals,
- promotes fairness for all in distribution of scarce goods,
- encourages trust and respects everyone,
- creates a caring and considerate atmosphere,
- is tolerant and sensitive towards individual differences, needs and interests,

- fosters reflection on the consequences of personal actions and collective responsibility, and
- stimulates the growth of a constructive sense of the person through one's interactions and relationships with others,

we need to create the conditions that generate collegiality and solidarity.

All of this is based on an understanding that, within a community, teachers need to adopt a caring pedagogy which encompasses a set of procedural principles to guide one's practice and which will protect and promote children's interests and welfare. There needs to be a school and department policy in which pupils and teachers have been involved in framing guidelines. This process of negotiation is central to providing a support for the personal development of every child. Thus, the climate, ethos, or the environment of PE in a school needs to formulate:

- teacher expectations of acceptable behaviour
- rules that govern conduct (pupils need to be involved in their creation)
- models of morally acceptable standards of behaviour
- models of caring behaviour
- reward structures that support/reinforce caring and morally acceptable standards of behaviour.

Without these a community cannot exist and children's learning will be impoverished.

CONCLUSION

I have attempted to sketch out a vision to inform deliberations about the kind of aspirations that PE should pursue. This vision contains three interrelated dimensions: first, a concern to promote active living for all our pupils; second, a desire to make available cultural practices that many people value highly, traditions within sport, dance and adventurous pursuits; and third, within PE, there are numerous challenges in which people want to push back personal limits and boundaries. However, these interrelated elements take place in an educational environment in which teachers help young people to make informed choices about what to do with their lives through the initiation of activities within PE which can generate satisfactions that help to enrich the quality of people's lives.

Teachers are the shapers of uninformed and unformed minds, therefore decisions about what to do and how to achieve it are grounded in ethical decisions. This makes the process of planning and mapping opportunities for young people to encounter the goods of accomplishment an important event and worthy of our best deliberations and the need for informed debate. In the same way, our deliberations need to take into account how the context of PE is a powerful medium for promoting interpersonal competence.

In this process of shaping, significant others (teachers and pupils) within the school's community become important dimensions. They can help either to distort how young people feel about themselves as persons or they can be positive agents. But, this can only be accomplished in a community in which there is shared committed action with common understanding of the tasks in hand. In the same way, our profession needs to generate a sense of shared committed action in which common understanding of the value of PE is an aspiration worth striving for.

NOTES

1. This aspect of Physical Education emerged as an idea during the 1980s but more recently Mike McNamee reinforced and strengthened my understanding of this feature of our work. McIntyre (1985) has been a strong influence in the development of thinking about 'cultural practices of significance'.

REFERENCES

Almond, L. (1989) *The Place of Physical Education in Schools*. London: Kogan Page.
Lawton, D. (1975) *Class, Culture and the Curriculum*. London: Routledge and Kegan Paul.
McIntyre, A. (1985) *After Virtue* (2nd edn). London: Duckworth.
Skilbeck, M. (1984) *School-based Curriculum Development*. London: Harper and Row.
Strike, K.A. (1990) 'The legal and moral responsibility of teachers', in Goodlad, J.I., Soder, R. and Sirotnik, K.A. (eds), *The Moral Dimensions of Teaching*. San Francisco: Jossey-Bass, pp. 188–223.

Index